Complete
BASIC
FOR THE SHORT COURSE

The Boyd & Fraser Programming Language Series includes these fine titles:

BASIC Fundamentals and Style
Beginning Structured COBOL
Advanced Structured COBOL: Batch and Interactive
Comprehensive Structured COBOL
Fortran 77 Fundamentals and Style
Pascal

Other outstanding programming language texts from Boyd & Fraser include:

BASIC Programming with Structure and Style
Complete BASIC: For the Short Course
Standard BASIC Programming: For Business and Management Applications
Structured Fortran 77 Programming
Structured Fortran 77 Programming: For Hewlett-Packard Computers
Pascal Programming: A Spiral Approach

Also available from Boyd & Fraser are these quality texts:

Data Communications Software Design
The Business Computing Primer: Using Microcomputer Software
Computers and Man

Cover Photo: David S. Hughes, Stock/Boston

Complete BASIC

FOR THE SHORT COURSE

James S. Quasney

John Maniotes

Purdue University Calumet

Boyd & Fraser Publishing Company

Boston

To our wives: Linda and Mary
The Quasney tribe: Lisa, Jeff, Marci, Jodi, Amanda and Nikole
The Maniotes clan: Dionne, Sam and Andrew

Editor: Tom Walker
Production manager: Erek Smith
Development editor: Sharon Cogdill
Associate editor: Donna Villanucci
Production editor: Toni Rosenberg
Design: Rafael Millán
Cover: Carol Rose

Manufactured in the United States of America

Library of Congress Cataloging in Publication Data

Quasney, James S.
   Complete BASIC.

   Includes index.
   1. Basic (Computer program language) I. Maniotes,
John. II. Title.
QA76.73.B3Q373 1985   001.64'24   84-29298
ISBN 0-87835-151-5

3 4 5 6 7 SZ 3 2 1 0 9

PREFACE

People in almost every walk of life will come into contact with computers and BASIC, the most popular language used to program them. BASIC has emerged as the most widely used programming language in the world. BASIC has gained strong support from the manufacturers of personal computer and timesharing systems because it is easy to learn, powerful and flexible.

THE BASIC PROGRAMMING LANGUAGE

Complete BASIC: For the Short Course is ideally suited for use in a short introductory programming course. The text was specifically designed, however, to meet the needs of instructors teaching an Introductory Data Processing course in which BASIC programming is a component. *Complete BASIC: For the Short Course* is a perfect complement to such texts as: Capron and Williams, COMPUTERS AND DATA PROCESSING, Second Edition (Benjamin-Cummings); Kroenke, BUSINESS COMPUTER SYSTEMS: AN INTRODUCTION, Second Edition (Mitchell); Long, INTRODUCTION TO COMPUTERS AND INFORMATION PROCESSING (Prentice-Hall); Mandell, COMPUTERS AND DATA PROCESSING TODAY (West); Sanders, COMPUTERS TODAY (McGraw-Hill); Shelly and Cashman, COMPUTER FUNDAMENTALS: FOR AN INFORMATION AGE (Anaheim); Stern and Stern, COMPUTERS AND SOCIETY (Prentice-Hall); and similar texts.

ABOUT THIS BOOK

The book was developed with the following objectives:

1. to instill good problem-solving habits
2. to acquaint the reader with the syntax of the BASIC programming language
3. to introduce the reader to the proper and correct way to design and write programs
4. to encourage independent study and help those working alone on their own systems

OBJECTIVES OF THIS BOOK

No previous experience with a computer is assumed, and no mathematics beyond the freshman high-school level is required. The book is specifically written for the student with average ability, for whom continuity, simplicity and practicality are essential.

LEVEL OF INSTRUCTION

DISTINGUISHING FEATURES

The distinguishing features of this book include the following:

Problem-oriented Approach

Over 100 BASIC programs plus many partial programs, representing a wide range of practical applications, are used to introduce specific statements and the proper and correct way to write programs.

Emphasis on the Program Development Cycle

The program development cycle is presented early in Chapter 1 and is used throughout the book. Good design habits are reinforced, and special attention is given to testing the design before attempting to implement the logic in a program.

Machine Specificity

Various dialects of BASIC are consistently highlighted throughout the book, which accentuates microsoft BASIC. General Forms or footnotes are used to indicate the availability and form of BASIC statements for the following computer systems: Apple, COMMODORE, DEC Rainbow/MBASIC-86, DEC VAX-11, IBM PC/MICROSOFT, Macintosh/MICROSOFT and TRS-80 Model 4. Other requirements that differ among systems, such as how to get a hard copy, clearing the screen, the composition of variable names and precision, are presented in tables.

Flowcharts Illustrating Program Design

Flowcharting is an excellent pedagogical aid and one of the tools of an analyst or programmer. Many of the program examples include program flowcharts of the logic to demonstrate programming style, design and documentation considerations. Line numbers have been placed on the top left corner of the symbols to better illustrate the relationship between the flowchart and the program.

BASIC at Work

The book contains 13 completely solved and annotated actual case studies, illuminating the use of BASIC and computer programming in the real world. Emphasis is placed on problem analysis, program design and an in-depth discussion of the program solution.

Programming Exercises with Sample Input and Output

Over 30 challenging Programming Exercises with sample Input and Output are included at the end of the chapters. These problems are in order from most simple to most difficult. All the problems include sample input data and the corresponding output results. Solutions to these exercises are given in the *Instructor's Manual and Answer Book* and are also available to instructors from our publisher on an IBM PC-compatible diskette.

Structured Programming Approach

Particular attention is given to designing proper programs using the three logic structures of structured programming: Sequence, Selection (If-Then-Else and Case) and Repetition (Do-While and Do-Until). Consistent use of the IF–THEN–ELSE statement, logical operators and the WHILE and WEND statements helps minimize dependence on the GOTO statement.

Complete Coverage of Sequential File Processing

Complete coverage of sequential files provides students with knowledge central to a real programming environment. Topics include creating sequential files and writing reports to auxiliary storage.

Interactive Applications (Menu-Driven Programs)

Although batch processing is discussed in detail, the primary emphasis is on interactive processing. The INPUT, PRINT and Clear Screen statements are introduced early in Chapter 2. Menu-driven programs are illustrated to familiarize students with the type of programming proliferating in today's world.

Debugging Techniques

Characteristic of a good programmer is confidence that a program will work the first time it is executed. This confidence implies that careful attention has been given to the design and that the design has been fully tested. Still, errors do occur, and they must be corrected. Throughout the book, especially in Appendix A, efficient methods for locating and correcting errors are introduced. Both TRON and TROFF, as well as other techniques, are discussed in detail.

Concise Introduction to Computers

A concise discussion of how computers operate is included at the beginning of the book. Equal attention is given to personal computers and timesharing.

Use of Second Color

The effective use of a second color throughout the book enhances readability, highlights key concepts and facilitates easy reference. This is especially important for readers using this book in a self-study environment or as a reference.

Solutions to Programming Exercises on IBM PC Diskette

An IBM PC-compatible diskette with all the program solutions to the 30 Programming Exercises is available upon request from our publisher, Boyd & Fraser, for instructors who adopt this book.

INSTRUCTOR'S MANUAL AND ANSWER BOOK

The *Instructor's Manual and Answer Book*, available to instructors upon request from Boyd & Fraser, includes transparency masters from each chapter of the text, chapter-by-chapter objectives and vocabulary lists, lecture outlines, program solutions to all 30 programming assignments in the book, answers to the odd-numbered BASIC Self-Text Exercises, and a test bank that includes true/false, short-answer, fill-in and multiple-choice questions for quizzes and tests.

ACKNOWLEDGMENTS   We were fortunate in having a group of reviewers whose critical evaluations of earlier drafts of the manuscript were of great value. Special thanks go to Professors Chester Bogosta of Saint Leo College, John J. Couture of San Diego City College, Syed Shahabuddin of Central Michigan University, Sumit Sircar of the University of Texas at Arlington, Marilyn Markowicz of Purdue University Calumet and Mick L. Watterson of Drake University. No book is possible without the motivation and support of an editorial staff. Therefore, our final acknowledgment and greatest appreciation is reserved for the following at Boyd & Fraser: to Tom Walker, editor in chief, for the opportunity to write this book and his constant encouragement; to Sharon Cogdill, a talented development editor, whose creative ideas and organizational abilities are visible throughout the book; to Toni Rosenberg, the production editor, who did a marvelous job editing the book under a tight production schedule, and to Donna Villanucci, associate editor, who was an invaluable asset during the writing and production of this book as well as of the accompanying *Instructor's Manual and Answer Book*.

Hammond, Indiana   James S. Quasney
January 1985   John Maniotes

CONTENTS

COMPUTERS AND PROBLEM-SOLVING: AN INTRODUCTION

A **computer** is a machine that can accept data, process the data at high speeds, and give the results of these processes in an acceptable form. A more formal definition of a computer is given by the American National Standards Institute (ANSI), which defines a computer as a device that can perform substantial computation, including numerous arithmetic or logic operations, without intervention by a human operator.

Advantages of a Computer

The major advantages of a computer are its speed, its accuracy, and its ability to store and have ready for immediate recall vast amounts of data. Modern computers can also accept data from anywhere via telephone lines or satellite communications. They can generate usable output, like reports, paychecks, and invoices, at several thousand lines per minute.

Computers can handle large amounts of data and tedious and time consuming work without ever tiring, which makes them indispensable for most businesses. In fact, computers have been among the most important forces in the modernization of business, industry and society since World War II. Keep in mind, however, that with all their capabilities, computers are not built to think or reason. They extend our intellect, but they do not replace thinking.

Computer **hardware** is the physical equipment of a computer system. The equipment may consist of any combination of mechanical, magnetic, optical, electrical and electronic devices. Although many computers have been built in different sizes, speeds, and costs, and with different internal operations, most of them have the same basic subsystems (see Figures 1.1, 1.2 and 1.3).

Input

An **input unit** is a device that allows **programs** (instructions to the computer) and **data** (like rate of pay, hours worked, and number of dependents) to enter the computer system. This device converts the incoming data into electrical impulses which are sent to the other units of the computer. A computer system usually has a **keyboard** for input. Other common input devices include a joystick, mouse, and floppy diskette unit.

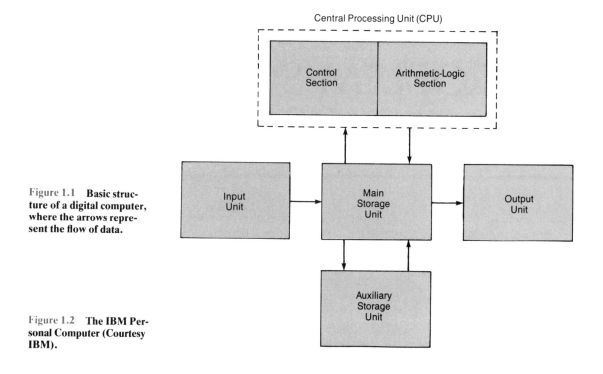

Figure 1.1 **Basic structure of a digital computer, where the arrows represent the flow of data.**

Figure 1.2 **The IBM Personal Computer (Courtesy IBM).**

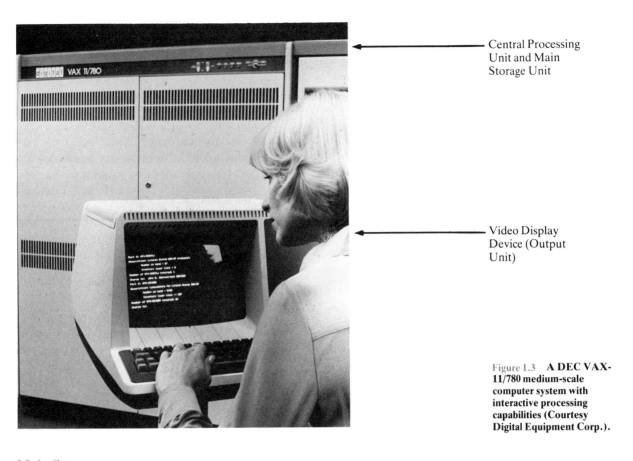

Central Processing Unit and Main Storage Unit

Video Display Device (Output Unit)

Figure 1.3 **A DEC VAX-11/780 medium-scale computer system with interactive processing capabilities (Courtesy Digital Equipment Corp.).**

Main Storage

After the instructions and data have entered the computer through an input unit, they are stored in the computer's **main storage** unit. Since computers can process vast amounts of data in a short time and since some can perform millions of calculations in just one second, the storage unit must be able to retain large amounts of data and make any single item rapidly available for processing.

Main storage in a computer is divided into locations, each having an **address**. When instructions and data are entered, they are stored in various locations of main storage. The computer leaves data in a storage location until it is instructed to replace it with new data. While a data item is in storage, the computer can "look it up" as often as it is needed. Thus, when data is retrieved from a storage location, the stored contents remain unaltered. When you instruct the computer to put new data in that location, it replaces old data.

Central Processing Unit (CPU)

The **CPU** controls and supervises the entire computer system and performs the actual arithmetic and logic operations on data as specified by the written program. The CPU is divided into the **arithmetic-logic section** and the **control section** (see Figure 1.1).

The arithmetic-logic section performs such operations as addition, subtraction, multiplication, division, transferring, storing, and setting the algebraic sign of the results. Depending on the cost and storage capacity of the computer, the speed of the arithmetic unit will range from several thousand to many millions of operations per second.

The arithmetic-logic section also carries out the decision-making operations required to change the sequence of instruction execution. These operations include testing various conditions, such as deciding the algebraic sign of a number or comparing two characters for equality. The result of these tests causes the computer to take one of two or more alternate paths through the program.

The control section directs and coordinates the entire computer system according to the program developed by the programmer and placed in main storage. Its primary function is to analyze and initiate the execution of instructions. This means that the control section has control over all other subsystems in the computer system. It can control the input of data and output of information and routing of data and information between auxiliary storage and main storage or between main storage and the arithmetic-logic section.

Auxiliary Storage

The function of the **auxiliary storage** unit is to store data and programs that are to be used over and over again. Common auxiliary storage devices are the **magnetic tape, hard disk** and **floppy diskette.**

Both magnetic tape and disk can be used to store programs and data for as long as desired. A new program entering the system erases the previous program and data in main storage, but the previous program and data may be permanently stored on an auxiliary storage device for recall by the computer.

In a business, files containing employee records, customer records, accounts receivable or payable data, and inventory data are stored on magnetic tape or disk. Programs written to print paychecks, invoices and management reports are also stored on these auxiliary storage devices. Without auxiliary storage, all programs and data would have to be manually entered through an input device every time an application was processed.

Output

When instructed by a program, the computer can communicate the results of a program to **output units.** A computer usually has a video display device for output. Other common output devices include a printer, plotter, and floppy diskette unit.

The **video display device**, also called a **CRT** or **VDT**, is similar to the tube in a television set and can be used to display the output results in the form of words, numbers, graphs, or drawings (see Figures 1.2 and 1.3).

High-speed line printers, some of which can operate at speeds of more than 2,000 lines per minute, can prepare invoices, checks, report cards, and other output. If the results of a program are to be processed further, the information can also be placed on magnetic disk, diskette or tape. The information can be used later as data for the next problem or sent over telephone lines to another computer for further processing.

In order for a computer to take action and produce a desired result, it must have a step-by-step description of the task to be accomplished. The step-by-step description is a series of precise instructions called a **program.** When these instructions are placed into the main storage unit of a computer, they are called the **stored program**. Main storage not only stores data but also the instructions which tell the computer what to do with the data. The stored program gives computers a great deal of flexibility. Without it the computer's ability to handle tasks would be reduced to that of a desk calculator.

Once the program is stored, the first instruction is located and sent to the control section, where it is interpreted and executed. Then the next instruction is located, sent to the control section, interpreted and executed. This process continues automatically, instruction by instruction, until the program is completed or until the computer is instructed to halt.

In order for the computer to perform still another job, a new program must be stored in main storage. Hence, a computer can be easily used to process a large number of different jobs.

Computer software is a set of programming languages and programs concerned with the operation of a computer system.

Programming languages are classified as **low-level languages** (like machine language and assembly language) and **high-level languages** (like Ada, BASIC, Pascal, COBOL, FORTRAN and PL/I). Early generation computers required programmers to program in **machine language**, and this language was different for each computer manufacturer's system.

Currently, most applications are programmed in one of the many popular high-level languages listed in Table 1.1. A high-level language is generally machine or computer independent; this means that programs written in a high-level language like BASIC are portable—they can be transferred from one computer system to another with little or no change in the programs.

Program 1.1 illustrates a program written in BASIC. It instructs the computer to compute the average of three numbers, 17, 23, and 50.

BASIC at Work

Computing an
Average

Program 1.1

```
100 REM PROGRAM 1.1
110 REM COMPUTING AN AVERAGE
120 REM ********************
130 LET A = (17 + 23 + 50)/3
140 PRINT "THE AVERAGE IS"; A
150 END
```

BASIC Program

System Command   `RUN`

Displayed Result   `THE AVERAGE IS 30`

The displayed answer, found below the word RUN, is 30. Even though we are deferring detailed explanations about this program until the next chapter, Program 1.1 gives you some indication of instructing a computer to calculate a desired result using the BASIC language.

TABLE 1.1   Some Popular High-Level Languages and Their Appropriate Area of Usefulness

Language	Area of Usefulness
Ada	A programming language that encourages structured programming. Ada is named in honor of Ada Lovelace, considered by many to be the world's first programmer, a close friend of Charles Babbage, a computer pioneer.*
BASIC	**B**eginner's **A**ll-purpose **S**ymbolic **I**nstruction **C**ode is a very simple problem-solving language used with personal computers or with terminals in a timesharing environment. BASIC is used for both business and scientific applications.
COBOL	The **CO**mmon **B**usiness **O**riented **L**anguage is an English-like language suitable for business data processing applications. It is especially useful for file and table handling and extensive input and output operations. COBOL is a very widely used programming language.
FORTRAN	**For**mula **Tran**slation is a problem-solving language designed primarily for scientific data processing and process control applications.
Pascal	Pascal, named in honor of the French mathematician Blaise Pascal, is a programming language that allows for the formulations of algorithms and data in a form which clearly exhibits their natural structure. It is primarily used for scientific applications, systems programming, and to some extent for business data processing.
PL/I	**P**rogramming **L**anguage/**I** is a problem-solving language designed for both business and scientific data processing. This language incorporates some of the best features of FORTRAN, COBOL and other languages.
RPG	**R**eport **P**rogram **G**enerator is a popular report generator designed for business data processing applications on small computer systems.

* Ada is a trademark of the United States Department of Defense (Ada Joint Program Office).

**1.5
PROBLEM-
SOLVING
AND PROGRAM
DEVELOPMENT**

Every action the computer is expected to make towards solving a problem must be spelled out in detail in the program. The step-by-step procedures listed below will help you set problems up for the computer to solve. These procedures make up what is called the **program development cycle.**

1. **Problem Analysis** • Define the problem to be solved precisely, including the form of the input, the form of the output and a description of the transformation of input to output.

2. **Program Design** • Devise an **algorithm**, or method of solution, the computer will use. This method must be a complete procedure for solving the specified problem, in a finite number of steps. There must be no ambiguity, no chance that something can be interpreted two ways.

    Develop a detailed logic plan using flowcharts or logic diagrams to describe each step that the computer must perform to arrive at the solution. As far as possible, the flowcharts or logic diagrams must describe *what* job is to be done and *how* that job is to be done.

    Develop good test data. As best you can, select data that will test for erroneous input and exceptions.

3. **Test the Design** • Step by step, go through the logic diagram using the test data, as if you were the computer. If the logic plan does not work, repeat steps 1 through 3.
4. **Code the Program** • Code the program according to the logic diagram. Include program documentation, like comments and explanation, within the program.
5. **Review the Code** • Carefully review the code. Put yourself in the position of the computer and step through the program.
6. **Enter the Program** • Submit the program to the computer via a keyboard or terminal.
7. **Test the Program** • Test the computer program until it is error-free and until it contains enough safeguards to ensure the desired results.
8. **Formalize the Solution** • Run the program, using the input data to generate the results. Review, and if necessary, modify the documentation for the program.

Flowcharts

A **program flowchart** is a popular logic tool used for showing an algorithm in graphic form. Figure 1.4 shows a flowchart which illustrates the computations that are required to compute the average commission paid to a company's sales personnel.

In constructing a flowchart, start at the top (or left-hand corner) of a page. The main flow should be top to bottom or left to right. A **flowchart template** can be used to draw the flowchart symbols.

Eight basic symbols are used in flowcharting a program. They are given in Table 1.2 with their respective names, meanings, and some of the BASIC statements that are represented by them.

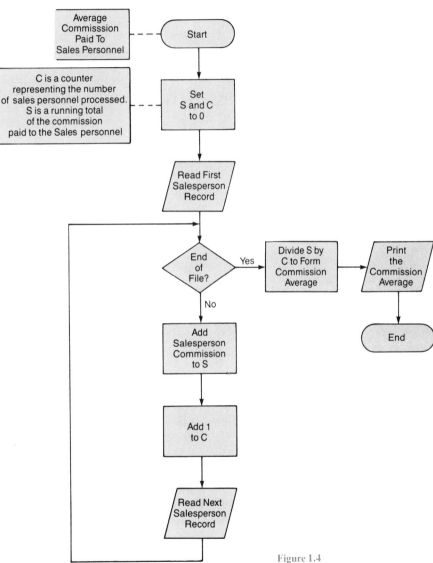

Figure 1.4

1.6
INTERACTIVE
PROCESSING

Programs are entered in one of three modes depending on the computer hardware available. First, a programmer may use a video display device connected to a central computer to enter programs, as shown in Figure 1.3. Second, a programmer may enter programs on a personal computer. These two modes are **interactive**, because

TABLE 1.2   **Flowchart Symbols and Their Meanings**

Symbol	Name	Meaning
	Process symbol	Represents the process of executing a defined operation or group of operations resulting in a change in value, form, or location of information. Examples: LET, DIM, RESTORE, RANDOMIZE, DEF and other processing statements. Also functions as the default symbol when no other symbol is available.
	Input/Output symbol	Represents an I/O function, which makes data available for processing (input) or displaying (output) of processed information. Examples: READ, INPUT, PRINT, and other I/O statements.
Left to right Right to left Top to bottom Bottom to top	Flowline symbol	Represents the sequence of available information and executable operations. The lines must connect two other symbols, and the arrowheads are mandatory only for right to left and bottom to top flow.
	Annotation symbol	Represents the addition of descriptive information, comments, or explanatory notes as clarification. The vertical line and the broken line may be placed on the left as shown or on the right. Example: REM.
	Decision symbol	Represents a decision that determines which of a number of alternative paths is to be followed. Examples: WHILE, IF and ON-GOTO statements.
	Terminal symbol	The beginning, end, or a point of interruption or delay in a program. Examples: STOP, RETURN and END statements.
	Connector symbol	Any entry from, or exit to, another part of the flowchart. Also serves as off-page connector.
	Predefined Process symbol	Represents a named process consisting of one or more operations or program steps that are specified elsewhere. Examples: GOSUB and ON-GOSUB statements.

the results will appear immediately. The third mode, **batch**, often means a delay in seeing the results of a program. This book assumes that you are programming in one of the interactive modes.

Timesharing Systems

A distinguishing feature of some interactive computer systems is their ability to provide **timesharing** between many users at terminals and the central computer. In Figure 1.5, the computer is serving eleven users, each seated at a terminal and communicating with the system. Of these eleven users, four are running programs in

BASIC, two in COBOL, one in FORTRAN, two in Pascal; two are in the Editor, which enables them to write, correct and modify the program itself.

Under timesharing, two or more users can access the central computer. They all receive what seem to be simultaneous results and enjoy what seems to be total control of the computer through their terminals. In reality, the computer assigns each user a small portion or **slice** of its processing **time** and allocates service among different programs until each program has been completed. The computer schedules these slices of time, sometimes in a round-robin fashion, so that each user receives one at short intervals.

Personal Computers

A **personal computer**, also called a **microcomputer**, is a computer with a CPU which is miniaturized on a **silicon chip**, typically a fraction of an inch long. The CPU, or **microprocessor**, controls the various operations of the personal computer and performs the necessary arithmetic and logic operations (see Figure 1.2).

As a program or data is entered through a keyboard, it is transferred to main storage and displayed on the video display device.

Results may be displayed on the video display device or printed on a printer. If the results and/or programs are to be saved for future reference, they may be stored in the personal computer's auxiliary storage unit, like the floppy diskette, or hard disk unit.

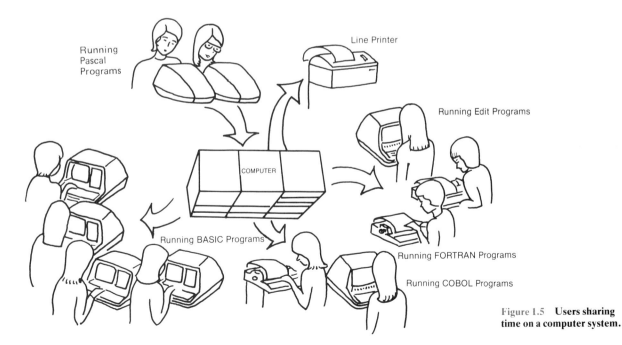

Running Pascal Programs

Line Printer

Running Edit Programs

COMPUTER

Running BASIC Programs

Running FORTRAN Programs

Running COBOL Programs

Figure 1.5   Users sharing time on a computer system.

1.7
**BASIC SELF-TEST
EXERCISES**
**(Even-numbered
answers in the
back of the book.)**

1. State three major advantages that computers have over the manual computation of problems.
2. What are the basic subsystems of a computer system? Briefly describe the function of each subsystem.
3. What makes up the central processing unit?
4. Name two devices that serve as both input and output devices.
5. Draw one flowchart which enables the Mechanical Man to accomplish efficiently the objectives in both phases 1 and 2 as illustrated in Figure 1.6.
   The Mechanical Man possesses the following properties:

   - He does *nothing* unless given a specific instruction.
   - His abilities are restricted to carrying out a limited repertoire of these instructions.
   - He can carry out such instructions *one at a time*.
   - He understands the following instructions:

   a. *Physical Movement:*
      1) Stand up (into an erect position without moving feet)
      2) Sit down (into a sitting position without moving feet)
      3) Take one step (forward only; steps are always a fixed integer length and can be made only if Man is standing up)
      4) Raise arms (into one fixed position, straight ahead)
      5) Lower arms (into one fixed position, straight down at his sides)
      6) Turn right (in place without taking a step and can be made only if Man is standing up; all right turns are 90 degree turns)

   b. *Arithmetic:*
      1) Add one (to a total that is being developed)
      2) Subtract one (from a total that is being developed)
      3) Record total (any number of totals can be remembered in this way)

   c. *Logic:* The Man can decide what instruction he will carry out next, based on the following:
      1) Arithmetic results
         a) Is the result positive?
         b) Is the result negative?
         c) Is the result zero?
         d) Is the result equal to a predetermined amount?
      2) Physical status
         a) Are the raised arms touching anything?

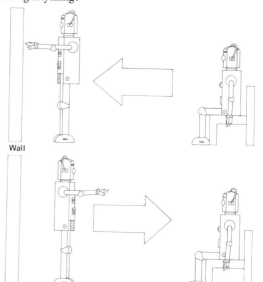

Phase 1: The Mechanical Man is seated at an unknown integer number of steps from the wall. He will stand up and walk forward until he touches the wall with his fingertips. In a seated position with arms raised, his fingertips are aligned with the tips of his shoes.

Wall

Phase 2: After touching the wall, the Mechanical Man will return to his chair. Since the chair is too low for him to sense by touch, he can get to it only by going back exactly as many steps as he came forward.

Figure 1.6

Wall

6. Selecting test data and carefully reviewing the design before coding the program are important steps to ensure that the program will work. Consider the flowchart in Figure 1.7 and the following list of test data items:

1, 2, 3, 2, 1, 1, 2, 2, 1, 3

   Assume that each time you come across the input symbol the next data item, beginning at the left, is assigned to Code.

   a. How many data items are used before the program ends?
   b. What is the value of Switch when the program ends?
   c. What is the value of Total when the program ends?

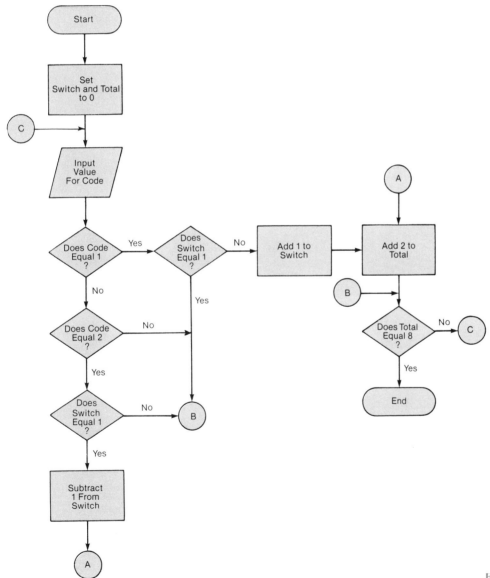

Figure 1.7

7. Draw one flowchart that will cause the Mechanical Mouse to go through any of the four mazes shown in Figure 1.8. At the beginning, an operator will place the mouse on the entry side of the maze, in front of the entry point, facing "up" toward the maze. The instruction "Move to next cell" will put the mouse inside the maze. Each maze has four cells. After that, the job is to move from cell to cell until the mouse emerges on the exit side. If the mouse is instructed to "Move to next cell" when there is a wall in front of it, it will hit the wall and blow up. Obviously, the mouse must be instructed to test if it is "Facing a wall?" before any "Move." The Mechanical Mouse's instruction set consists of the following:

a. *Physical Movement:*
   1) Move to next cell (the mouse will move in the direction it is facing)
   2) Turn right
   3) Turn left
   4) Turn around (all turns are made in place, without moving to another cell)
   5) Halt

b. *Logic:*
   1) Facing a wall? (Through this test, the mouse determines whether there is a wall *immediately* in front of it, that is, on the border of the cell it is occupying and in the direction it is facing.)
   2) Outside the maze?
   If the mouse is outside the maze, it can also make the following decisions:
   3) On the entry side?
   4) On the exit side?

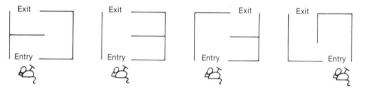

Figure 1.8

BASIC: AN INTRODUCTION

The purpose of Chapter 2 is to develop some of the rules of the BASIC programming language that are common to all BASIC programs and to introduce some fundamental BASIC statements. This chapter concentrates on "simple" program illustrations, input/output operations and system commands. Upon successful completion of Chapter 2 you should be able to write some elementary BASIC programs to run on a computer.

2.1 COMPOSING A BASIC PROGRAM

General Characteristics of a BASIC Program

A BASIC program is composed of:

1. A sequence of lines
2. The last of which contains the END statement

Each line contains a unique **line number** which serves as a label for the statement (see Figure 2.1). A line number followed by a statement is a **line**, as indicated by the example below:

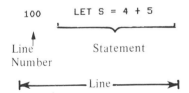

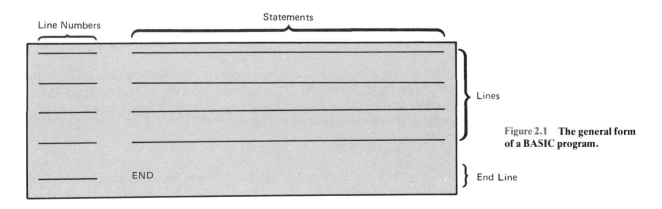

Figure 2.1 **The general form of a BASIC program.**

BASIC at Work

Determining a Salesperson's Commission

The following problem illustrates the composition of a BASIC program.

Most salespeople work on a commission basis. Their earned commissions are often determined by multiplying their assigned commission rate by the amount of dollar sales. The dollar sales amount is computed by deducting any returned sales from the sum of their weekly sales. Assuming a biweekly period, the earned commission can be determined from the following formula:

Earned Commission = Rate × (Week 1 Sales + Week 2 Sales − Returns)

For the biweekly period, a salesperson's assigned commission rate is 15% and sales are $1200 the first week, $1500 the second week. The returned sales are $75.

BASIC Program 2.1 instructs the system to compute the earned amount and display it on an output device. The earned commission of 393.75 is just below a **system command** RUN.

Program 2.1

BASIC Program
```
100 LET E = 0.15 * (1200 + 1500 - 75)
110 PRINT E
120 END
```

System Command ` RUN `

Displayed Result ` 393.75 `

Keywords

There are three lines in this program. The first statement is a LET statement. The LET statement consists of the **keyword** LET, a **variable name** E, an **equal sign**, four **constants** (0.15, 1200, 1500 and 75), and three **arithmetic operators** (* , + and −).

A keyword has special meaning to BASIC. It informs BASIC of the type of statement to be executed. In Program 2.1, there are three keywords—LET, PRINT and END.

Variable Names and Constants

In programming, a **variable** is a storage location in main memory whose value can change as the program is executed. In Program 2.1, the variable name E references the storage location assigned to it by BASIC. Line 100 instructs the system to complete the arithmetic operations and assign the resulting value of 393.75 to E.

All BASIC systems allow variable names to be one or two characters in length. The first character must be a letter (A–Z). If a second character is used, this character must be numeric (0–9). X, Y, E, A1, C2 and F0 are valid variable names. Many BASIC systems expand on these rules to allow for more meaningful variable names.

The equal sign in any LET statement means that the value of the variable to the left of the equal sign is to be replaced by the final value to the right of the equal sign.

Constants, like 0.15, 1200, 1500 and 75, represent ordinary numbers that do not change during the execution of a program.

Arithmetic Operators

The plus sign (+) in Program 2.1 signifies addition between the two constants representing the weekly sales. The minus sign (−) indicates subtraction of the returned sales from the sum of the weekly sales. The asterisk (*) indicates multi-plication between the rate and the actual sales. The set of parentheses in line 100 is used to override the normal sequence of arithmetic operations. All five arithmetic operators are summarized in Table 2.1.

TABLE 2.1 **The Five Arithmetic Operators**

Arithmetic Operator	Meaning	Examples of Usage	Meaning of the Examples
+	Addition	3.14 + 2.9	Add 3.14 and 2.9
−	Subtraction	S − 35.4	Subtract 35.4 from the value of S
*	Multiplication	600.00 * A1	Multiply the value of A1 by 600.00
/	Division	H/10	Divide the value of H by 10
∧	Exponentiation	2 ∧ 3	Raise 2 to the third power

The PRINT Statement

The second statement in Program 2.1 is called a PRINT statement. PRINT statements instruct the system to bring a result out from main storage and display it on an output device. The statement causes the computer to display 393.75, the value of E.

The END Statement

The last line of Program 2.1, the **end line**, includes the END statement. When executed, the END statement instructs the system to stop executing the program. While most BASIC systems do not require an end line, it is recommended that you always include one. The end line serves the following two purposes:

1. It marks the physical end of a program.
2. It terminates the execution of the program.

Line Numbers

Every line in a BASIC program must begin with a unique line number. In this book, a line number must be an integer between 1 and 32767, though some BASIC systems allow for a greater range. A line number must not contain a leading sign, embedded spaces, commas, decimal points or any other punctuation. Line numbers are used in BASIC to:

1. Indicate the **sequence** of statement execution
2. Provide control points for branching
3. Add, change and delete statements

Many experienced BASIC programmers begin with 100, as in Program 2.1, and then increase each new statement's line number by 10. This leaves room to insert up to 9 possible extra statements between the numbers at a later time.

The system command RUN, found just below Program 2.1, is *not* a BASIC statement, but instructs the system to execute the program.

> **Line Number Rule 1:** BASIC statements have line numbers, and system commands don't.

Some Relationships Between Statements

The PRINT statement in Program 2.1 would display a result of zero if, earlier in the program, we had failed to instruct the system to assign a value to the variable E. In other words, the system cannot correctly display the value of E before it determines this value. Therefore, if Program 2.1 were incorrectly *written*, as below, it would not be correctly *executed* by the system, unless by chance the earned commission was zero.

Invalid
```
100 PRINT E
110 LET E = 0.15 * (1200 + 1500 - 75)
120 END
```

This program is incorrect for the same reason:

Invalid
```
100 LET D = 0.15 * (1200 + 1500 - 75)
110 PRINT E
120 END
```

The variable E in line 110 has not been assigned a value earlier in the program. The system will calculate a value of 393.75 for D, but display a result of zero. BASIC automatically assigns all variables in a program a value of zero when the system command RUN is issued.

The relationship between output statements, like the PRINT statement, and other statements in the program can now be stated as follows:

> **Output Rule 1:** Every variable appearing in an output statement should have been previously defined in the program.

Structured Style

Although the flexibility of the language permits certain statements to be placed anywhere in a program, logic, common sense and **structured style** dictate where these statements are placed. Structured style is disciplined, consistent programming. Discipline and consistency help programmers construct readable, maintainable and reliable programs.

2.2 THE INPUT STATEMENT

One of the major tasks of any computer program is to integrate the data to be processed into the program. In Program 2.1 the data was included directly in the LET statement as constants.

Program 2.1
```
100 LET E = 0.15 * (1200 + 1500 - 75)
110 PRINT E
120 END
```
Data as Constants

This technique has its limitations. For example, line 100 must be completely re-entered for each new salesperson processed. An alternative method of integrating the data into the program is shown in Program 2.2.

In this new program, data in the form of constants has been assigned to the variables C, S1, S2 and R. Line 140, used to calculate the earned commission, contains the variables that have been assigned the data in lines 100 through 130. When it executes Program 2.2, the system must be informed of the numeric values for C, S1, S2 and R before it can calculate a value for E. This can be generalized as:

Program 2.2
```
100 LET C = 0.15
110 LET S1 = 1200
120 LET S2 = 1500        Data as constants
130 LET R = 75
140 LET E = C * (S1 + S2 - R)
150 PRINT E
160 END

RUN

393.75
```

> **Arithmetic Rule 1:** Every variable appearing to the right of the equal sign in a LET statement should have been previously defined in the program.

This second method of integrating the data into the program has the same limitations as Program 2.1. That is, lines 100 through 130 would have to be modified in order to process a new salesperson. The only advantage to Program 2.2 is that the LET statement in line 140 will work for any salesperson.

A third way to integrate data into the program is through the use of the INPUT statement. The INPUT statement provides for assignment of data to variables from a source outside the program during execution. The data is supplied to the program *after* the command RUN has been executed.

Through the use of the INPUT statement, Program 2.1, Determining a Salesperson's Commission, can be made more general for calculating the earned commission for any salesperson, no matter what his or her commission rate, weekly sales or returned sales. One version of the rewritten program is shown as Program 2.3.

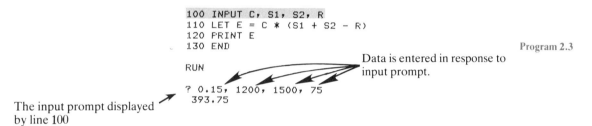

```
100 INPUT C, S1, S2, R
110 LET E = C * (S1 + S2 - R)
120 PRINT E
130 END

RUN

? 0.15, 1200, 1500, 75
 393.75
```

Program 2.3

Data is entered in response to input prompt.

The input prompt displayed by line 100

The function of the INPUT statement in line 100 is to display an **input prompt** and suspend execution of the program until data has been supplied. Most BASIC systems display a question mark (?) followed by a single space for the input prompt. Then it is up to the user to supply the data for each of the required variables. It is necessary that the return key, also called the Enter key, be pressed following entry of the data.

Once the necessary data is supplied, line 110 determines the earned commission, line 120 prints the earned commission and, finally, line 130 terminates the program.

This third alternative of integrating data into a program is far more efficient than the other two alternatives, because we can process any number of salespeople without changing the program. For example, to determine the earned commission for three salespeople, we can run the program three times, as shown below.

```
100 INPUT C, S1, S2, R
110 LET E = C * (S1 + S2 - R)
120 PRINT E
130 END

RUN

? 0.15, 1200, 1500, 75
 393.75


RUN

? 0.10, 1000, 1300, 30
 227

RUN

? 0.20, 2000, 4500, 0
 1300
```

Program 2.3

Execute program for salesperson 1.

Execute program for salesperson 2.

Execute program for salesperson 3.

It is important that the variables in the INPUT statement and the data supplied in response to the input prompt be separated by commas. In BASIC, a comma is used to establish a **list**, which is a set of distinct elements, each separated from the next by a comma. The punctuation must be used so that the system can distinguish how many variables or data elements occur in each list.

Input Prompt Message

To ensure that the data is entered in its proper order, most computer systems allow for an **input prompt message** to be placed in the INPUT statement. When the system executes an INPUT statement containing an input prompt message, the message is displayed on the output device. Execution is then suspended until the data is supplied. To simplify the entries, the following program requests one entry per INPUT statement:

```
100 INPUT "WHAT IS THE COMMISSION RATE"; C
110 INPUT "WHAT IS THE WEEK 1 SALES"; S1
120 INPUT "WHAT IS THE WEEK 2 SALES"; S2
130 INPUT "WHAT IS THE RETURN SALES"; R
140 LET E = C * (S1 + S2 - R)
150 PRINT E
160 END

RUN

WHAT IS THE COMMISSION RATE? 0.15
WHAT IS THE WEEK 1 SALES? 1200
WHAT IS THE WEEK 2 SALES? 1500
WHAT IS THE RETURN SALES? 75
 393.75
```

Program 2.4

When line 100 is executed in Program 2.4, the system displays the input prompt message:

```
WHAT IS THE COMMISSION RATE?
```

After displaying the input prompt message, the system suspends execution of the program until a response is entered. The system processes lines 110 through 130 as it did line 100.

After the data is entered for line 130, line 140 determines the earned commission. Line 150 displays the earned commission and line 160 terminates the program.

The quotation marks surrounding the input prompt message and the semicolon separating the message from the variable in lines 100 through 130 are required punctuation. Here is the rule for determining the placement of the INPUT statement in a program:

> INPUT **Rule 1:** Every variable appearing in the program whose value is directly obtained through input must be listed in an INPUT statement before it is used elsewhere in the program.

Table 2.2 gives the general form of the INPUT statement. The INPUT statement consists of the keyword INPUT followed by an optional input prompt message followed by a list of variables separated by mandatory commas.

TABLE 2.2 **The** INPUT **Statement**

General Form: INPUT variable, . . . , variable
or
INPUT "input prompt message"; variable, . . . , variable

Purpose: Provides for the assignment of values to variables from a source external to the program.

Examples:

Input Statements	*Data from an External Source*
100 INPUT A	23.5
115 INPUT X, Y, Z	2, 4, 6
300 INPUT A$, B	GROSS, -2.73
400 INPUT "PLEASE ENTER THE SALES TAX"; T	0.05
500 INPUT "WHAT IS YOUR NAME"; N$	JOHN
600 INPUT "ENTER PART NUMBER"; P	1289

Note: In the second General Form, a question mark is displayed when a semicolon is used after the INPUT prompt message. In Microsoft BASIC, using a comma instead of a semicolon suppresses the question mark.

One of the functions of the PRINT statement is to display the values of variables defined earlier in a program. You should understand by now that the following:

```
100 LET X = 10
110 PRINT X
```

displays 10, the *value* of X, and not the letter X. The PRINT statement can also be used to display messages that identify a program result, as it is here:

2.3 THE PRINT AND CLEAR SCREEN STATEMENTS

```
100 INPUT "WHAT IS THE COMMISSION RATE"; C
110 INPUT "WHAT IS THE WEEK 1 SALES"; S1
120 INPUT "WHAT IS THE WEEK 2 SALES"; S2
130 INPUT "WHAT IS THE RETURN SALES"; R
140 LET E = C * (S1 + S2 - R)
150 PRINT "THE EARNED COMMISSION IS"; E
160 END

RUN

WHAT IS THE COMMISSION RATE? 0.15
WHAT IS THE WEEK 1 SALES? 1200
WHAT IS THE WEEK 2 SALES? 1500
WHAT IS THE RETURN SALES? 75
THE EARNED COMMISSION IS 393.75
```

Program 2.5

Line 150 in Program 2.5 instructs the computer to display the message THE EARNED COMMISSION IS followed by the value of E. As with the INPUT statement, it is necessary in a PRINT statement to begin and end a message with quotation marks. The quotation marks in a PRINT statement serve to inform BASIC that the item to be displayed is a message rather than a variable.

The semicolon following the message in line 150 instructs the system to keep the **cursor** on the same line instead of positioning it on the next line. The cursor is a movable, blinking marker (like a line or block) on the video screen that indicates where the next point of character entry, change or display will be.

BASIC displays a numeric value which consists of a sign, the decimal representation and a **trailing space**. Appearing immediately before the number, the sign is a **leading space** if the number is positive and a leading minus sign if the number is negative.* The space following the message displayed by line 150 in Program 2.5 represents the sign of the variable E.

```
THE COMMISSION EARNED IS 393.75
```

A space here indicates that 393.75 is positive.

The Clear Screen Statement

One of the responsibilities of the programmer is to ensure that the prompt messages and results are meaningful and easy to read. This is especially true of video display devices found on personal computer systems. A cluttered screen on a video display device can make it difficult for you to locate necessary information. Most personal computer systems include a BASIC statement to clear the screen, which erases all the information on the screen and places the cursor in the upper left corner of the screen.

The general form of the Clear Screen statement is found in Table 2.3, which shows that different computer manufacturers use different statements to clear the screen.

TABLE 2.3   The Clear Screen Statement

General Form:	Depends on the computer system you have.

Computer	*General Form*
Apple	HOME
COMMODORE	PRINT "Press Shift and CLR HOME keys"
DEC Rainbow	PRINT CHR$(27); "[H"; CHR$(27); "[OJ"
DEC VAX-11	PRINT CHR$(27); "[H"; CHR$(27); "[OJ"
IBM PC	CLS
Macintosh	CLS
TRS-80	CLS

Purpose:	Erases all the information on the screen and places the cursor in the upper left corner of the screen.
Examples:	For the IBM, Macintosh and TRS-80:

```
100 CLS
600 CLS
```

The following program incorporates the Clear Screen statement, CLS.

Program 2.6

```
100 CLS
110 INPUT "WHAT IS THE COMMISSION RATE"; C
120 INPUT "WHAT IS THE WEEK 1 SALES"; S1
130 INPUT "WHAT IS THE WEEK 2 SALES"; S2
140 INPUT "WHAT IS THE RETURN SALES"; R
150 LET E = C * (S1 + S2 - R)
160 PRINT
170 PRINT "THE EARNED COMMISSION IS"; E
180 END

RUN

WHAT IS THE COMMISSION RATE? 0.15
WHAT IS THE WEEK 1 SALES? 1200
WHAT IS THE WEEK 2 SALES? 1500
WHAT IS THE RETURN SALES? 75

THE EARNED COMMISSION IS 393.75
```

*The Apple computer does not display a leading space when the number is positive; nor does it automatically display a trailing space after the number.

When the RUN command is issued for Program 2.6, the system clears the screen and then displays the input prompt message WHAT IS THE COMMISSION RATE at the top of the screen. After obtaining a response through the keyboard, the system displays the next input prompt message on line 2, and the rest of the program is executed.

The Clear Screen statement clears the screen, but it does not clear main storage. After you have entered the RUN command and the output results are displayed, you may again display the program by entering the LIST command.

Line 160, which contains a PRINT statement without a list, shows how to instruct the system to display a blank line to separate the input prompt messages from the results. A **null list** like this causes the PRINT statement to display a blank line.

Documentation is the readable description of what a program or procedure within a program is supposed to do. BASIC programmers usually support the programs they write with **internal comments**. Documentation is used to identify programs and clarify parts of a program that would otherwise be difficult for others to understand.

The REM Statements in Program 2.7, lines 100 through 140, 160, 210 and 230, are called **remark lines.** The remark line consists of some comment or explanation intended solely for humans. The keyword REM, when present after a line number, designates the line as a remark line. A REM statement can be located anywhere before the END statement.

2.4 DOCUMENTING A PROGRAM— THE REM STATEMENT

```
100 REM PROGRAM 2.7
110 REM J. S. QUASNEY
120 REM DETERMINING A SALESPERSON'S COMMISSION
130 REM *****************************************
140 REM CLEAR SCREEN
150 CLS
160 REM REQUEST DATA FROM OPERATOR
170 INPUT "WHAT IS THE COMMISSION RATE"; C
180 INPUT "WHAT IS THE WEEK 1 SALES"; S1
190 INPUT "WHAT IS THE WEEK 2 SALES"; S2
200 INPUT "WHAT IS THE RETURN SALES"; R
210 REM CALCULATE THE EARNED COMMISSION (E)
220 LET E = C * (S1 + S2 - R)
230 REM DISPLAY THE EARNED COMMISSION
240 PRINT
250 PRINT "THE EARNED COMMISSION IS"; E
260 END

RUN

WHAT IS THE COMMISSION RATE? 0.15
WHAT IS THE WEEK 1 SALES? 1200
WHAT IS THE WEEK 2 SALES? 1500
WHAT IS THE RETURN SALES? 75

THE EARNED COMMISSION IS 393.75
```

Program 2.7

REM statements have no effect on the execution of a BASIC program. Program 2.7, which includes REM statements, and Program 2.6, which does not, both produce the same results. The general form for the REM statement is found in Table 2.4.

TABLE 2.4   **The REM Statement**

General Form: REM comment.
Purpose: To insert explanatory comments in a program for documentary purposes.
Examples:
```
110 REM J. S. QUASNEY
160 REM DETERMINE THE BALANCE DUE
200 REM PROGRAM 2.7
250 REM
300 REM ***********************
```

Another method of documenting a program is to place remarks or comments on the right-hand side of a BASIC statement. In order to distinguish between a BASIC statement and a comment on the same line, some BASIC systems require the insertion of an apostrophe (') or an exclamation point (!) before the comment. For example, line 220 in Program 2.7 may be written as follows:

```
220 LET E = C * (S1 + S2 - R)        ' E IS THE EARNED COMMISSION
```

Indicates the beginning of a comment

When the BASIC system encounters an apostrophe in a line, it stops processing that line and ignores any comments that follow.

**2.5
SYSTEM
COMMANDS**

As indicated earlier, two types of instructions are used with BASIC systems. One type is the BASIC statement itself, like the LET statement, the PRINT statement and the INPUT statement. The second type is the system command associated with the BASIC system, like the RUN command.

The RUN and LIST Commands

Perhaps the most important system command to a beginner is the command RUN. If this command is not issued, the BASIC program will not be executed.

Another useful system command is the LIST command. It instructs the computer to display all or part of the BASIC program. This command is especially useful in situations where changes have been made to the program statements and a new listing of the program is desired. Program 2.8 illustrates the use of the RUN and LIST system commands.

Program 2.8

```
100 REM PROGRAM 2.8
110 INPUT A, B
120 LET C = A - B
130 PRINT "THE DIFFERENCE IS:"; C
140 END

RUN

? 159, 62
THE DIFFERENCE IS: 97
```

If line 120 is changed by entering the following statement

```
120 LET C = B - A
```

this new line 120 replaces the original line 120. If a LIST command is issued followed by RUN, Program 2.8 appears:

Program 2.8
revised

```
LIST
100 REM PROGRAM 2.8
110 INPUT A, B
120 LET C = B - A
130 PRINT "THE DIFFERENCE IS:"; C
140 END

RUN

? 159, 62
THE DIFFERENCE IS:-97
```

```
LIST 130
130 PRINT "THE DIFFERENCE IS:"; C
```

```
LIST 120-140
120 LET C = B - A
130 PRINT "THE DIFFERENCE IS:"; C
140 END
```

The command LIST can be used to list any part of a program. For example, LIST 130 lists line 130 only. LIST 120−140 lists lines 120 through 140, inclusive.

The NEW Command

Another system command that is of considerable importance is the command NEW. This command instructs the system to erase or delete the last program keyed into the main storage. Without this command, statements from the old program may mix with the statements of the new one.

Table 2.5 summarizes the system commands discussed thus far.

TABLE 2.5   Summary of Some Common System Commands Found with BASIC Systems

System Command	Function
LIST	Causes all or part of the BASIC program currently in main storage to be displayed.
NEW	Causes deletion of the BASIC program currently in main storage and indicates the beginning of a new program to be created in main storage.
RUN	Causes the BASIC program currently in main storage to be executed.

Additional System Commands

The system commands summarized in Table 2.5 are common to all BASIC systems. The syntax of the remaining commands varies from system to system. Table 2.6 lists several **systems functions,** actions taken by the computer when a system command is entered. Also listed in Table 2.6, on page 24, are the system commands that correspond to most BASIC system functions. A column has been left blank for you to fill in the system commands for your BASIC system. You will have to rely on your instructor or find in the user's manual the exact syntax of the system commands that correspond to the functions listed.

Two of the more important system functions listed in Table 2.6 are saving BASIC programs into auxiliary storage for later use and loading BASIC programs from auxiliary storage into main storage.

2.6 PROGRAMMING TIPS

You are ready to write your first program to use a computer for solving a problem. At the end of Chapter 2 are several BASIC Programming Problems. Each one includes a short statement of the problem, suggested input data and the corresponding output results. Collectively, these items are the **program specifications.** After the sample BASIC Programming Problem below, we have suggested a step-by-step procedure for solving it. You will find this helpful when you begin solving problems on your own. You will also find it helpful to review Section 1.5, Problem-Solving and Program Development.

TABLE 2.6 **Additional System Functions**

Common System Function	System Command Used with Microsoft BASIC	System Command on Your BASIC System You may write them in this column .
Saves or files the current program into auxiliary storage for later use. Most BASIC systems require that a file-name be 8 characters or less and begin with a letter.	SAVE "filename"	
Loads a previously stored program from auxiliary storage into main storage.	LOAD "filename"	
Deletes a previously stored program from auxiliary storage.	KILL "filename"	
Lists the names of all programs and files in auxiliary storage that belong to the user.	FILES	
Terminates your session with BASIC.	SYSTEM	
Lists the current program on the printer (valid only if you have a personal computer with a printer attached).	LLIST	
Renumbers the entire current program uniformly.	RENUM starting line,, increment	
Automatically starts a BASIC line with a line number. Each new line is assigned a systematically incremented line number.	AUTO starting line, increment	
Changes the name of a file in auxiliary storage to a new name.	NAME "old fn" AS "new fn"	
Terminates a system activity, such as execution of a program, listing of a program or automatic line numbering.	Press both CTRL key and Break key	

Sample BASIC Programming Problem: Computation of State Tax

Problem: Construct a program that will compute the state tax owed by a taxpayer. The state determines the amount of tax by taking a person's yearly income, subtracting $500.00 for each dependent and then multiplying the result by 2% to determine the tax due. Use the following formula:

$$\text{Tax} = 0.02 * (\text{Income} - 500 * \text{Dependents})$$

Code the program so that it will request the taxpayer's income and the number of dependents.

Input Data: Use the following sample input data:

Taxpayer's income — $73,000.00
Number of dependents — 8

Output Results: The following results are displayed:

```
WHAT IS THE TAXPAYER'S INCOME? 73000
WHAT IS THE NUMBER OF DEPENDENTS? 8

THE STATE TAX DUE IS 1380
```

The following systematic approach to solving this exercise as well as the other programming problems in this textbook is recommended. In essence, this list is the same as the program development cycle outlined in Section 1.5.

Step 1: Problem Analysis

Review the program specifications until you thoroughly understand the problem to be solved. Ascertain the form of input, the form of output and the type of processing that must be performed. For this exercise, you should have determined the following:

Input—The program must allow for the user to supply the data through the use of INPUT statements. There are two data items—taxpayer's income and number of dependents.
Processing—The formula Tax = 0.02 * (Income − 500 * Dependents) will determine the state tax.
Output—The required results include the input prompt messages and the state tax due.

Step 2: Program Design

Develop a method of solution the computer will use. One way to develop a method of solution is to list the program tasks sequentially. For this exercise, the program tasks are:

1. Clear screen.
2. Prompt the user for the necessary data.
3. Calculate the state tax.
4. Display the state tax.

Next, draw a program flowchart that shows how the program will accomplish the program tasks. The flowchart for the sample programming problem is shown in Figure 2.2, on page 26.

Step 3: Test the Design

Carefully review the design by stepping through the program flowchart to ensure that it is logically correct.

Step 4: Code the Program

Code the program, as shown in Figure 2.3, on page 26, according to the flowchart.

Step 5: Review the code

Carefully review the coding. Put yourself in the position of the computer and step through the program. This is sometimes referred to as **desk checking** your code. Be sure the syntax of each instruction is correct. Check to be sure that the sequence of the instructions is logically correct. *You want to be confident that the program will work the first time it is executed.*

Step 6: Enter the Program

Enter the program into the computer system, as shown in Figure 2.4, on page 26.

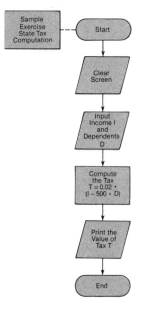

Figure 2.2   Flowchart for Sample Programming Exercise.

```
  1 2 3 4 5 6 7 8 9 10 11 12 13 14 15 16 17 18 19 20 21 22 23 24 25 26 27 28 29 30 31 32 33 34 35 36 37 38 39 40 41 42 43 44 45 46 47 48 49 50 51 52 53 54 5
100 REM CIS 160, DIV. 01, BASIC PRØGRAMMING
110 REM J. S. QUASNEY
120 REM SEPTEMBER 20, 1988
130 REM SAMPLE PRØGRAMMING EXERCISE
140 REM CØMPUTATIØN ØF STATE TAX
150 REM ****************************************
160 CLS
170 INPUT "WHAT IS THE TAXPAYER'S INCOME"; I
180 INPUT "WHAT IS THE NUMBER ØF DEPENDENTS"; D
190 REM CALCULATE THE TAX (T)
200 LET T = 0.02 * (I - 500 * D)
210 PRINT
220 PRINT "THE STATE TAX DUE IS"; T
230 END
```

Figure 2.3   Sample Programming Exercise entered on coding form.

```
100 REM CIS 160, DIV. 01, BASIC PROGRAMMING
110 REM J. S. QUASNEY
120 REM SEPTEMBER 20, 1988
130 REM SAMPLE PROGRAMMING EXERCISE
140 REM COMPUTATION OF STATE TAX
150 REM ***********************************
160 CLS
170 INPUT "WHAT IS THE TAXPAYER'S INCOME"; I
180 INPUT "WHAT IS THE NUMBER OF DEPENDENTS"; D
190 REM CALCULATE THE TAX (T)
200 LET T = 0.02 * (I - 500 * D)
210 PRINT
220 PRINT "THE STATE TAX DUE IS"; T
230 END
```

Figure 2.4   Sample Programming Exercise entered in the computer system.

```
RUN

WHAT IS THE TAXPAYER'S INCOME? 73000
WHAT IS THE NUMBER OF DEPENDENTS? 8

THE STATE TAX DUE IS 1380
```

Figure 2.5   The display from executing the Sample Programming Exercise.

Step 7:   Test the Program

Test the program by executing it, using the RUN command, as shown in Figure 2.5. If the input data does not produce the expected results, the program must be **debugged;** reviewed and corrected. (See Appendix A for debugging techniques.)

Step 8: Formulize the Solution

After debugging the program, obtain a **hard copy,** a listing of the source program and the output results. If the program logic was modified in Steps 4 through 7, revise the documentation and redraw the program flowchart to include the changes.

2.7 HARD COPY OUTPUT

Most BASIC programmers use a keyboard for input and a video display device for output. In many instances, it is desirable to list the program and/or the results on a printer. A listing of this type is **hard copy output**. Table 2.7 illustrates procedures for obtaining hard copy output for some of the more popular computer systems. The procedures involve issuing system commands.

TABLE 2.7   **Procedures for Obtaining Hard Copy Output**

Computer Systems	List the Program	List the Program and Output Results
Apple	PR#1 LIST PR#0	PR#1 LIST RUN PR#0
COMMODORE	OPEN 4, 4 CMD 4 LIST PRINT# 4 CLOSE 4	OPEN 4, 4 CMD 4 LIST RUN PRINT# 4 CLOSE 4
DEC Rainbow	LLIST	Simultaneously press the CTRL and P keys. LIST RUN Simultaneously press the CTRL and P keys.
DEC VAX-11*	SAVE LAB1.BAS EXIT PRINT LAB1.BAS	SAVE LAB1.BAS EXIT PRINT LAB1.BAS BASIC LAB1 LINK LAB1 ASSIGN/USER LAB1OUT.LIS SYS$OUTPUT RUN LAB1 PRINT LAB1OUT
IBM PC	LLIST	Simultaneously press the CTRL and Prt Sc keys. LIST RUN Simultaneously press the CTRL and Prt Sc keys.
Macintosh	LLIST	Simultaneously press the Shift, Special Feature and key 4.
TRS-80	LLIST	Varies from system to system.

*Check the user's manual for the rules regarding filenames.

1. Put yourself in the place of the computer and record for each line number the current values of W, X, and Y. (*Hint:* The value of a variable does not change until the program instructs the computer to change it.)

```
100 LET W = 4
110 LET X = 2
120 LET Y = 6
130 PRINT Y, X, W
140 LET W = W + 1
150 LET X = W * Y
160 PRINT X
170 LET X = 9
180 LET Y = Y - 2
190 PRINT X, Y
200 LET X = X/100
210 PRINT X
220 END
```

W	X	Y	Displayed
4	2	6	6 2 4
5	30		30
	9	4	9 4
	.09		.09

**2.8
BASIC
SELF-TEST
EXERCISES
(Even-numbered
answers in the
back of the book.)**

2. What will be displayed when the following programs are executed?

```
a. 100 PRINT "CALCULATE DISCOUNT"
   110 LET P = 4162.50
   120 LET D = 0.10
   130 LET N = D * P
   140 LET S = P - N
   150 PRINT "ORIGINAL PRICE"; P
   160 PRINT "DISCOUNT"; N
   170 PRINT "SALE PRICE"; S
   180 PRINT "END OF PROGRAM"
   190 END
```

```
b. 100 LET A = -2
   110 LET B = -3
   120 LET C = A * B
   130 PRINT "THE VALUE OF A IS"; A
   140 PRINT "THE VALUE OF B IS "; B
   150 PRINT
   160 PRINT "THE VALUE OF C IS"; C
   170 END
```

3. For each program below, construct a table similar to the one in Exercise 1. Record for each line number the current values of the variables and the results displayed by the PRINT statements.

```
a. 100 LET A = 1
   110 LET B = 3
   120 PRINT A, B
   130 LET A = A + 1
   140 LET B = B - 1
   150 PRINT A, B
   160 LET A = A + 1
   170 LET B = B - 1
   180 PRINT A, B
   190 END
```

c. Assume A and B are assigned the values of 7 and 2, respectively.

```
   100 INPUT A, B
   110 LET C = A^B
   120 PRINT C
   130 LET D = A - B
   140 PRINT D
   150 LET E = 1
   160 PRINT E
   170 LET D = D - 3
   180 LET X = E/D
   190 PRINT X
   200 END
```

b. Assume A and B are assigned the values 4 and 2, respectively.

```
   100 LET C = 4
   110 PRINT C
   120 INPUT A, B
   130 LET C = A/B + C
   140 LET A = A - 3
   150 LET B = C^A
   160 PRINT A, B
   170 END
```

d. Assume P and R are assigned the values 500 and 10, respectively.

```
   100 INPUT P, R
   110 LET R = R/100
   120 LET D = P * R
   130 LET R = R * 100
   140 REM PRINT RESULTS
   150 PRINT "DISCOUNT RATE"; R; "%"
   160 PRINT "PRICE"; P; "DOLLARS"
   170 PRINT "DISCOUNT"; D; "DOLLARS"
   180 END
```

4. Correct the errors in the following programs.

```
a. 100 PRINT Y
   110 END
   120 LET Y = 21.0
```

```
b. 100 LET S = 3/5000
   110 PRINT S
   120 END
```

```
c. 100 LET X = 3003 * 4004
   110 PRINT X
```

```
d. 100 LET S = 23 - 901
   95 PRINT S
   110 END
```

```
e. 100 LET A1 = 999/888
   110 PRINT S
   120 DEND
```

```
f. 100 LET Z = 1
   110 PRINT Z1
   120 END
```

5. Fill in the missing word in each of the following:

   a. An output statement must contain the word _____.

   b. Every BASIC program must have as its last the _____ line.

   c. Every LET statement must contain an _____ sign.

6. Explain in one sentence each the purpose of the following system commands: RUN, LIST, NEW.

7. How many times can you retype a BASIC line?

8. Is it possible to issue a RUN command more than once for the same program?

9. How do you instruct the computer to display two consecutive blank lines in a program?

In order to document computer programs properly, the following identification format may be used at the beginning of each BASIC source program:

```
100 REM DEPARTMENT, COURSE NUMBER, DIVISION, COURSE NAME
110 REM YOUR NAME
120 REM DATE
130 REM PROBLEM OR EXERCISE NUMBER
140 REM A SHORT DESCRIPTION OF THE PROBLEM
150 REM *****************************************************
```

Upon completion of each exercise, turn in to your instructor:

1. A logic diagram
2. A listing of the source program
3. The output results

Whenever possible, meaningful variable names should be used in all the programs. Each major section of the source program should be documented with appropriate remark lines.

> **NOTE:** All BASIC Programming Problems in this book include partial or complete sample output results and, when applicable, sample input data. Learn to select good test data to evaluate the logic of your program. Check your design and program against the sample output, and also select your own data for additional testing purposes.

Purpose: To become familiar with elementary uses of the INPUT, PRINT and LET statements.

**1:
Determining the
Selling Price**

Problem: Merchants are in the retail business to buy goods from producers, manufacturers and wholesalers and to sell the merchandise to their customers. To make a profit they must sell their merchandise for more than the cost plus the overhead (taxes, store rent, upkeep, salaries, and so forth). The margin is the sum of the overhead and profit. The selling price is the sum of the margin and cost. Write a program that will determine the selling price of an item that costs $48.27 and has a margin of 25%. Use the formula:

$$\text{Selling Price} = \left(\frac{1}{1 - \text{Margin}} \right) \text{Cost}$$

Input Data: Use the following data in response to INPUT statements:

Cost—$48.27
Margin—25%

Output Results: The following results are displayed:

```
WHAT IS THE COST? 48.27
WHAT IS THE MARGIN IN PERCENT? 25

THE SELLING PRICE IS 64.36
```

**2:
Payroll
Problem I—
Gross Pay
Computations**

Purpose: To become familiar with some of the grammatical and logical rules of BASIC and to demonstrate the basic concepts of executing a BASIC program.

Problem: Construct three programs that will compute and display the gross pay for an employee working 80 hours during a biweekly pay period at an hourly rate of $12.50.

Version A: Insert the data, 80 and 12.50, directly into a LET statement that determines the gross pay.

Version B: Assign the data, 80 and 12.50, to variables in LET statements and then compute the gross pay in a separate LET statement.

Version C: Enter the data, 80 and 12.50, in response to INPUT statements containing input prompt messages.

Output Results: The following results are displayed for Version B.

```
HOURS===> 80
RATE OF PAY====> 12.5
GROSS PAY======> 1000
```

PROGRAMS WITH CALCULATIONS AND STRINGS

3

In Chapter 2, you were introduced to some simple computer programs that showed some of the rules of the BASIC language. Included were examples of programs that interact with the user through the use of the INPUT and PRINT statements. This chapter continues to develop straight-line programs, with more complex computations and manipulation of data.

This chapter concentrates on constants, variables, expressions, functions, and statements which assign values. It also introduces **string** values, like a word, phrase or sentence. Upon successful completion of this chapter you should be able to write programs that manipulate string and numeric expressions.

Program 3.1 determines the average neck, hat and shoe sizes of a male customer. The program uses the following formulas:

BASIC at Work

Tailor's Calculations

$$\text{Neck Size} = 3 \left(\frac{\text{Weight}}{\text{Waistline}} \right)$$

$$\text{Hat Size} = \frac{\text{Neck Size}}{2.125}$$

$$\text{Shoe Size} = 50 \left(\frac{\text{Waistline}}{\text{Weight}} \right)$$

```
100 REM PROGRAM 3.1
110 REM TAILOR'S COMPUTATIONS
120 REM H = HAT SIZE,   S = SHOE SIZE
130 REM N = NECKSIZE, N$ = CUSTOMER'S NAME
140 REM ********************************
150 INPUT "CUSTOMER'S FIRST NAME"; N$
160 INPUT "WAISTLINE"; W
170 INPUT "WEIGHT"; P
180 LET N = 3 * P/W
190 LET H = N/2.125
200 LET S = 50 * W/P
210 PRINT
220 PRINT N$; "'S NECK SIZE IS"; N
230 PRINT N$; "'S HAT SIZE IS"; H
240 PRINT N$; "'S SHOE SIZE IS"; S
250 END

RUN

CUSTOMER'S FIRST NAME? MIKE
WAISTLINE? 36
WEIGHT? 190

MIKE'S NECK SIZE IS 15.8333
MIKE'S HAT SIZE IS 7.45098
MIKE'S SHOE SIZE IS 9.47368
```

Program 3.1

31

Program 3.1 computes the average neck size (15.8333), hat size (7.45098) and shoe size (9.47368) for Mike, who has a 36-inch waistline and weighs 190 pounds. Not used in the computations, the customer name helps identify the measurements when more than one set of computations is involved.

Program 3.1 contains a sequence of LET statements (lines 180 through 200) with expressions that are more complex than those encountered in Chapter 2. Furthermore, line 150 contains a variable N$ that is assigned a string of letters MIKE rather than a numeric value. The value of N$ is displayed along with the results because of lines 220 through 240. The following pages introduce some formal definitions and special rules for constructing LET statements and manipulating strings.

3.1 CONSTANTS

Recall from Chapter 2 that constants are values that do not change during the execution of a program. Two different kinds of constants are valid for use in BASIC programs, **numeric constants** and **string constants.**

Constants are common in the LET statement and the PRINT statement. Numeric constants represent ordinary numbers. A string constant is a sequence of letters, digits, and special characters enclosed in quotation marks. They are used for such non-numeric purposes as representing an employee name, social security number, address or telephone number.

Numeric Constants

A numeric constant can have one of these three forms in BASIC:

1. **Integer:** a positive or negative whole number with no decimal point, like -174 or 5903 or 0 or -32768.
2. **Fixed Point:** a positive or negative real number with a decimal point, like 713.1417 or 0.0034 or 0.0 or -35.1 or 19235475957463.34.
3. **Floating Point:** a positive or negative real number written in **exponential form.** A constant written in this form consists of an integer or fixed point constant, followed by the letter E and an integer. E stands for "times ten to the power." The usual range for floating point constants is 10^{-38} to 10^{+38}. Valid floating point constants include 793E19, 62E-23, 1E0, -2.3E-3, $+12.34$E$+7$.

Examples of numeric constants in Program 3.1 are 3, 2.125 and 50, found in lines 180, 190 and 200. The numeric data items 36 and 190, entered in response to the input statements in lines 160 and 170, must take the form of numeric constants. This leads to the following rule:

> INPUT **Rule 2:** Numeric data assigned to numeric variables through the use of the INPUT statement must take the form of numeric constants.

A number entered in response to the INPUT statement may have as many digits as required, up to a maximum of 38. However, only the first several digits are significant. The exact number of digits that is significant is dependent on the precision of the computer system and the type of numeric variable being assigned the value.

Computer Precision

We tell BASIC how to store a value, like a numeric constant, by the way we write it. For example, a numeric constant is stored as an integer if it is between -32768 and

+32767 and does not contain a decimal point. A numeric constant is stored in **single-precision** if it is outside the range for an integer, or contains a decimal point, or is written in exponential form. Some systems that allow for **double-precision** store a numeric constant in this form if the number of significant digits exceeds that of single-precision. Table 3.1 shows the **precision** with which a numeric constant may be stored and the **accuracy** with which it may be displayed.

TABLE 3.1   Numeric Precision and Accuracy of Some Computer Systems

Computer System	Single-Precision		Double-Precision	
	Stored With a Precision of	Displayed With an Accuracy Up To	Stored With a Precision of	Displayed With an Accuracy Up To
Apple	10 digits	9 digits	Not Available	
COMMODORE	10 digits	9 digits	Not Available	
DEC Rainbow	7 digits	6 digits	16 digits	16 digits
DEC VAX-11	7 digits	6 digits	16 digits	16 digits
IBM PC	7 digits	7 digits, last digit may not be accurate	17 digits	16 digits
Macintosh	6 digits	6 digits	14 digits	14 digits
TRS-80	7 digits	6 digits	16 digits	16 digits

For the most part, you can let the computer handle the precision with which it stores numeric values. However, you should be aware that not all computers store values to the same precision, and for this reason, identical programs executed on different computers will not always generate identical results.

Numeric Constants in Exponential Form

Numeric constants may also be written in **exponential (E-type)** or **scientific notation**. This form is a shorthand way of representing very large and very small numbers in a program. If a result exceeds the precision under which it is stored, the system displays it in exponential form.

Using exponential notation, a number, regardless of its magnitude, is expressed as a value between 1 and 10 times a power of 10. For example, 1,500,000 can be expressed as 1.5×10^6 in exponential notation or written as an E-type constant in the form of 1.5E6. The *positive* power of ten in the exponential notation of 1.5×10^6 shows that the decimal point was previously moved 6 places to the *left*. That is,

1.500000.

6 places to left

In order to write 1.5×10^6 as an E-type constant in BASIC, the letter E, which stands for "times ten to the power," is substituted for the "$\times$ 10." Hence, the E-type constant is 1.5E6.

In the same way, a small number like 0.000000001234 can be expressed in exponential notation as 1.234×10^{-9} or 1.234E−9. The *negative* power of ten in

1.234×10^{-9} shows that the decimal point was moved 9 places to the *right.* That is,

$$0.\underbrace{000000001.\ 234}_{\text{9 places to right}}$$

String Constants

A string constant has as its value the string of all characters between surrounding quotation marks. In this book we will adopt the rule that the length of a string constant may be from 0 to 255 characters. Some BASIC systems are more restrictive, while others allow for string constants to be longer. Quotation marks indicate the beginning and end of the string constant and are not considered to be part of the value.

The messages that have been incorporated in INPUT statements to prompt for the required data and in PRINT statements to identify results are examples of string constants. A string with a length of zero is a **null** or **empty string.**

String constants can be assigned to variables in a LET statement, as is shown in the following program.

```
100 REM PROGRAM 3.2
110 REM EXAMPLES OF STRING CONSTANTS
120 REM ****************************
130 LET M$ = "Q1937A"
140 LET P$ = "12AB34"
150 LET D$ = "NYLON, DISC"
160 PRINT "MODEL NUMBER: "; M$
170 PRINT "PART NUMBER: "; P$
180 PRINT "DESCRIPTION: "; D$
190 END

RUN

MODEL NUMBER: Q1937A
PART NUMBER: 12AB34
DESCRIPTION: NYLON, DISC
```

Program 3.2

In line 130 of Program 3.2, the variable M$ is assigned the value Q1937A. In line 140, P$ is assigned the value 12AB34, and in line 150, D$ the value NYLON, DISC.

3.2 VARIABLES

In programming, a **variable** is a storage location in main memory whose value can change as the program is executed. In a program, the variable is referenced by a variable name. Variables are declared in a BASIC program by incorporating variable names in statements. Unlike a constant, a variable may be redefined (that is, its value may be changed) during the execution of a program. For example, in the following partial program

```
100 LET A = 15
110 LET B$ = "PURDUE"
120 LET A = 20
```

the variable A, which was assigned the value 15 by line 100, is now assigned the value 20 when line 120 is executed. BASIC recognizes that the two variable names are the same and does not attempt to create another storage location for the second variable name A. In other words, there can only be one variable in a program with the name A; however, it can be referenced and the value changed as often as needed.

Types of Variables

As with constants, there are two types of variables: **numeric** and **string**. A numeric variable may only be assigned a number and a string variable may only be assigned a string of characters.

When the system command RUN is issued for a program, all numeric variables are assigned an initial value of zero and all string variables are assigned a null value. The LET statement may be used to assign a variable a constant value or the result of a calculation. Variables may also be assigned values through INPUT statements.

Selection of Variable Names

Although all BASIC systems allow variable names to be one or two characters in length, many allow them to be considerably longer. Table 3.2 illustrates the rules regarding the composition of variable names for some of the more popular computer systems.

TABLE 3.2 **Variable Naming Conventions for Some of the More Popular Computer Systems**

Computer System	Naming Convention	Valid Forms	Invalid Forms and Reason	
Apple COMMODORE TRS-80	A variable name begins with a letter and may be of any length. The letter may be followed by letters and digits. However, only *the first two characters* of the variable name are used to distinguish one name from another. Keywords like LET, PRINT and END or any other word that has special meaning to BASIC may not be included in the variable name. It is important to note that the variable name *COUNT* and *COT* represent the same variable.	S D1 SUM COUNTER NAME$ CUST$ DAYNAME$ G6$	IFTAL F T$ FILET VALUE$ 1AB	IF is a keyword. Blank character not allowed. LET is a keyword. VAL is a function name and has special meaning to BASIC. Must begin with a letter.
DEC Rainbow IBM PC Macintosh In general, any system running Microsoft BASIC.	A variable name begins with a letter and may be of any length. The letter may be followed by letters, digits and decimal points. Only *the first 40 characters* are significant. A variable name may not be a keyword or any other word that has special meaning to BASIC, but the variable name may contain embedded keywords or words that have special meaning to BASIC.	D F4 CUST. COUNT WEEK. 1. SALES TOTAL FILET$ F5$	GOTO %RATE$ A B 1AB IF$	GOTO is a keyword. Must begin with a letter. Blank character not allowed. Must begin with a letter. IF is a keyword.
DEC VAX-11 In general, any system running BASIC-PLUS-2.	A variable name begins with a letter followed by up to 29 letters, digits, underscores and decimal points. For a string variable name, the $ at the end counts as one of the 29 characters.	S J3 SUMMATION TOTAL. COUNT CUST_NAME$ SALESPERSON$ DO$ J$	1AB A#B _S	Must begin with a letter. Number sign is invalid. Must begin with a letter.

When you compose variable names, make them as meaningful as possible. It is far easier to follow the various statements in a program if meaningful names are used.

For example, assume the formula for gross pay is given by:

Gross Pay = Rate × Hours

The following BASIC statement represents the formula:

```
150 LET A = B * C
```

However, it is more meaningful to write:

```
150 LET G = R * H
```

And if your BASIC system allows it, it is even more meaningful to say:

```
150 LET GROSS = RATE * HOURS
```

Assigning String Variables Values Through the INPUT Statement

The following program requests that string data be entered in response to the INPUT statements.

```
100 REM PROGRAM 3.3
110 REM ENTERING STRING DATA IN
120 REM RESPONSE TO THE INPUT STATEMENT
130 REM ********************************
140 INPUT "MODEL NUMBER"; M$
150 INPUT "PART NUMBER"; P$
160 INPUT "DESCRIPTION"; D$
170 PRINT
180 PRINT "THE MODEL NUMBER IS "; M$
190 PRINT "THE PART NUMBER IS "; P$
200 PRINT "THE DESCRIPTION IS "; D$
210 END
```

Program 3.3

```
RUN

MODEL NUMBER? "Q1937A"          Quoted string data entered
PART NUMBER? "345123"           in response to the program's
DESCRIPTION? "NYLON, DISC"      INPUT statements

THE MODEL NUMBER IS Q1937A
THE PART NUMBER IS 345123
THE DESCRIPTION IS NYLON, DISC
```

In Program 3.3 the string variables M$, P$ and D$ are assigned quoted strings following the rules for string constants. In general, surrounding a string with quotation marks is optional when using an INPUT statement to assign the string to a string variable. Examine the following output from Program 3.3 when quoted and unquoted strings are entered.

```
RUN

MODEL NUMBER? Q1937A            Unquoted strings
PART NUMBER? 345123
DESCRIPTION? "NYLON, DISC"      Quoted strings

THE MODEL NUMBER IS Q1937A
THE PART NUMBER IS 345123
THE DESCRIPTION IS NYLON, DISC
```

The first two string data items Q1937A and 345123 are entered as unquoted strings. The third data item NYLON, DISC is entered within quotes because it contains an embedded comma. The following rule summarizes the assignment of string data items through the use of the INPUT statement.

INPUT **Rule 3:** String data assigned to string variables through the use of the INPUT statement may be entered with or without surrounding quotation marks, provided the string contains no leading or trailing blanks or embedded commas. If the string contains leading or trailing blanks or embedded commas, it must be surrounded with quotation marks.

Displaying String Variables

BASIC does not add leading or trailing spaces when it displays a string value. Therefore, when the semicolon is used as the separator between string items in a PRINT statement, a space should be included to separate the values displayed, as illustrated below:

```
180 PRINT "THE MODEL NUMBER IS "; M$
      .
      .
      .
RUN

THE MODEL NUMBER IS Q1937A
```

The LET statement in BASIC is used to assign a value to a variable. The general form of the LET statement is given in Table 3.3. Each LET statement consists of the keyword LET, followed by a variable, followed by an equal sign, and then by an expression.

**3.3
THE LET
STATEMENT**

TABLE 3.3   **The LET Statement**

General Form:	LET numeric variable = numeric expression
	or
	LET string variable = string expression
Purpose:	Causes the evaluation of the expression, followed by the assignment of the resulting value to the variable to the left of the equals sign.
Examples:	100 LET H = A + 7
	150 LET Q = (B + A)/2 - Q + R
	200 LET C = C + 1
	250 LET X = -X
	300 LET A(Y, 4) = 0
	350 LET D$ = "PRICE"
	400 LET F$ = G$
	450 LET P(I) = C(K) + P(J)
	500 LET E = M * C^2
	550 LET A$ = B$ + "001"
Note:	The keyword LET is optional.

The execution of the LET statement is not a one-step process for the computer. The execution of a LET statement requires two steps, evaluation and assignment.

Although the = sign is employed in BASIC, it does not carry all the properties of the = sign in mathematics. For example, the = sign in BASIC does not allow for the symmetric relationship. That is,

```
100 LET A = B
```

cannot be written as

```
100 B = LET A
```

The = sign in BASIC can best be described as meaning "is replaced by." Therefore,

```
160 LET I = P * R * T/360
```

means: replace the old value of I with the value determined from the expression to the right of the equal sign.

BASIC at Work

Finding the Single Discount Rate

Program 3.4 determines the single discount rate equal to the series of discount rates of 25%, 10% and 10% using the following formula:

$$R = 1 - (1 - r_1)(1 - r_2)(1 - r_3)\cdots(1 - r_n)$$

where R is the single discount rate, and r_1, r_2 ... r_n is the series of discount rates. The number of factors of $(1 - r_n)$ that are used to determine the single discount rate is dependent on the number of discounts. Program 3.4 is written to find the single discount rate of a series of *three* discount rates.

```
100 REM PROGRAM 3.4
110 REM FINDING THE SINGLE DISCOUNT RATE
120 REM R = SINGLE DISCOUNT RATE
130 REM ********************************
140 PRINT "ENTER IN DECIMAL FORM THE:"
150 INPUT "            FIRST DISCOUNT"; R1
160 INPUT "            SECOND DISCOUNT"; R2
170 INPUT "            THIRD DISCOUNT"; R3
180 LET R = 1 - (1 - R1) * (1 - R2) * (1 - R3)
190 PRINT
200 PRINT "THE SINGLE DISCOUNT IS"; R
210 END

RUN

ENTER IN DECIMAL FORM THE:
            FIRST DISCOUNT? 0.25
            SECOND DISCOUNT? 0.10
            THIRD DISCOUNT? 0.10

THE SINGLE DISCOUNT IS .3925
```

Program 3.4

After the three discount rates are assigned their decimal values, the LET statement in line 180 determines the value of the single discount from the expression found to the right of the equal sign. Specifically, the expression is evaluated and the final value 0.3925 is assigned to the variable R. Line 200 displays the value for the R before the program ends.

When dealing with rates that usually occur in percent form, it is often preferable to have the program accept the data and display the results in percent form. Program 3.5 shows how you can write a solution to Finding the Single Discount Rate that accomplishes this task.

In Program 3.5, the INPUT statements (lines 150 through 170) prompt the user to enter the discount rates in percent form. In lines 180 through 200, the rates are changed from percent form to decimal form by dividing R1, R2 and R3 by 100. The single discount is then determined by line 210. Line 220 changes the value of R from decimal form to percent form. Line 240 then displays the value of R. The string constant % found at the end of line 240 helps identify the result as a percent value.

Program 3.5 includes two concepts that many beginners have difficulty understanding. The first is that the same variable—R1 for example, in line 180—can be found on both sides of the equal sign. The second concerns the reuse of a variable that had been assigned a value through computations in an earlier LET statement. In

Program 3.5, R1, R2 and R3 are reused in line 210 after being assigned values in earlier LET statements.

```
100 REM PROGRAM 3.5
110 REM FINDING THE SINGLE DISCOUNT RATE
120 REM R = SINGLE DISCOUNT RATE
130 REM *******************************
140 PRINT "ENTER IN PERCENT FORM THE:"
150 INPUT "              FIRST DISCOUNT"; R1
160 INPUT "              SECOND DISCOUNT"; R2
170 INPUT "              THIRD DISCOUNT"; R3
180 LET R1 = R1/100
190 LET R2 = R2/100
200 LET R3 = R3/100
210 LET R = 1 - (1 - R1) * (1 - R2) * (1 - R3)
220 LET R = 100 * R
230 PRINT
240 PRINT "THE SINGLE DISCOUNT IS"; R; "%"
250 END

RUN

ENTER IN PERCENT FORM THE:
              FIRST DISCOUNT? 25
              SECOND DISCOUNT? 10
              THIRD DISCOUNT? 10

THE SINGLE DISCOUNT IS 39.25 %
```

Program 3.5

3.4 EXPRESSIONS

Expressions may be either numeric or string. **Numeric expressions** consist of one or more numeric constants, numeric variables and numeric function references, all of which are separated from each other by parentheses and arithmetic operators. **String expressions** consist of one or more string constants, string variables and string function references separated by the **concatenation operator** (+).

Formation of Numeric Expressions

The definition of a numeric expression dictates the manner in which a numeric expression is to be validly formed. For example, it may be perfectly clear to you that the following *invalid* statement has been formed to assign A twice the value of B.

Invalid   `100 LET A = 2B`

However, the computer will reject the statement because a constant and a variable witin the same expression must be separated by an arithmetic operator. The statement can validly be written as

```
100 LET A = 2 * B
```

Evaluation of Numeric Expressions

Formation of complex expressions involving several arithmetic operations can sometimes create problems. For example, consider the statement:

```
100 LET A = 8/4/2
```

Does this assign a value of 1 or 4 to A? The answer depends on how the BASIC system evaluates the expression. If it completes the operation 8/4 first and only then 2/2, the expression yields the value 1. If the system completes the second operation, 4/2, first and only then 8/2, it yields 4.

In BASIC the **evaluation** of an expression—the assigning of a value to that expression—follows the normal algebraic rules, which are given by the following rule:

> **Precedence Rule 1:** Unless parentheses dictate otherwise, reading from left to right in a numeric expression, all exponentiations are performed first, then all multiplications and/or divisions, and finally all additions and/or subtractions.

This order of operations is sometimes called the **rules of precedence,** or the **hierarchy of operations.** The meaning of these rules can be made clear with some examples.

For example, the expression $18/3 \wedge 2 + 4 * 2$ is evaluated as follows (Recall from Table 2.1 that $3 \wedge 2 = 3^2$).

$$
\begin{aligned}
18/3 \wedge 2 + 4 * 2 &= 18/9 + 4 * 2 \\
&= 2 \quad + 4 * 2 \\
&= 2 \quad + 8 \\
&= 10
\end{aligned}
$$

If you had trouble following the logic behind this evaluation, use the following technique. Whenever a numeric expression is to be evaluated, "look" or "scan" from *left* to *right* three different times applying the Precedence Rule 1.

The expression below yields the value of -2.73, as follows:

$$
\begin{aligned}
2 - 3 * 4/5 \wedge 2 + 5/4 * 3 - 2 \wedge 3 &= 2 - 3 * 4/25 + 5/4 * 3 - 8 \text{ (at end of first scan)} \\
&= 2 - 0.48 + 3.75 - 8 \text{ (at end of second scan)} \\
&= -2.73 \text{ (at end of third scan)}
\end{aligned}
$$

The Effect of Parentheses in the Evaluation of Numeric Expressions

Parentheses may be used to change the order of operations. In BASIC, parentheses are normally used to avoid ambiguity and to group terms in a numeric expression; they do *not* imply multiplication. The order in which the operations in an expression containing parentheses are evaluated is given in the following rule:

> **Precedence Rule 2:** When parentheses are inserted into an expression, the part of the expression within the parentheses is evaluated first and then the remaining expression is evaluated according to Precedence Rule 1.

If the first example contained parentheses, as $(18/3) \wedge 2 + 4 * 2$ does, then it would be evaluated in the following manner:

$$
\begin{aligned}
(18/3) \wedge 2 + 4 * 2 &= 6 \wedge 2 + 4 * 2 \\
&= 36 + 4 * 2 \\
&= 36 + 8 \\
&= 44
\end{aligned}
$$

A rule of thumb for utilizing parentheses in your first programs is: *use parentheses freely when in doubt as to the formation and evaluation of a numeric expression.* For example, if you wish to have the computer divide $8 * D$ by $3 \wedge P$, the expression may correctly be written as $8 * D/3 \wedge P$, but you may also write it as $(8 * D)/(3 \wedge P)$ and feel more certain of the result.

For more complex expressions, BASIC allows parentheses to be contained within other parentheses. When this occurs, the parentheses are said to be **nested.** In this case the BASIC system evaluates the innermost parenthetical expression first and then goes on to the outermost. Thus, $18/3 \wedge 2 + (3 * (2 + 5))$ would be broken down in the following manner:

$$
\begin{aligned}
18/3 \wedge 2 + (3 * (2 + 5)) &= 18/3 \wedge 2 + (3 * 7) \\
&= 18/3 \wedge 2 + 21 \\
&= 18/9 + 21 \\
&= 2 + 21 \\
&= 23
\end{aligned}
$$

String Expressions

The ability to process strings of characters is an essential part of any programming language that is to be used for business applications. Letters, words, names, and a combination of letters and numbers can play an important role in generating readable reports and easing communication between non-data-processing personnel and the computer.

In BASIC, string expressions include string constants, string variables, string function references and a combination of the three separated by the concatenation operator ($+$). Consider the following program:

```
100 REM PROGRAM 3.6
110 REM EXAMPLES OF STRING EXPRESSIONS
120 REM *****************************
130 INPUT "AREA CODE"; A$
140 INPUT "LOCAL NUMBER"; T$
150 LET B$ = A$
160 LET C$ = "TELEPHONE NUMBER "
170 LET D$ = A$ + "-" + T$
180 PRINT
190 PRINT C$; D$
200 PRINT "AREA CODE "; B$
210 END

RUN

AREA CODE? 219
LOCAL NUMBER? 844-0520

TELEPHONE NUMBER 219-844-0520
AREA CODE 219
```

Program 3.6

Examples of string expressions in Program 3.6 include:

1. The string variable A$ in line 150, which is assigned to B$.
2. The string TELEPHONE NUMBER in line 160, which is assigned to C$.
3. The expression A$ + "−" + T$ in line 170, which is assigned to D$.

In line 170 the plus sign is the concatenation operator. When strings are concatenated, the resultant expression combines the value of each term in the order they are found in the expression to yield a single string. The value of D$, which is displayed by line 190, is illustrated in the output results of Program 3.6.

Note that in BASIC the operator ($+$) has two meanings. When it appears in a string expression, it represents concatenation. When it appears in a numeric expression, it represents addition.

Use of LEFT$, LEN, MID$ and RIGHT$ **String Functions**

Although concatenation is the only valid string operation, most BASIC systems include functions that allow for additional string manipulation. The string functions most commonly found in BASIC systems are presented in Table 3.4.

TABLE 3.4   Some Common String Functions

Function	Function Value
LEFT$ (X$, N)	Extracts the leftmost N characters of the string argument X$
LEN (X$)	Returns the length of the string argument X$
MID$ (X$, P, N)	Extracts N characters of the string argument X$ beginning at P
RIGHT$ (X$, N)	Extracts the rightmost N character of the string argument X$

Where X$ is a string expression, and N and P are numeric expressions.

The following program illustrates the use of the functions found in Table 3.4.

Program 3.7

```
100 REM PROGRAM 3.7
110 REM EXAMPLE OF REFERENCING STRING FUNCTIONS
120 REM ****************************************
130 REM ****REQUEST TELEPHONE NUMBER*****
140 INPUT "COMPLETE TELEPHONE NUMBER"; T$
150 LET A$ = LEFT$(T$, 3)
160 LET P$ = MID$(T$, 5, 3)
170 LET N$ = RIGHT$(T$, 4)
180 LET N = LEN(T$)
190 PRINT
200 PRINT "THE AREA CODE IS "; A$
210 PRINT "THE PREFIX NUMBER IS "; P$
220 PRINT "THE LAST FOUR DIGITS ARE "; N$
230 PRINT "THE NUMBER OF CHARACTERS IN "; T$; " IS"; N
240 END

RUN

COMPLETE TELEPHONE NUMBER? 219-844-0520

THE AREA CODE IS 219
THE PREFIX NUMBER IS 844
THE LAST FOUR DIGITS ARE 0520
THE NUMBER OF CHARACTERS IN 219-844-0520 IS 12
```

In Program 3.7, the function LEFT$ in line 150 assigns the three leftmost characters of T$ to A$. A$ is assigned the string 219. In line 160, the MID$ function assigns 3 characters beginning with the fifth character 8 in T$ to P$. P$ is assigned the string 844. In line 170, the function RIGHT$ assigns the last four characters of T$ to N$. N$ is assigned the string 0520. Finally, in line 180, the numeric variable N is assigned a value equal to the number of characters in T$. N is assigned the numeric value 12.

**3.5
BASIC
SELF-TEST
EXERCISES**

1. Which of the following are invalid constants if each appeared exactly as written in a valid location in a BASIC statement?

   a. 6.4
   b. 7/8
   c. +.319
   d. 0

   e. 1,976
   f. 1792164
   g. 9.613
   h. $1.75

   i. 1E1
   j. 987.6E−25

2. Write the number 8,962,482,176 to the greatest possible accuracy using a precision of 7 significant digits. What is the error in this value?
3. Consider the valid programs below. What is displayed if each is executed?

a.
```
100 REM EXERCISE 3.3A
110 LET A = 2.5
120 LET B = 4 * A/2 * A + 5
130 PRINT B
140 LET B = 4 * A/(2 * A + 5)
150 PRINT B
160 LET A = -A
170 PRINT A
180 LET A = -A
190 PRINT A
200 END
```

c.
```
100 REM EXERCISE 3.3C
110 LET Y = 50
120 LET A$ = "INDIANA"
130 LET B = 4 * Y * (Y - 10)
140 LET C = (B - Y + 5 * Y)/(Y - 39 + B/2000)
150 LET B$ = A$
160 PRINT Y
170 PRINT B
180 PRINT C
190 PRINT B$
200 END
```

b.
```
100 REM EXERCISE 3.3B
110 LET E = 0
120 LET E = E + 1
130 PRINT E
140 LET E = E + 1
150 PRINT E
160 LET E = E + 1
170 PRINT E
180 LET E = E - 3
190 PRINT E
200 END
```

d.
```
100 REM EXERCISE 3.3D
110 LET A$ = "A"
120 LET T$ = "T"
130 LET B$ = "B"
140 LET W$ = B$ + A$ + T$
150 PRINT W$
160 LET W$ = T$ + A$ + B$
170 PRINT W$
180 END
```

4. Calculate the numeric value for each of the following valid numeric expressions if $X = 2$, $Y = 3$ and $Z = 6$.
   a. $X + Y \wedge 2$
   b. $Z/Y/X$
   c. $12/(3 + Z) - X$
   d. $X \wedge Y \wedge Z$
   e. $X * Y + 2.5 * X + Z$
   f. $(X \wedge (2 + Y)) \wedge 2 + Z \wedge (2 \wedge 2)$
5. Repeat Exercise 4 for the case of $X = 4$, $Y = 6$, $Z = 2$.
6. Write a valid LET statement for each of the following algebraic statements.
   a. $q = (d + e)^{1/3}$
   b. $d = (A^2)^{3.2}$
   c. $b = \dfrac{20}{6 - S}$
   d. $Y = a_1 x + a_2 x^2 + a_3 x^3 + a_4 x^4$
   e. $e = X + \dfrac{X}{X - Y}$
   f. $S = 19.2 X^3$
   g. $V = 100 - (2/3)^{100-B}$
   h. $t = \sqrt{76,234/(2.37 + D)}$
   i. $V = 0.12340005 M - \left[\dfrac{(0.123458)^3}{M - N} \right]$
   j. $Q = \dfrac{(F - M1000)^{2B}}{4M} - \dfrac{1}{E}$
7. Which arithmetic operation is performed first in the following numeric expressions?
   a. $9/5 * 6$
   b. $X - Y + A$
   c. $3 * (A + 8)$
   d. $(X * (2 + Y)) \wedge 2 + Z \wedge (2 \wedge 2)$
   e. $X/Y/Z$
   f. $(B \wedge 2 - 4 * A * C)/(2 * A)$
8. Which of the following are invalid LET statements?
   a. `100 LET X = 9/B(A + C)`
   b. `200 LET X + 5 = Y`
   c. `0 LET X = 17`
   d. `750 LET P = 4 * 3-+6`
   e. `260 LET US = GO`
   f. `140 LET X = -X * (((1 + R)^2 - N)^2 + (2 + X)`
   g. `300 GET Q = R^S^Q^T`
   h. `400 LET P = +4`
   i. `500 LET G = 4(-2 + A)`
   j. `120 LET X = X + 1`
9. Given the LET statement:

   `100 LET B$ = "BASIC IS NOT EASY"`

   write a LET statement that will assign A$ the following substrings:
   a. BASIC
   b. IS NOT
   c. EASY
   d. BASIC IS EASY
10. If necessary, insert parentheses so that each numeric expression results in the value indicated.
    a. $8/2 + 2 + 12 \longrightarrow 14$
    b. $8 \wedge 2 - 1 \longrightarrow 8$
    c. $3/2 + 0.5 + 3 \wedge 1 \longrightarrow 5$
    d. $1 \wedge 2 + 1 * 2 * 3/4 - 3/2 \longrightarrow 0$
    e. $12 - 2 - 3 - 1 - 4 \longrightarrow 10$
    f. $7 * 3 + 4 \wedge 2 - 3/13 \longrightarrow 28$
    g. $3 * 2 - 3 * 4 * 2 + 3 \longrightarrow -60$
    h. $3 * 6 - 3 + 2 + 6 * 4 - 4/2 \wedge 1 \longrightarrow 33$

3.6
BASIC
PROGRAMMING
PROBLEMS
1:
**Computing the
Two-Week Dow-Jones
Average**

Purpose: To become familiar with entering data items in response to an INPUT statement and calculating an average.

Problem: Construct a program to input the last 10 Dow-Jones closings, compute the average from these ten numbers and print the average.

Input Data: Use the following sample data:

Week 1 Closings: 1285.45, 1276.45, 1260.50, 1263.80, 1267.95
Week 2 Closings: 1269.34, 1275.29, 1280.34, 1287.46, 1290.58

Output Results: The following results are displayed:

```
FIRST WEEK FIVE CLOSINGS
? 1285.45, 1276.45, 1260.50, 1263.80, 1267.95
SECOND WEEK FIVE CLOSINGS
? 1269.34, 1275.29, 1280.34, 1287.46, 1290.58

THE TWO WEEK DOW-JONES AVERAGE IS 1275.72
```

2:
**Present Value of
an Annuity Fund**

Purpose: To become familiar with the hierarchy of operations in a complex LET statement.

Problem: The present value of an annuity fund is defined as the amount of money required on hand to pay out a given sum of money (for example, to a beneficiary) over a period of years where interest is earned on the amount left after each payment. The following formula determines the present value of an annuity:

$$A = R \left[\frac{1 - \left(1 + \frac{J}{M}\right)^{-MN}}{P\left[\left(1 + \frac{J}{M}\right)^{M/P} - 1\right]} \right]$$

where

A = Present value of the annuity   M = Conversions per year
R = Payment per year   N = Duration of payments in years
P = Number of payments per year   J = Normal interest rate

Write a program that determines the amount of money to be placed in an annuity fund for a beneficiary to receive $300 a month for 15 years. An interest rate of 11.85% is earned on the annuity fund converted quarterly.

Input Data: Use the following sample data in response to the appropriate INPUT statements.

Payment per year   — $3600   Conversion per year — 4
Number of payments per year — 12   Interest   — 11.85%
Duration of payments   — 15 years

Output Results: The following results are displayed:

```
WHAT IS:
        THE PAYMENT PER YEAR? 3600
        NUMBER OF PAYMENTS PER YEAR? 12
        DURATION OF PAYMENTS? 15
        CONVERSIONS PER YEAR? 4
        INTEREST RATE? 11.85

THE PRESENT VALUE OF THE ANNUITY IS $ 25355.67
```

Purpose: To become familiar with executing a program a multiple number of times.

Problem: Modify Payroll Problem I in Problem 2, Chapter 2, to accept by means of INPUT statements an employee number, number of dependents, hourly rate of pay and hours worked during a biweekly pay period. Use the following formulas to compute the gross pay, federal withholding tax and net pay:

1.   Gross pay = hours worked × hourly rate of pay
2.   Federal witholding tax = 0.2 × (gross pay − dependents × 38.46)
3.   Net pay = gross pay − federal withholding tax

Execute the program for each employee described under Input Data.

Input Data: Use the following sample data:

Employee Number	Number of Dependents	Hourly Rate of Pay	Hours Worked
123	2	$12.50	80
124	1	8.00	100
125	1	13.00	80
126	2	4.50	20

Output Results: The following results are displayed for employee number 123:

```
EMPLOYEE NUMBER? 123
NUMBER OF DEPENDENTS? 2
HOURLY RATE OF PAY? 12.50
HOURS WORKED? 80

GROSS PAY=================> 1000
FEDERAL WITHHOLDING TAX===> 184.62
NET PAY===================> 815.38
```

MORE ON INPUT/OUTPUT PROCESSING 4

The programs discussed in the previous chapters are classified as straight-line coding programs. Up to this point, therefore, we have not utilized the complete power of the computer. We have merely used the computer to function essentially as a high-speed calculator. However, the power of a computer is derived both from its speed and its ability to deviate from sequential execution. One of the purposes of this chapter is to introduce the GOTO statement, which allows the computer to **branch** backward or forward to other statements in a program.

In this chapter we will also present a technique for integrating data into a program through the use of the READ and DATA statements. The READ and DATA statements are usually preferred over the INPUT statement when a program has to process large amounts of data that are to be a permanent part of the program itself.

The third topic to be discussed in this chapter is the generation of tabular reports. To write programs that can produce meaningful information in an easily readable and understandable form, you need to know more about the PRINT statement and the PRINT USING statement, a statement that gives you even more control over the output than the PRINT statement does.

BASIC at Work

Determining the Sale Price

Program 4.1 computes the discount amount and sale price for each of a series of products. The discount amount is determined from the following formula:

$$D = \frac{R}{100} \times P$$

where:

D = discount amount
R = discount rate in percent
P = original price

The sale price S is determined from the following formula:

$$S = P - D$$

The product data includes a product identification number, original price and discount rate, as follows:

Product Number	Original Price	Discount Rate in Percent
112841A	$115.00	14
213981B	100.00	17
332121A	98.00	13
586192X	88.00	12
714121Y	43.00	8

The flowchart corresponding to Program 4.1 is given in Figure 4.1, on page 48. Line numbers have been placed on the top left-hand corner of the symbols to illustrate the relationship between the flowchart and the program.

```
100 REM PROGRAM 4.1
110 REM DETERMINING THE SALE PRICE
120 REM N$ = PRODUCT NO.    P = ORIGINAL PRICE
130 REM R  = DISCOUNT RATE  D = DISCOUNT AMOUNT
140 REM S  = SALES PRICE
150 REM *****************************************
160 PRINT 'PRODUCT', 'ORIGINAL', 'DISCOUNT', 'DISCOUNT', 'SALE'
170 PRINT 'NUMBER', 'PRICE', 'RATE IN %', 'AMOUNT', 'PRICE'
180 REM ***********PROCESS A RECORD***********
190 READ N$, P, R
200 REM DETERMINE THE DISCOUNT AMOUNT AND SALE PRICE
210 LET D = R/100 * P
220 LET S = P - D
230 PRINT N$, P, R, D, S
240 GOTO 190
250 REM *************DATA FOLLOWS***************
260 DATA 112841A, 115, 14
270 DATA 213981B, 100, 17
280 DATA 332121A, 98, 13
290 DATA 586192X, 88, 12
300 DATA 714121Y, 43, 8
310 END
```

Loop ↓ (lines 190–240)

Program 4.1

```
RUN

PRODUCT        ORIGINAL       DISCOUNT       DISCOUNT       SALE
NUMBER         PRICE          RATE IN %      AMOUNT         PRICE
112841A        115            14             16.1           98.9
213981B        100            17             17             83
332121A        98             13             12.74          85.26
586192X        88             12             10.56          77.44
714121Y        43             8              3.44           39.56

---OUT OF DATA LINE 190
```

Lines 100 through 150 of Program 4.1 are remark lines, which simply give information about the program to the reader. Lines 160 and 170 are PRINT statements which display the column headings. Note that the first two PRINT statements contain a comma after each string constant or variable. Using a comma separator in PRINT statements, instead of the semicolon separator used in previous programs, causes the system to produce output that is automatically positioned in a tabular format.

Line 190 is a READ statement which instructs the computer to assign values to N$, P, and R from the sequence of data created from DATA statements that begin at line 260. Note that this data is part of Program 4.1 itself.

Lines 210 and 220 are LET statements which assign values to the variables D and S. Line 230 causes the display of the output in tabular format.

Lines 190 through 240 establish a **loop**. In looping, a control statement, like that represented by line 240, is used to return control to the first of a series of

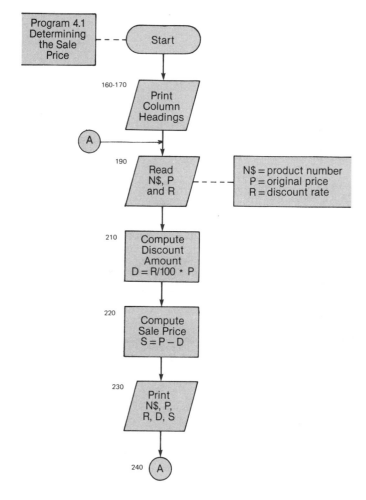

Figure 4.1   **Flowchart for Program 4.1.**

statements that are executed repeatedly until a specified condition is met or satisfied. One execution of the loop is called a **pass.**

4.1 THE UNCONDITIONAL GOTO STATEMENT

By now the potential of the GOTO statement should be apparent. In Program 4.1, after the first three values in line 260 are read by the READ statement and the values of the discount amount and sales price are computed and displayed along with the product number N$, the assigned price P and the discount rate R, the system executes the GOTO 190 statement represented by line 240. This in turn causes line 190, the READ statement, to be executed next.

As a result, the system reads in the next three values represented by line 270. These newly read values for N$, P, and R therefore replace the three original values in the main storage unit. Next, the system calculates values for D and S, displays them along with the values of N$, P and R, and executes the GOTO 190 statement for the second time, which again transfers control back to line number 190. The system continues this looping operation until all the values in the DATA statements have been read by the READ statement and all the computations and output have been completed.

Lines 260 through 300 contain data for only five products. When the system branches back to the READ statement for the sixth time, there are no data items left in the DATA statements to be assigned to the three variables in the READ statement. Therefore, the program terminates execution after printing a diagnostic message regarding the unavailability of additional data, like ---OUT OF DATA LINE 190.

In Program 4.1 a discount amount and sale price can be calculated for almost an unlimited number of products by adding more DATA statements after line 300. Each pass through the loop, lines 190 through 240, produces the desired product information from the data processed. The general form of the unconditional GOTO statement is given in Table 4.1.

TABLE 4.1 The GOTO Statement

General Forms:	GOTO line number
Purpose:	Causes the execution of the program to be continued starting at the specified line number
Examples:	500 GOTO 300
	700 GOTO 900
	800 GOTO 100

Upon execution, the GOTO statement interrupts the sequential execution of statements in a program by transferring control to a line number in that same program. For this reason, the GOTO statement is sometimes called a **transfer statement** or an **unconditional branch statement.**

There are several important points to watch for in the application of the GOTO statement. For example, if Program 4.1 is rewritten by changing the READ statement to

```
188 READ N$, P, R
```

then the GOTO statement in line 240 must be changed to

```
240 GOTO 188
```

A GOTO statement can transfer control to any statement in a BASIC program, regardless of whether the statement has a higher or lower line number than the GOTO statement itself. When control transfers to a statement with a higher line number, the intervening statements skipped will not be executed. Additional statements must be included in the program to execute the statements skipped and also to prevent the occurrence of never-ending loops.

4.2 THE READ, DATA AND RESTORE STATEMENTS

In Section 4.1 the READ and DATA statements were briefly introduced. This section will illustrate the rules of the READ, DATA and RESTORE statements and will give further examples of their use, as well as their limitations.

The DATA Statement

The DATA statement provides for the creation of a sequence of data items for use by the READ statement. The general form of the DATA statement and some examples are given in Table 4.2.

TABLE 4.2   **The** DATA **Statement**

General Form:	DATA data item, . . . , data item
	where each data item is either a numeric constant or a string constant.
Purpose:	Provides for the creation of a sequence of data items for use by the READ statement

Examples (with READ statements):

```
110 DATA 2, -3.14, 0.025, -95
120 READ A, B, C, D2

------------------------------------

130 DATA 0.24E33, 0, -2.5E-12
140 READ E, F, G(J)

------------------------------------

150 DATA 15, CENTS, ",", "YES", "2 + 7", NO, 2.2, "15.47"
160 READ H(3), A$, B$, C$, D$, E$, I, F$
```

The DATA statement consists of the keyword DATA followed by a list of data items separated by mandatory commas. The data items may be numeric or string and formulated according to the following rules:

> DATA **Rule 1:** Numeric data items placed in a DATA statement must be formulated as numeric constants.

> DATA **Rule 2:** String data items placed in a DATA statement may be formulated with or without surrounding quotation marks, provided the string contains no trailing or leading blanks or embedded commas or colons. If the string contains a trailing or leading blank or an embedded comma or colon, it must be surrounded with quotation marks.

Data items from all DATA statements in a program are collected in main storage into a single **data sequence holding area.** The order in which the data items appear among all DATA statements determines the order of the data items in the single data sequence. In other words, the ordering of the data items is based on:

1. The ascending line numbers of the DATA statements
2. The order from left to right of the data items within each DATA statement

The DATA statement, like the REM statement, is a **non-executable statement**; that is, if the execution of a program reaches a line containing a DATA statement, it proceeds to the next line with no other effect.

> DATA **Rule 3:** The DATA statement may be located anywhere before the end line in a program.

The DATA statement permits a great deal of leeway in its placement in the program. Some BASIC programmers prefer to place all of the program's DATA statements first. Others prefer to place the DATA statement immediately after the first READ statement that refers to it, so that it is easier to see the connection between the READ statement and the DATA statement. We prefer to place all the program's DATA statements just before the end line, as shown in Program 4.1.

The READ Statement

The READ statement provides for the assignment of values to variables from a sequence of data items created from DATA statements. The general form of the READ statement is given in Table 4.3. The READ statement consists of the keyword READ followed by a list of variables separated by mandatory commas. The variables may be numeric or string variables.

TABLE 4.3   The READ Statement

General Form:	READ variable, . . . , variable
	where each variable is either a numeric variable or a string variable.
Purpose:	Provides for the assignment of values to variables from a sequence of data items created from DATA statements.
Examples: (with DATA statements): See Table 4.2.	

The READ statement causes the variables in its list to be assigned specific values, in order, from the data sequence formed by all of the DATA statements. In order to visualize the relationship between the READ statement and its associated DATA statement, you may think of a **pointer** associated with the data sequence holding area. When a program is first executed, this pointer points to the first data item in the data sequence. Each time a READ statement is executed, the variables in the list are assigned specific values from the data sequence, beginning with the data item indicated by the pointer; then the pointer is advanced one value per variable.

Program 4.2, on page 52, illustrates the data sequence holding area and pointer for a program containing multiple READ and multiple DATA statements. The pointer initally points to the location of 565.33 in the holding area. When line 150 is executed, the value of 565.33 is assigned to the variable M, the pointer is advanced to the location of the next value, 356.45, which is assigned to the variable T, and the pointer is advanced to the location of the next value, 478.56. When line 160 is executed, the variable W is assigned the value of 478.56, T1 the value of 756.23, and F the value of 342.23.

As this assignment occurs, the pointer advances one value per variable to point to a location beyond the data used, which is recognized by the system as the end of the data sequence holding area. In Program 4.2, the system is unable to calculate A correctly until it has the value of M, T, W, T1 and F. The READ statement should occur somewhere *before* the LET statement in the program. This example can be generalized to give the following:

> READ **Rule 1:** Every variable appearing in the program whose value is directly obtained by a READ should be listed in a READ statement before it is used elsewhere in the program.

While the placement of the DATA statements in a program is immaterial, the placement of the READ statement is important. Furthermore, more than one DATA statement may be used to satisfy one READ statement and more than one READ statement may be satisfied from one DATA statement.

> READ **Rule 2:** A program containing a READ statement must also have at least one DATA statement with values to be assigned to the variables listed in the READ statement.

```
100 REM PROGRAM 4.2
110 REM DETERMINING THE AVERAGE DAILY SALES
120 REM WITH MULTIPLE READ AND
130 REM MULTIPLE DATA STATEMENTS
140 REM ************************************
150 READ M, T
160 READ W, T1, F
170 LET A = (M + T + W + T1 + F)/5
180 PRINT M, T
190 PRINT W, T1, F
200 PRINT A
210 REM ***********DATA FOLLOWS***********
220 DATA 565.33, 356.45, 478.56
230 DATA 756.23, 342.23
240 END
```

Program 4.2

```
RUN

565.33      356.45
478.56      756.23      342.23
499.76
```

Data Sequence Holding Area

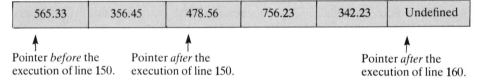

| 565.33 | 356.45 | 478.56 | 756.23 | 342.23 | Undefined |

Pointer *before* the execution of line 150.   Pointer *after* the execution of line 150.   Pointer *after* the execution of line 160.

Finally, the type of data item in the data sequence must correspond to the type of variable to which it is to be assigned.

> READ **Rule 3:** Numeric variables in READ statements require numeric constants as data items in DATA statements, and string variables require quoted strings or unquoted strings as data.

The RESTORE Statement

Usually data items from a DATA statement are processed by a READ statement only once. If you want the system to read these same data items later, you must use the RESTORE statement to restore the data.

The RESTORE statement allows the data in a given program to be reread as often as desired by other READ statements. The general form of the RESTORE statement is given with an example in Table 4.4. The RESTORE statement consists simply of the keyword RESTORE.

TABLE 4.4   The RESTORE Statement

General Forms:	RESTORE
Purpose:	Allows the data in the program to be reread.
Example:	500 RESTORE
Note:	On the IBM PC, Macintosh and in general with Microsoft BASIC, a line number may optionally follow the keyword RESTORE. If a line number is present, the data pointer is reset to the first data item in the DATA statement with that line number.

The RESTORE statement causes the pointer to be moved back to the beginning of the data sequence holding area. This is done so that the next READ statement executed will read the data from the beginning of the sequence once again.

The RESTORE statement is generally used when it is necessary to perform several types of computations on the same data items.

The execution of the PRINT statement generates a string of characters for transmission to an external device like a video display device. The PRINT statement is commonly used to display the results from computations, to display headings and labeled information, and to plot points on a graph. In addition, the PRINT statement allows you to control the spacing and the format of the desired output.

The general form of the PRINT statement is given with examples in Table 4.5. The PRINT statement consists of the keyword PRINT. It may also have an optional list of **print items** separated by mandatory commas and/or semicolons. The print items may be numeric or string constants, variables, expressions, or null items.

TABLE 4.5   The PRINT **Statement**

General Form:	PRINT item pm item pm . . . pm item where each item is a constant, variable, expression, function reference or null and where each punctuation mark pm is a comma or semicolon.
Purpose:	Provides for the generation of labeled and unlabeled output or of output in a consistent tabular format from the program to an external device.
Examples:	100 PRINT 110 PRINT X 120 PRINT A, B, C 130 PRINT A; B; C; D, E, F 140 PRINT H, I; J(2); A$, B$ 150 PRINT "THE ANSWER IS"; M 160 PRINT "X = "; X, "Y = "; Y, N 170 PRINT (M + N)/4,,, P; Q, B * B - 4 * A * C 180 PRINT TAB(5); A$; TAB(40); B$; "END"

Print Zones and Print Positions

The most common use of the PRINT statement is to output values defined earlier in a program. Every sample program presented thus far has included a PRINT statement. Listing several variables separated by commas within a PRINT statement, like this line

```
230 PRINT N$, P, R, D, S
```

in Program 4.1, causes the values of N$, P, R, D and S to be displayed on a *single* line. BASIC displays the values of N$, P, R, D and S into **print zones.** On most computer systems, there are five print zones per line. Each print zone has 14 positions, for a total of 70 positions per line. The print positions are numbered consecutively from the left, starting with position one, as shown in Figure 4.2.

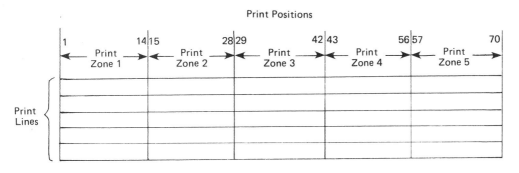

Figure 4.2   The print line is divided into five print zones.

Representation of Numeric Output

Numeric constants, variables, expressions, and function references are evaluated to produce a string of characters consisting of:

1. a sign
2. the decimal representation of the number
3. a trailing space

The sign is a leading space if the number is positive or a leading minus sign if the number is negative.*

Use of the Comma Separator

Punctuation marks like the comma and the semicolon are placed between print items. In this section the role of the comma, or **comma separator**, is examined. As illustrated in Program 4.3 of Figure 4.3, the comma separator allows you to produce output that is automatically positioned in a tabular format determined by the print zones. Each PRINT statement executed displays one line of information,

1. *Unless* the number of print zones required by the PRINT statement exceeds 5 (see Figure 4.3, line 270).
2. *Unless* the PRINT statement ends with a punctuation mark like a comma or semicolon (see Figure 4.3, lines 280 and 290).

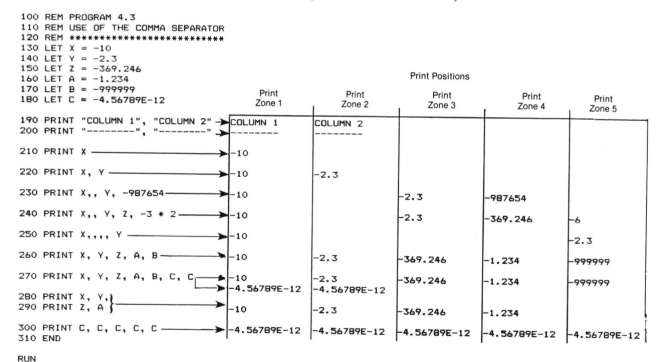

RUN

Figure 4.3   **The effect of commas with numeric and string expressions in** PRINT **statements.**

*The Apple computer does not display a leading space when the number is positive, nor does it display a trailing space.

Use of the Semicolon Separator

In this section, the role of the **semicolon separator** in the PRINT statement is examined.* The semicolon does not allow you to tab to a fixed print position as the comma does. The semicolon enables you to display more than 5 items on a line.

Some possible formats for the representation of string and numeric expressions like constants and variables are shown by Program 4.4 in Figure 4.4. Each numeric representation is preceded by a leading sign and followed by a trailing space. Hence, the statement

```
190 PRINT A; B; C; D; E
```

can be used to generate numeric output in a compressed form without having the numeric representations run into one another.

```
100 REM PROGRAM 4.4
110 REM USE OF THE SEMICOLON SEPARATOR
120 REM ****************************
130 LET A = -10
140 LET B = -20
150 LET C = -30
160 LET D = -40
170 LET E = -50
180 PRINT "THE"; "VALUE"; "OF E IS "; E
190 PRINT A; B; C; D; E
200 PRINT A, B; C; D, E
210 PRINT A; B; C;
220 PRINT D; E
230 END
```

RUN

Print Zone 1	Print Zone 2	Print Zone 3
THEVALUEOF E IS -50		
-10 -20 -30 -40 -50		
-10	-20 -30 -40	-50
-10 -20 -30 -40 -50		

Figure 4.4   **The effect of semicolons with numeric and string expressions in PRINT statements.**

When the semicolon is used to separate strings, no trailing space occurs between the strings in the output, as shown by line 180. Line 190, which contains semicolon separators, compresses the values of A, B, C, D, and E starting at print position 1. Comma and semicolon separators can be mixed in a PRINT statement, as shown by line 200. If a PRINT statement ends with a semicolon, as in line 210, the first item in the next PRINT statement (220) displays on the same line in compressed form.

The use of semicolons in PRINT statements may prevent the output from lining up in neat, vertical columns. If you want the output aligned, use commas between the items in the PRINT statements.

Use of the TAB Function

Thus far, PRINT statements have contained the comma and semicolon as separators among numeric and string expressions in order to display the values of these expres-

*With Microsoft BASIC, typing one or more spaces has the same effect as typing a semicolon.

sions in a readable format with correct spacing. Compact and exact spacing of output results can also be achieved by the use of the TAB function.

The TAB function is used in PRINT statements to specify the exact print positions for the various output results on a given line. In effect, the TAB function allows you to move the cursor to a specified position. The positions are numbered from left to right, usually starting with position one. The TAB function is similar to the tabulator key on a typewriter.

The form of the TAB function is:

TAB (numeric expression)

where the numeric expression, the argument, may be a numeric constant, variable, expression, or function reference. The value of the argument determines the position on the line of the next character to be displayed, relative to the starting position of the line.

Consider the following PRINT statement:

```
160 PRINT TAB(25); "ABC COMPANY"
```

The function TAB(25) causes the system to tab to print position 25 and display the string ABC COMPANY in positions 25 to 35.

Multiple TAB functions are allowed in a PRINT statement. For example:

```
190 PRINT TAB(5); "EMP NO"; TAB(21); "RATE"; TAB(36); "HOURS"
```

displays the strings EMP NO, beginning at print position 5, RATE beginning at print position 21, and HOURS beginning at print position 36, displaying three centered column headings.

The TAB function can also be used in PRINT statements for graphic purposes. BASIC Self-Test Exercises 9 and 10 are designed to illustrate this point.

Calculations Within the PRINT Statement

BASIC systems permit calculations to be made within the PRINT statement. For instance, the sum, difference, product, quotient, and exponentiation of two numbers, like 2 and 4, may be made in the conventional way by using LET statements or by using the PRINT statement, as is done in Program 4.5.

Program 4.5

```
100 REM PROGRAM 4.5
110 REM CALCULATIONS WITHIN THE PRINT STATEMENT
120 REM ****************************************
130 PRINT 2 + 4; 2 - 4; 2 * 4; 2/4; 2^4
140 END

RUN

 6 -2  8  .5  16
```

Using the Immediate Mode in BASIC

Many BASIC systems have an **immediate mode** or a **calculator mode** of operation which permits the computer to appear to the user as a powerful desk calculator. You are in the immediate mode when you type a BASIC statement without a line number. In this mode, BASIC statements like the PRINT statement can be executed individually without being a part of a program. You merely enter the keyword PRINT followed by any numeric expression. As soon as you press the Enter key, the BASIC system *immediately* computes and displays the value of the expression.

The following example of calculating a complex expression uses the immediate mode of a BASIC system:

```
PRINT (2 - 3 * 4/5)^2 + 5/(4 * 3 - 2^3)
```

The value displayed is 1.41.

BASIC also allows you to use the immediate mode to debug programs. If a fatal error occurs in a program, the PRINT statement can be used to display the values of variables used in that program. Appendix A discusses methods of debugging.

Similar to the PRINT statement, the PRINT USING statement is far more useful in controlling the format of a program's output. In Section 4.3 you were introduced to the comma, semicolon and TAB function for print control purposes. For most applications, these print control methods will suffice. However, when you are confronted with generating readable reports for non-data-processing personnel, more control over the format of the output is essential. Through the use of the PRINT USING statement, you can:

**4.4
THE** PRINT USING
STATEMENT

1. Specify the exact image of a line of output.
2. Force decimal point alignment when printing numeric tables in columns.

TABLE 4.6   The PRINT USING **Statement**

General Form:	PRINT USING string expression; list where the string expression (sometimes called the format field) is either a string constant or a string variable. The format field is an exact image of the line to be displayed. list is a list of items to be displayed in the format specified by the format field.
Purpose:	Provides for controlling exactly the format of a program's output by specifying an image to which that output must conform.
Examples:	150 PRINT USING "THE ANSWER IS #,###.##"; Y 200 PRINT USING "## DIVIDED BY # IS #.#"; A, B, C 200 LET A$ = "THE TOTAL IS $$,###.##-" 210 PRINT USING A$; T 350 LET C$ = "**,###.##" 360 PRINT USING C$; X; 900 PRINT USING "\ \"; Q$ 950 PRINT USING "!, !, \ \"; F$, M$, L$ 999 PRINT USING "#.##^^^^"; S$,
Caution:	The PRINT USING statement is not available on Apple and COMMODORE systems. Large timesharing systems, like the DEC VAX-11, use a comma instead of a semicolon after the string expression in the PRINT USING statement.

3. Control the number of digits displayed for a numeric result.
4. Specify that commas be inserted into a number. (Starting from the units position of a number and progressing toward the left, digits are separated into groups of 3 by a comma).
5. Specify that the sign status of the number be displayed along with the number (+ or blank if positive, − if negative).
6. Assign a fixed or floating dollar sign ($) to the number displayed.
7. Force a numeric result to be displayed in exponential notation.
8. **Left-** or **right-justify** string values in a formatted field (i.e., align the left or rightmost characters, respectively).
9. Specify that only the first character of a string be displayed.
10. Round a value automatically to a specified number of decimal digits.

The general form of the PRINT USING statement is given with examples in Table 4.6.

Declaring the Format of the Output

To control the format of the values displayed, the PRINT USING statement is used in conjunction with a string expression that specifies the desired format of the print line. Consider the two methods shown below.

Method 1:

```
100 REM FORMAT SPECIFIED AS A STRING IN THE PRINT USING STATEMENT
110 PRINT USING "EMPLOYEE ### HAS EARNED $#,###.##"; I, B
```

Method 2:

```
100 REM FORMAT SPECIFIED EARLIER AND ASSIGNED TO A STRING VARIABLE
110 LET A$ = "EMPLOYEE ### HAS EARNED $#,###.##"
      .
      .
      .
170 PRINT USING A$; I, B
```

In Method 1, the string constant following the keywords PRINT USING in line 110 instructs the system to display the values of I and B using the format found in that statement. In Method 2, the string constant has been replaced by the string variable A$ which was assigned the desired format in line 110. If I is equal to 000105 and B is equal to 4563.20, then the results displayed from the execution of line 110 in Method 1 or line 170 in Method 2 are:

```
EMPLOYEE 105 HAS EARNED $4,563.20
```

Format Symbols

Table 4.7 includes the **format symbols** available on most BASIC systems. One or more consecutive format symbols appearing in a string expression is a **descriptor field**, or **field format**.

The Number Sign Symbol

The number sign (#) is the format symbol used to define a numeric field. Grouped number signs indicate exactly how many positions are desired in a numeric result

TABLE 4.7   Format Symbols

Symbol	Function	Examples
#	The number sign defines a numeric field. Grouped number signs indicate how many positions are desired in a numeric result during output. For each # in the field, a digit (0 to 9) or sign is substituted.	# ### ###.## #.#
.	The period is used for decimal point placement. The internal value is automatically aligned with the assigned format.	#.## ###.
,	A comma in the descriptor field places a comma in the output record at that character position unless all digits prior to the comma are zero. In that case, a space is displayed in that character position.	#,### ###,###.##
+ or −	A single plus or minus sign to the right or left in the descriptor field causes the sign status (positive or negative) of the number to be displayed. A plus or minus sign to the left in the descriptor field causes the sign status to be displayed to the left of the first significant nonzero digit.	+## −### #,###.##+ $$#.##−
$	A single dollar sign as the first character in the descriptor field causes a dollar sign to be displayed in that position. Two dollar signs ($$) cause a dollar sign to be placed to the left of the first significant nonzero digit. One of the two dollar signs reserves a position for a digit.	$$,###.## $$##.##− $##.##
**	Two leading asterisks cause the number to be displayed with leading asterisks filling any unused positions to the left in the displayed result. Each asterisk reserves a position for a digit.	**,###.## **###.### **.##−
∧ ∧ ∧ ∧	Four consecutive circumflexes to the right of a set of grouped number signs indicate that the numeric value is to be displayed in exponential notation.	##∧∧∧∧ ##.##∧∧∧∧ #.###∧∧∧∧
&	The ampersand specifies a variable length descriptor field for a string value. The string value is aligned in the descriptor field left-justified. If the string value has more than one character, the ampersand causes expansion to the right to display the entire string value in the output line. (DEC VAX-11 uses the characters 'L in place of the ampersand.)	&
\\	Two backslashes separated by n spaces reserves a fixed number of positions (n + 2) for a string value. The internal string value is aligned left-justified with the assigned format. If the string value is made up of more characters than the number specified in the descriptor field, the rightmost characters in the string value are truncated. If the string value has fewer characters than the number specified in the descriptor field, the result is filled on the right with spaces. (The TRS-80 uses percent signs instead of backslashes.)	\ \ \\
!	An exclamation point specifies a one-character field for a string value. The exclamation point causes the first character of a string value to be displayed. (The DEC VAX-11 uses the characters 'E in place of the exclamation point.)	!

during output. A number sign reserves space for a digit or sign. For example,

$$\#\#$$ indicates two positions in a numeric result
$$\#\#\#\#.\#\#$$ indicates six positions, two of which are decimal fractional positions

It is your responsibility to ensure that enough number signs are in the descriptor field to fit the output results in the prescribed format.

Consider the following example, where A = 10, B = −11, C = 12.75, and D = 4565.

```
100 REM FORMAT SPECIFIED EARLIER AND ASSIGNED TO A STRING VARIABLE
110 LET S$ = " ####        ####       ##       ###"
    .
    .
    .
190 PRINT USING S$; A, B, C, D
```

The results that are displayed from the above sequence are as follows:

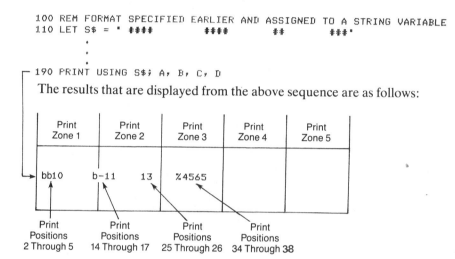

The fields are spaced exactly as indicated in the string expression. The value of A, which is 10, is displayed right-justified as bb10 with leading spaces b. The value of B, which is −11, is displayed with the minus sign positioned next to the first significant digit.

The value of C, 12.75, is automatically rounded to 13 in order to agree with the ## field format. In other words, the value of C is rounded to an integer. The value of D, 4565, is too large to be displayed using the ### field format. Hence, the value is displayed but preceded by a percent sign (%) to indicate that an insufficient number of positions were reserved for this field.

TABLE 4.8   Use of the Decimal Point (Period) in a Descriptor Field

Field Format	Data	Output	Remarks
####.##	217.5	b217.50	Unspecified decimal fraction positions are filled with trailing zeros.
#####.##	40	bbb40.00	
#####.##	23.458	bbb23.46	Decimal fractional digits are rounded.
#####.##	0.027	bbbb0.03	The last leading zero before the decimal point is not suppressed.

The Decimal Point (Period) Symbol

The period (.) in a descriptor field places a decimal point in the output record at that character position in which it appears, and the format of the numeric result is aligned with the position of the decimal point. When number signs (#) precede the decimal point in a descriptor field, any leading zeros appearing in the data are replaced by spaces, except for a single leading zero immediately preceding the decimal point.

When number signs follow the decimal point, unspecified decimal fractional positions are filled with trailing zeros. When the data contains more decimal fractional digits than the descriptor field allows, the decimal fraction is rounded to the limits of the field. Table 4.8 illustrates the use of the decimal point in various descriptor fields.

The Comma Symbol

A comma (,) in a descriptor field places a comma in the output record at that character position unless all digits before the comma are zero. In that case, a space is printed in that character position. Table 4.9 illustrates the use of the comma in various descriptor fields.

TABLE 4.9   Use of the Comma (,) in a Descriptor Field

Field Format	Data	Output	Remarks
#,###	4000	4,000	Comma displayed
###,###	999999	999,999	Comma displayed
#,###.##	30.5	bbb30.50	Space displayed for comma with leading digits blank.

Formatted Character String Output

Descriptor field for string values are defined in terms of the ampersand (&), two backslashes (\\) or the exclamation point (!), rather than the number sign (#). Some systems use other characters to define these functions. Table 4.7 summarizes these three symbols.

TABLE 4.10   Use of the Backslash (\) in a Descriptor Field

Field Format	Number of Spaces Between Backslashes	Data	Output	Remarks
\ \	3	ABCDE	ABCDE	Size of descriptor field and string value the same.
\ \	1	ABCDE	ABC	The last two characters are truncated.
\\	0	ABCDE	AB	The last three characters are truncated.
\ \	6	ABCDE	ABCDEbbb	Three spaces are appended to the right of the string value in the print line.

The exact number of positions to use for displaying a string value can be specified by using two backslashes separated by zero or more spaces. The number of positions in the descriptor field, *including* the two backslashes, indicates how many positions are to be used to display the string value. The string value is aligned in the descriptor field left-justified. If the internal value of the string contains fewer characters than the descriptor field, the string value is filled with spaces on the right in the print line. If the internal value of the string contains more characters than the descriptor field, the string value is truncated on the right. Table 4.10 summarizes the use of the backslash, and Program 4.6 gives examples of its use.

Program 4.6

```
100 REM PROGRAM 4.6
110 REM USE OF TWO BACKSLASHES IN A DESCRIPTOR FIELD
120 REM *********************************************
130 PRINT    "NAME      ADDRESS      CITY-STATE      ZIP CODE"
140 PRINT    "_____    _____    _____    _____"
150 LET A$ = "\         \  \        \  \           \  \       \"
160 READ N$, D$, C$, Z$
170 PRINT USING A$; N$, D$, C$, Z$
180 REM *****************DATA FOLLOWS*****************
190 DATA JONES J, 451 W 173, "GARY, IN", 46327
200 END

RUN

NAME      ADDRESS      CITY-STATE      ZIP CODE
_____    _____    _____    _____
JONES J    451 W 173    GARY, IN         46327
```

Study closely the method used in lines 130 through 150 in Program 4.6 to align the fields. The string constants in line 130 and 140 are purposely started five positions to the right of the keyword PRINT so that the column headings align with the string constant in line 150. This technique will be used throughout this book.

LPRINT and LPRINT USING Statements

While the PRINT and PRINT USING statements display results on your video display device, the LPRINT and LPRINT USING statements print the results on the printer of your personal computer system. Everything that has been presented with respect to the PRINT and PRINT USING statements in this chapter applies to the LPRINT and LPRINT USING statements as well. Obviously, to use these two statements you must have a printer attached to your personal computer.

4.5 BASIC SELF-TEST EXERCISES

1. Consider the valid programs listed below. What is displayed if each is executed?

a.
```
100 REM EXERCISE 4.1A
110 REM MPG COMPARISON
120 READ C$, M, G
130 LET A = M/G
140 PRINT "VEHICLE "; C$
150 PRINT "MILES"; M
160 PRINT "GALLONS"; G
170 PRINT "MPG"; A
180 PRINT
190 GOTO 120
200 REM ****DATA FOLLOWS****
210 DATA A, 1275, 41.7
220 DATA B, 685, 23.2
230 DATA C, 1650, 62.5
240 END
```

b.
```
100 REM EXERCISE 4.1B
110 REM DETERMINING PRODUCTS
120 READ X, Y
130 LET C = X * (Y + 1)
140 PRINT "C IS EQUAL TO C"
150 PRINT "C IS EQUAL TO"; C
160 GOTO 120
170 REM ****DATA FOLLOWS****
180 DATA 3, 4
190 DATA 3
200 DATA 2, 1
210 DATA 7, 8
220 END
```

```
c. 100 REM EXERCISE 4.1C
   110 REM ACCUMULATED LOAN PAYMENTS
   120 LET C = 0
   130 LET A = 0
   140 READ N$
   150 PRINT "NAME "; N$
   160 READ P
   170 LET C = C + 1
   180 LET A = A + P
   190 PRINT
   200 PRINT "WEEK"; C
   210 PRINT "PAYMENT"; P
   220 PRINT "ACCUMULATED PAYMENTS"; A
   230 GOTO 160
   240 REM ****DATA FOLLOWS****
   250 DATA LAURA GOODLY, 120, 50
   260 DATA 30, 60, 500.25
   270 END
```

```
d. 100 REM EXERCISE 4.1D
   110 REM DETERMINING SQUARE FOOTAGE
   120 PRINT "ROOM", "SQ FT", "ACC SQ FT"
   130 LET T = 0
   140 READ R$, L, W
   150 LET A = L * W
   160 LET T = T + A
   170 PRINT R$, A, T
   180 GOTO 140
   190 REM ****DATA FOLLOWS****
   200 DATA KITCHEN, 13, 15
   210 DATA FAMILY ROOM, 25, 17.5
   220 DATA HALL 1, 6, 12.5
   230 DATA HALL 2, 6.5, 8
   240 DATA WASHROOM, 8, 9
   250 DATA BEDROOM 1, 16, 18
   260 DATA BEDROOM 2, 13, 15
   270 DATA FRONT ROOM, 20, 18
   280 END
```

2. Correct the errors in the following programs:

```
a. -95 REM EXERCISE 4.2A
    100 READ S, B,
    110 LET D = S - B
    120 PRANT D
    130 END
    140 DATA 4, 6
```

```
b. 100 REM EXERCISE 4.2B
   110 DATA 1, 2, 5, 6, 8, 7, 1, 3, 2
   120 READ X, Y, Z
   130 LET X1 = X * Y
   140 LET X1 = X1 * Z
   150 GOTO 130
   160 PRINT X2
   170 END
```

3. How many values will be read from a DATA statement by the following READ statement?

   a. 100 READ Q, R, S, T, U
   b. 110 READ A, B
   c. 120 READ J, K, K, J
   d. 130 READ U * V - W, S, X

4. Write valid DATA statements for the READ statements in 3.

5. Write a correct PRINT statement to display your name in the first position of:
   a. The first print zone
   b. The third print zone

6. Write a sequence of PRINT statements that will display the value of A on the first line and the value of B on the fourth line.

7. Write a single PRINT statement to compute and display:
   a. $\sqrt{Y}$ b. $\sqrt[3]{Y}$ c. $\sqrt[4]{Y}$

8. Which of the following are true?
   a. Every PRINT statement displays one line of information.
   b. The END statement is mandatory.
   c. Every program must have a PRINT statement.
   d. The semicolon in a print statement causes spacing to the next print zone.
   e. It is invalid to have more data items in a DATA statement than required by a READ statement.

9. Write a program that will generate the following graphic output.

```
*************
* B A S I C *
B L       N B
A   E   R   A
S       A   S
I   E   R   I
C L       N C
* B A S I C *
*************
```

10. What kind of graphic output displays from this program?

```
100 REM EXERCISE 4.10
110 PRINT TAB(34); "VVVVV"
120 PRINT TAB(33); "X"; TAB(39); "X"
130 PRINT TAB(32); "X"; TAB(35); "O"; TAB(37); "O"; TAB(40); "X"
140 PRINT TAB(32); "X"; TAB(40); "X"
150 PRINT TAB(32); "X"; TAB(36); "U"; TAB(40); "X"
160 PRINT TAB(32); "X"; TAB(34); "("; TAB(38); ")"; TAB(40); "X"
170 PRINT TAB(32); "X"; TAB(36); "-"; TAB(40); "X"
180 PRINT TAB(33); "X"; TAB(39); "X"
190 PRINT TAB(34); "XXXXX"
200 END
```

11. For each of the following descriptor fields and corresponding data, indicate what the computer displays. Use the letter b to indicate the space character.

	Descriptor Field	Data	Output
a)	###	25	
b)	#,###.##	38.4	
c)	$$,###.##-	-22.6	
d)	$#,###.##-	425.89	
e)	**#,###.##	88.756	
f)	#,###.#	637214	
g)	##.##-	3.975	
h)	###.##	-123.8	
i)	##,###.###	12.6143	
j)	#.##^^^^	265.75	
k)	!	ABCD	
l)	&	ABCD	
m)	\\ (zero spaces)	ABCD	
n)	\ \ (2 spaces)	ABCD	

4.6 BASIC PROGRAMMING PROBLEMS 1: Determining the P/E Ratio

Purpose: To become familiar with I/O statements and the GOTO statement.

Problem: Construct a program to print the Price/Earnings (P/E) ratio for companies whose current stock prices and earnings per share are known. The P/E ratio is a useful tool employed by stock market analysts in evaluating the investment potential of various companies. The P/E ratio is determined by dividing the price of a share of stock by the company's latest earnings per share.

Input Data: Prepare and use the following sample data:

Stock Name	Price per Share	Latest Earnings
DIGITAL	113.5	5.98
DATAGN	57	1.06
IBM	121.75	8.12
APPLE	34	1.42
TANDY	54.5	2.51

Output Results: The following results are displayed:

```
STOCK          PRICE PER     LATEST        P/E
NAME           SHARE         EARNINGS      RATIO
-----          ---------     --------      -----
DIGITAL        113.5         5.98          18.9799
DATAGN         57            1.06          53.7736
IBM            121.75        8.12          14.9939
APPLE          34            1.42          23.9437
TANDY          54.5          2.51          21.7132
```

Output Results Formatted: Use the PRINT USING statement to display all numeric fields to the nearest hundredth place. Right-justify and align all numeric fields on the decimal point. The fields must also be centered under the column headings.

2:
Determining the Point of Intersection

Purpose: To become familiar with using the computer to solve systems of equations and generate readable reports.

Problem: Maximum profit or minimum cost can often be determined from equations based on known facts concerning a product. The point of intersection of the equations is significant. Write a program to find the point of intersection for two first-degree equations in two variables (that is, two equations and two unknowns). The general form for two equatons is:

$$a_1x + b_1y = c_1$$
$$a_2x + b_2y = c_2$$

Its solutions are expressed as:

$$x = \frac{c_1b_2 - c_2b_1}{a_1b_2 - a_2b_1}$$

$$y = \frac{c_2a_1 - c_1a_2}{a_1b_2 - a_2b_1}$$

The program should read the coefficients (a_1, b_1, c_1, a_2, b_2 and c_2 in this order) from a DATA statement, solve for x and y, display the values of a_1, b_1 and c_1 on one line, a_2, b_2, c_2, x and y on the next line. The program should loop back to read a set of data for the next system of equations.

Input Data: Prepare and use the following sample data:

System	*Equation 1 Coefficients*			*Equation 2 Coefficients*		
	a	*b*	*c*	*a*	*b*	*c*
1	1	1	5	1	−1	1
2	2	−7	8	3	1	−8
3	.6	−.75	−8	.6	−.125	2

Output Results: The following results are displayed:

```
<-------------EQUATIONS----------->           <---INTERSECTION----->
 COEFF A           COEFF B           COEFF C      X VALUE        Y VALUE
------            ------            ------      -------        -------

   1                1                5
   1               -1                1            3              2

   2               -7                8
   3                1               -8          -2.08696       -1.73913

   .6              -.75             -8
   .6              -.125             2          6.66667         16
```

Output Results Formatted: Use the PRINT USING statement to display the results of x and y to the nearest thousandth place, right-justified with the decimal points aligned.

3:
Straight-Line
Depreciation
Calculations

Purpose: To become familiar with calculating the annual straight-line depreciation charges or allowances on potential or present capital investments.

Problem: As a corporate accountant you have been asked to write a program that calculates the annual depreciation expense under the straight-line method using the following formula:

$$\text{Depreciation} = \frac{\text{Asset Cost} - \text{Salvage Value}}{\text{Service Life}}$$

Input Data: Prepare and use the following sets of data:

Description	Data	
	Set 1	Set 2
I.D. No.	1486	2173
Asset Cost in $	325,000	42,000
Salvage Value in $	45,000	12,000
Years of Service Life	14	10

Execute the program with data from Set 1 and then replace the corresponding DATA statement with one incorporating the data from Set 2.

Output Results: The following results are displayed for Set 1 (Final results for Set 2 are not shown):

```
ITEM 1486 HAS AN ANNUAL DEPRECIATION OF $ 20000
FOR AN INVESTMENT OF $ 325000 FOR 14 YEARS
WITH A SALVAGE VALUE OF $ 45000.
```

Output Results Formatted: Use the PRINT USING statement to float the dollar sign, insert a comma and display each monetary amount to the nearest cent. The following formatted results are displayed for Set 1:

```
ITEM 1486 HAS AN ANNUAL DEPRECIATION OF  $20,000.00
FOR AN INVESTMENT OF  $325,000.00 FOR 14 YEARS
WITH A SALVAGE VALUE OF  $45,000.00.
```

Purpose: To become familiar with looping and the use of the READ and DATA statements.

Problem: Modify Payroll Problem II in Problem 3, Chapter 3, to generate a report with column headings and a line of information for each employee. Each line is to include employee number, gross pay, federal withholding tax and net pay.

Input Data: Use the sample data found in Problem 3, Chapter 3.

Output Results: The following results are displayed:

```
EMPLOYEE
NUMBER       GROSS PAY      FED. TAX      NET PAY
--------     ---------      --------      -------
  123        1,000.00        184.62       815.38
  124          800.00        152.31       647.69
  125        1,040.00        200.31       839.69
  126           90.00          2.62        87.38

---OUT OF DATA LINE 170
```

LOOPING AND DECISION-MAKING 5

**5.1
STRUCTURED
PROGRAMMING**

It is appropriate at this time to introduce you to some important concepts related to **structured programming**.

Structured programming is a methodology according to which all program logic can be constructed from a combination of the following three basic logic structures:

1. **Sequence.** The most fundamental of the logic structures. It provides for two or more actions to be executed in the order they appear.
2. **If-Then-Else** or **Selection.** Provides a choice between two alternative actions.
3. **Do-While** or **Repetition.** Provides for the repeated execution of a loop.

The following are two common extensions to these logic structures:

4. **Do-Until** or **Repeat-Until.** An extension of the Do-While logic structure.
5. **Case.** An extension of the If-Then-Else logic structure in which the choice includes more than two alternatives.

Logic Structures

The sequential flow of control used in previous programs and shown in Figure 5.1 is not sufficient to solve problems that involve **decision-making**. To develop an algorithm that requires deviation from sequential control we need another logic structure. This new structure, called If-Then-Else, is shown in Figure 5.2.

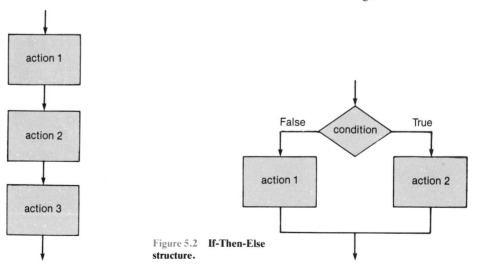

**Figure 5.1
Sequence
structure.**

**Figure 5.2   If-Then-Else
structure.**

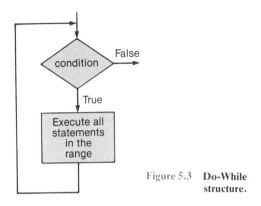

Figure 5.3   **Do-While structure.**

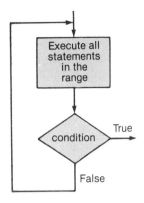

Figure 5.4   **Do-Until structure.**

The flowchart representation of a decision is the diamond-shaped symbol. One flowline will always be shown entering the symbol and two lines will always be shown leaving the symbol. A **condition** which must be true or false is written within the decision symbol. Such a condition asks, for example, if two variables are equal or if an expression is within a certain range. If the condition is true, one path is taken; if not, the other path is taken.

To instruct the computer to select actions based on a condition, as illustrated in Figure 5.2, BASIC includes three statements which are classified as decision statements: IF (IF-THEN and IF-THEN-ELSE), ON-GOTO, and ON-GOSUB. This chapter presents both forms of the IF statement and the ON-GOTO. The ON-GOSUB will be discussed in Chapter 6.

Most programs perform only simple calculations but repeat these calculations again and again until certain conditions are satisfied. It is necessary to include within the repeatedly executed process a decision to terminate the loop after a sufficient number of repetitions has occurred. Most computer scientists agree that the decision to terminate a loop should be located at the very top or very bottom of the loop. A loop that has the termination decision at the top is called a Do-While structure (see Figure 5.3). A loop that has the termination decision at the bottom is called a Do-Until structure (see Figure 5.4). BASIC has the following three pairs of statements to control the looping process illustrated in Figures 5.3 and 5.4:

1.   IF-THEN and GOTO
2.   WHILE and WEND
3.   FOR and NEXT

The IF statements are commonly regarded as the most powerful statements in the BASIC language. They have two primary functions in BASIC:

1.   They perform selection.
2.   They facilitate looping.

In selection, a statement is used to let a program choose between two alternative paths, as illustrated in Figure 5.2. The IF statements are used to specify conditional control, decision-making, in a program. Looping is illustrated in Figures 5.3 and 5.4.

5.2
THE IF-THEN AND IF-THEN-ELSE STATEMENTS

TABLE 5.1 **The** IF-THEN **Statement**

General Form:	IF condition THEN $\left\{\begin{array}{l}\text{line number}\\\text{statement}\end{array}\right\}$
	where braces { } signify choice between line number and statement; condition is a relationship that is either true or false.
Purpose:	Causes execution of a specified line number or statement if the condition is true. If the condition is false, control passes to the line following the IF-THEN statement.
Examples:	``` 125 IF X >= 0 THEN 50 190 IF Y + 5 > 8 THEN LET A = A + 1 290 IF C + B/A <= X + 9 THEN IF S >= 50 THEN 560 300 IF A$ = "YES" THEN GOTO 100 400 IF C$ <> B$ THEN PRINT C$ 500 IF C * (X - Y) + 8 < 45.7 THEN READ D, E$, F ```

BASIC has two types of IF statements. One is the IF-THEN statement and is illustrated in Table 5.1. The second is the IF-THEN-ELSE statement and is illustrated in Table 5.3.

As indicated in Table 5.1, the IF-THEN statement is used to specify a decision. The condition appears between the keywords IF and THEN. The condition specifies a relationship between expressions that is either true or false. The relationship is a comparison between one numeric expression and another or between one string expression and another. If the condition between IF and THEN is true and a *line number* follows the keyword THEN, control transfers to the stated line number. If the condition is true and a *statement* follows the keyword THEN, the statement is executed and control passes to the line following the IF-THEN. If the condition is false, regardless of what follows the keyword THEN, execution continues to the next line following the IF-THEN statement.

The condition between the keywords IF and THEN is made up of two expressions and a relational operator. Expressions may be associated with either numeric or string values. In determining whether a condition is true or not, BASIC first determines the single value of each expression and then evaluates them both with respect to the relational operator. Table 5.2 lists the six relational operators that are used to indicate this type of comparison.

TABLE 5.2 **Relational Operators Used in Conditions**

Relations	Math Symbol	BASIC Symbol	Examples
Equal to	$=$	=	`400 IF A = B THEN 200 ELSE 1400`
Less than	$<$	<	`500 IF A$ < "4" THEN 900 ELSE PRINT A`
Greater than	$>$	>	`600 IF X - Y > 9 THEN LET P = X * Y`
Less than or equal to	$\leqq$	<=	`700 IF X$ <= B$ THEN READ A$ ELSE READ A`
Greater than or equal to	$\geqq$	>=	`800 IF X + Y/Z >= C THEN 150`
Not equal to	$\neq$	<>	`900 IF S$ <> "NO" THEN READ A, B`

As is clear in Table 5.3, the IF-THEN-ELSE statement is similar to the IF-THEN statement. If the condition between IF and THEN is true, the system acts upon the line number or statement following the keyword THEN.

TABLE 5.3   **The IF-THEN-ELSE Statement**

General Form:	IF condition THEN $\left\{\begin{array}{l}\text{line number}\\\text{statement}\end{array}\right\}$ ELSE $\left\{\begin{array}{l}\text{line number}\\\text{statement}\end{array}\right\}$ where braces { } signify choice between line number and statement; condition is a relationship that is either true or false.
Purpose:	Causes execution of a line or statement following the keyword THEN if the condition is true. Causes execution of a line or statement following the keyword ELSE if the condition is false.
Examples:	``` 200 IF F > T THEN 210 ELSE 250 300 IF D$ = "Y" THEN LET A = A + 1 ELSE GOTO 310 400 IF X + Y <> S * Q THEN 450 ELSE LET C = C * 2 500 IF A * (B + C) <= S/G THEN LET G = G + 2 ELSE LET G = G + 1 600 IF L >= INT(L) THEN PRINT "THE VALUE IS"; L ELSE PRINT 2 * L 700 IF LEN(T$) < 5 THEN 710 ELSE 750 800 IF Z = Y THEN IF S > T THEN LET F = F + 1 ELSE 500 ELSE 750 900 IF D <= R THEN IF G = 5 THEN PRINT D ELSE PRINT R ```
Caution:	This statement is not available on the Apple and COMMODORE systems.

There is an important difference, however, between the IF-THEN-ELSE statement and the IF-THEN statement, which passes control to the next line when the condition is false. When the condition is false in the IF-THEN-ELSE statement, the system acts upon the line number or statement following the keyword ELSE. If a line number follows THEN or ELSE, control transfers to that line number. If a non-transfer statement follows the keyword THEN or ELSE, the statement is executed and control passes to the line following the IF-THEN-ELSE.

Figure 5.5 illustrates the use of the If-Then-Else structure to resolve a gross pay computation in which employees are paid a fixed rate per hour for hours worked less than or equal to 40 and time-and-a-half for hours worked greater than 40.

The gross pay computation illustrated in Figure 5.5 may be written in BASIC as follows:

```
100 REM GROSS PAY COMPUTATIONS
110 REM H = HOURS WORKED, R = RATE OF PAY, G = GROSS PAY
    .
    .
    .
200 IF H <= 40 THEN LET G = R * H ELSE LET G = R * H + 0.5 * R * (H - 40)
210 .
```

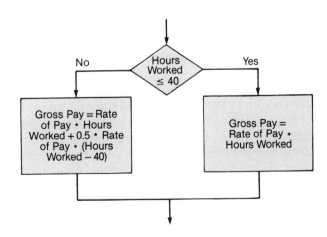

Figure 5.5   **Use of the If-Then-Else structure.**

Line 200 selects a LET statement to compute the gross pay G. If H (hours worked) is less than or equal to 40, the gross pay is computed using the LET statement immediately following the keyword THEN. If the condition, H $\leq$ 40, is false, then the gross pay is computed using the LET statement following the keyword ELSE. In either case, control passes to line 210.

Comparing Numeric Expressions

If the condition includes two numeric expressions, the comparison is based on the algebraic values of the two expressions. That is, the system evaluates not only the magnitude of each resultant expression, but also its sign.

Comparing String Expressions

If the condition includes two string expressions, the system evaluates the two strings from left to right, one character at a time. Two string expressions are considered equal if the two expressions have the same length and contain an identical sequence of characters. As soon as one character in an expression is different from the corresponding character in the other expression the comparison stops and the system decides which expression has a lower value, based in general on numerical and alphabetical order. In other words, the system evaluates two string expressions like you would.

Termination of a Loop Using an IF-THEN Statement

A useful function of the IF-THEN statement is to perform an end-of-file (**EOF**) test to terminate a looping process. An IF-THEN statement following a READ statement can be used to test for a final data item that is distinguishable from all the rest of the data assigned to a variable. This final data item is put in a **trailer record** that is placed in the last DATA statement. Since it guards against reading past the end-of-file, the extra record is also called a **sentinel record**. The data item selected for the EOF test is called the **sentinel value**. When the sentinel value is detected by the IF-THEN statement, control transfers to an end-of-job routine. This technique for terminating a program prevents the diagnostic messages which occurred in programs in Chapter 4 from being displayed at the conclusion of the programs, and it allows for final totals to be displayed prior to termination.

BASIC at Work

Determining the Sales Price with an EOF Test

Consider again the program solution presented for Determining the Sale Price in Chapter 4 (p. 46). Recall that the program read a record consisting of a product number, original price and discount rate. A discount amount and sale price were computed and displayed. The program then processed the next record and proceeded in this fashion until all the records were processed. Program 5.1 is similar to Program 4.1 except that it employs an EOF test and prevents a diagnostic message from being displayed upon termination.

To incorporate an EOF test, a variable must be selected and a sentinel record added to the data. In Program 5.1, we selected the product number as a test for the end-of-file and the sentinel value of EOF. The input data for Program 5.1 is the same as that processed by Program 4.1 except for the addition of the trailer record as shown below.

	Product Number	Original Price	Discount Rate in Percent
	112841A	$115.00	14
	213981B	100.00	17
	332121A	98.00	13
	586192X	88.00	12
	714121Y	43.00	8
Trailer Record ⟶	EOF	0	0

Note that for the trailer record we arbitrarily assigned zero values to the remaining data items.

```
100 REM PROGRAM 5.1
110 REM DETERMINING THE SALE PRICE WITH AN EOF TEST
120 REM N$ = PRODUCT NO.    P = ORIGINAL PRICE
130 REM R  = DISCOUNT RATE  D = DISCOUNT AMOUNT   S = SALES PRICE
140 REM **********************************************************
150 PRINT     "PRODUCT    ORIGINAL   DISCOUNT   DISCOUNT    SALE"
160 PRINT     "NUMBER     PRICE      RATE IN %  AMOUNT      PRICE"
170 PRINT     "-------    --------   ---------  --------    -----"
180 LET A$ = "\         \    #,###.##       ###       #,###.## #,###.##"
190 REM READ THE FIRST RECORD
200 READ N$, P, R
210 REM ***************PROCESS A RECORD***************
220 IF N$ = "EOF" THEN 290
230     LET D = R/100 * P
240     LET S = P - D
250     PRINT USING A$; N$, P, R, D, S
260     READ N$, P, R
270 GOTO 220
280 REM ***************EOF ROUTINE*******************
290 PRINT
300 PRINT "END OF REPORT"
310 REM ***************DATA FOLLOWS*****************
320 DATA 112841A, 115, 14
330 DATA 213981B, 100, 17
340 DATA 332121A, 98, 13
350 DATA 586192X, 88, 12
360 DATA 714121Y, 43, 8
370 DATA EOF, 0, 0
380 END
```

Program 5.1

```
RUN

PRODUCT    ORIGINAL   DISCOUNT   DISCOUNT    SALE
NUMBER     PRICE      RATE IN %  AMOUNT      PRICE
-------    --------   ---------  --------    -----
112841A     115.00       14        16.10     98.90
213981B     100.00       17        17.00     83.00
332121A      98.00       13        12.74     85.26
586192X      88.00       12        10.56     77.44
714121Y      43.00        8         3.44     39.56

END OF REPORT
```

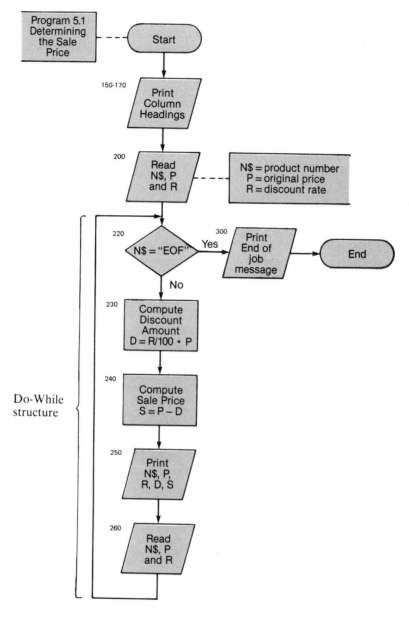

Figure 5.6   **Flowchart for Program 5.1.**

Program 5.1 and its flowchart in Figure 5.6 show that a Do-While structure is used to establish the looping process. The algorithm includes the use of two READ statements. The first READ statement before the loop is executed only once and is used to read the first record. The product number is then tested to determine if the loop should be executed. The second READ statement located at the bottom of the loop is used to read the remaining records. Each time the second READ statement is executed, control passes back to the decision statement to determine if the trailer record has been read. If the trailer record is read, the program terminates; otherwise, the loop is re-entered and the record is processed further. The statements in the loop, other than the first and last, should be indented by three spaces for the purpose of readability (see lines 230 through 260 in Program 5.1).

Most programs require the inclusion of **accumulators**. Accumulators are often used to develop totals. Accumulators are initialized to a value of zero before the execution of a loop, incremented within the loop and then manipulated or displayed after the looping process is complete. Although BASIC automatically initializes numeric variables to zero, good programming practice demands that it be done in the program. There are two types of accumulators—counters and running totals. Both types are discussed in the sections that follow.

5.3
ACCUMULATORS

Counters

A **counter** is an accumulator used to count the number of times some action is performed. Associated with a counter is a statement placed prior to the execution of the loop that initializes the counter to some value. In most cases the counter is initialized to zero. The following partial program illustrates the initialization and incrementation of a counter called C:

```
Set C to zero ──────────► 200 LET C = 0
before the loop.          210 READ N, A
                          220 IF N = -1 THEN 320
Add one to C. ──────────► 230    LET C = C + 1
                                   .
                                   .
                                   .
                          300    READ N, A
Display the value of C    310 GOTO 220
at end-of-job. ─────────► 320 PRINT "THE TOTAL COUNT IS"; C
```

Running Totals

A **running total** is an accumulator used to sum the different values that a variable is assigned during the execution of a program.

The following partial program illustrates the initialization and incrementation of a running total. Assume the variable S is assigned the monthly salary of an employee each time the READ statement is executed. Since the variable T is incremented by the employee salary S, at end-of-job T will represent the total monthly salary paid to all the employees in the file.

```
Initialization of T. ───► 200 LET T = 0
                          210 READ N$, S
                          220 IF N$ = "EOF" THEN 320
T increased by S. ──────► 230    LET T = T + S
                                   .
                                   .
                                   .
                          300    READ N$, S
Running total T           310 GOTO 220
displayed. ─────────────► 320 PRINT "THE TOTAL EMPLOYEE SALARY IS"; T
```

The second method for controlling a looping process in BASIC is through the use of the WHILE and WEND statements, which define a loop called a **While loop**. Like the IF-THEN and GOTO statements illustrated in Program 5.1, the WHILE and WEND statements can be used to implement the Do-While structure. The general forms of the WHILE and WEND statements are given in Tables 5.4 and 5.5, respectively.

To illustrate the similarity in programming between the looping concepts discussed in the previous sections of this chapter and the WHILE and WEND state-

5.4
THE WHILE
AND WEND
STATEMENTS

ments, look at Program 5.2 and Program 5.3, which includes a While loop. Both programs compute and display the sum of the first 100 integers.

Program 5.2 employs IF-THEN and GOTO statements to control the looping process. Lines 140 and 150 initialize the running total S to 0 and the counter I to 1, respectively. Line 160 tests to determine if the value of I is greater than 100. If the condition is false, control passes to line 170 where lines 170 through 190 are executed and control transfers back to line 160. When the condition in the IF-THEN statement is true, the program terminates the loop and displays the running total S in line 200.

TABLE 5.4 **The WHILE Statement**

General Form:	WHILE condition
Purpose:	Causes the statements between WHILE and WEND to be executed repeatedly while the condition is true. As long as the condition is false, control transfers to the line following the corresponding WEND statement.
Examples:	100 WHILE C = 0 200 WHILE M$ <> "EOF" 300 WHILE A + B > S 400 WHILE X >= 0 500 WHILE D < C * D + 4/S 600 WHILE F <= 0
Caution:	This statement is not available on the Apple or COMMODORE systems.

TABLE 5.5 **The WEND Statement**

General Form:	WEND
Purpose:	Identifies the end of a While loop.
Examples:	500 WEND 700 WEND
Caution:	The DEC VAX-II uses the keyword NEXT rather than WEND to identify the end of a While loop. This statement is not available on the Apple or COMMODORE systems.

```
100 REM PROGRAM 5.2
110 REM SUMMING A SERIES OF INTEGERS
120 REM USING A DO-WHILE STRUCTURE
130 REM ****************************
140 LET S = 0
150 LET I = 1
160 IF I > 100 THEN 200
170     LET S = S + I
180     LET I = I + 1
190 GOTO 160
200 PRINT "THE SUM IS"; S
210 END

RUN

THE SUM IS 5050
```

```
100 REM PROGRAM 5.3
110 REM SUMMING A SERIES OF INTEGERS
120 REM USING A WHILE LOOP
130 REM ****************************
140 LET S = 0
150 LET I = 1
160 WHILE I <= 100
170     LET S = S + I
180     LET I = I + 1
190 WEND
200 PRINT "THE SUM IS"; S
210 END

RUN

THE SUM IS 5050
```

Program 5.2
and
Program 5.3

Program 5.3 facilitates the construction of the loop by use of the WHILE and WEND statements. In executing the While loop in Program 5.3, the following occurs:

1. When the WHILE statement is executed for the first time, the While loop (lines 160 to 190) becomes activated.
2. Next, the condition is tested to determine if the statements in lines 170 and 180 in the loop should be executed. This test occurs *before* the first pass.

3. If the condition is true, the statements within the loop are executed. If the condition is false, control transfers to line 200, which follows the corresponding WEND.
4. The WEND statement is the last statement of a While loop. As long as the condition is true, control *automatically* returns to the top of the loop.

Note that the statements in the loop are indented to make the program more readable. In our opinion, Program 5.3 is easier to read and code than Program 5.2. With a While loop, you need not concern yourself with a GOTO as the last statement of a loop.

The following rules can be formulated about the placement of the WHILE and WEND statements:

> WHILE **Rule 1:** The WHILE statement may be located anywhere before the corresponding WEND statement.

> WEND **Rule 1:** The WEND statement may be located anywhere after the corresponding WHILE statement and before the end line.

The following example incorporates both a counter and a running total, as well as some of the concepts discussed earlier in this section. An analysis of the problem, a flowchart, and a BASIC program follow.

BASIC at Work

Weekly Payroll and Summary Report

Problem

A payroll application requires that the employee number, the hours worked, the rate of pay and the gross pay be displayed for each employee shown below.

Employee Number	Hours Worked	Rate of Pay
124	40	$5.60
126	56	5.90
128	38	4.60
129	48.5	6.10

Also, the total gross pay, the total number of employees, and the average gross pay for this payroll are displayed. The gross pay is determined by multiplying the hours worked by the hourly rate of pay. Overtime (hours in excess of 40) is paid at 1½ times the hourly rate.

Program Tasks

Consider the following analysis for this problem.

1. Display report and column headings.
2. Initialize a counter C and running total T to 0. Use the counter C to determine the total number of employees processed. Use the running total T to determine the total gross pay.
3. Read a record.
4. Test for end-of-file. If end-of-file, compute and display the average gross pay. If not end-of-file, proceed to the next step.
5. Establish a loop and do the following within the loop:
   a. Increment counter C by 1.
   b. Determine the gross pay.
   c. Increment the running total T by the gross pay.
   d. Read the next record.

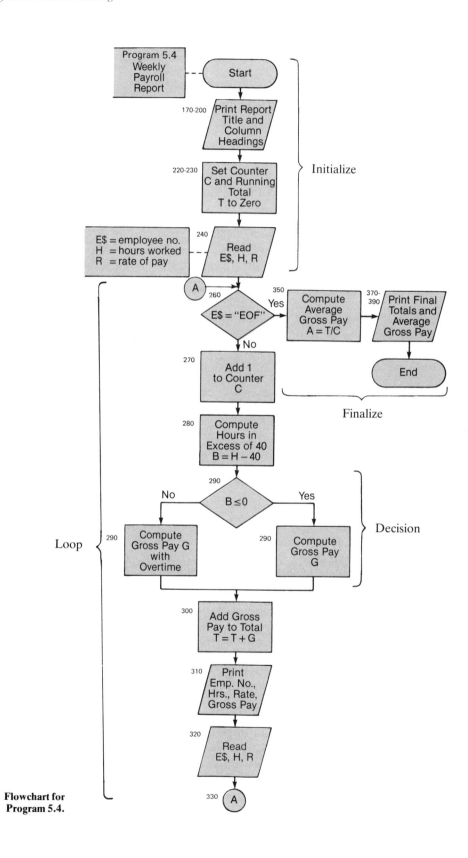

Figure 5.7   **Flowchart for Program 5.4.**

```
100 REM PROGRAM 5.4
110 REM WEEKLY PAYROLL AND SUMMARY REPORT
120 REM C  = EMPLOYEE COUNT    T = TOTAL GROSS PAY
130 REM E$ = EMPLOYEE NUMBER   H = HOURS WORKED
140 REM R  = RATE OF PAY       B = HOURS GREATER THAN 40
150 REM G  = GROSS PAY         A = AVERAGE GROSS PAY
160 REM ***************************************************
170 PRINT TAB(12); "WEEKLY PAYROLL REPORT"
180 PRINT
190 PRINT       "EMPLOYEE NO.    HOURS     RATE     GROSS PAY"
200 PRINT       "------------    -----     ----     ---------"
210 LET A$ = "   \    \        ###.#     ##.##    ##,###.##"
220 LET C = 0
230 LET T = 0
240 READ E$, H, R
250 REM *****************PROCESS A RECORD***************
260 WHILE E$ <> "EOF"
270    LET C = C + 1
280    LET B = H - 40
290    IF B <= 0 THEN LET G = H * R ELSE LET G = H * R +0.5 * B * R
300    LET T = T + G
310    PRINT USING A$; E$, H, R, G
320    READ E$, H, R
330 WEND
340 REM *****************EOF ROUTINE******************
350 LET A = T/C
360 PRINT
370 PRINT USING "THE TOTAL GROSS PAY IS $$#,###.##"; T
380 PRINT USING "THE TOTAL NUMBER OF EMPLOYEES IS ###"; C
390 PRINT USING "THE AVERAGE GROSS PAY IS $$#,###.##"; A
400 REM ****************DATA FOLLOWS*****************
410 DATA 124, 40, 5.60
420 DATA 126, 56, 5.90
430 DATA 128, 38, 4.60
440 DATA 129, 48.5, 6.10
450 DATA EOF, 0, 0
460 END
```

Initialize { (lines 170–240)
Loop { (lines 260–330)
Finalize { (lines 350–390)

Program 5.4

```
RUN
            WEEKLY PAYROLL REPORT

EMPLOYEE NO.    HOURS     RATE    GROSS PAY
------------    -----     ----    ---------
     124        40.0      5.60       224.00
     126        56.0      5.90       377.60
     128        38.0      4.60       174.80
     129        48.5      6.10       321.77

THE TOTAL GROSS PAY IS   $1,098.17
THE TOTAL NUMBER OF EMPLOYEES IS    4
THE AVERAGE GROSS PAY IS     $274.54
```

The solution to the Weekly Payroll Report as represented by the flowchart in Figure 5.7 and the corresponding Program 5.4 includes a few significant points which did not appear in previous programs. They are:

1. The loop (lines 260 through 330) is defined by the WHILE and WEND statements. The condition in line 260 tests for the sentinel value EOF. When E$ is assigned the value EOF by line 320, control passes to the EOF routine beginning at line 350.

2. The use of a counter C and a running total T, which are initialized to zero (lines 220 and 230). Both variables are incremented in the loop. The counter is used to keep track of the total number of employees and is incremented in line 270. The running total is used to sum the gross pay and is incremented by the individual employee gross pay in line 300.

3. A decision is made in line 290 to determine which of two formulas is to be used to compute the gross pay.
4. The EOF routine (lines 350 to 390) involves calculating an average based on the total gross pay and the number of employees and displaying these totals and the average.

5.5
IMPLEMENTING
THE IF-THEN-ELSE
STRUCTURE

This section will be a discussion of various forms of the If-Then-Else structure and their implementation in BASIC using the IF-THEN and IF-THEN-ELSE statements.

Consider the If-Then-Else structure in Figure 5.8 and the corresponding methods of implementing the logic in BASIC. Assume that R$ represents a person's voter registration status. If R$ is equal to "Y," the person is registered to vote. If R$ does not equal "Y," the person is not registered to vote. R1 and R2 are counters that are incremented as specified in the flowchart.

In the first method of solution in Figure 5.8 an IF-THEN-ELSE statement resolves the If-Then-Else structure in one line. If R$ is equal to "Y," then R2 is incremented by 1. If R$ is not equal to "Y," then R1 is incremented by 1. Regardless of the counter incremented, control passes to line 210. Line 210 is said to be the **structure terminator**, since both the true and false tasks pass control to this line.

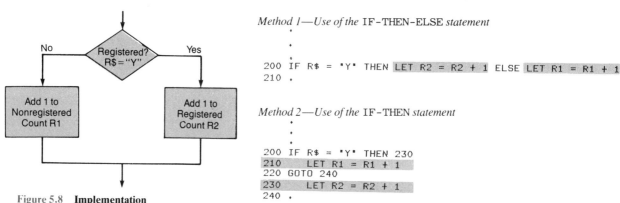

Method 1—Use of the IF-THEN-ELSE *statement*

```
        .
        .
200  IF R$ = "Y" THEN LET R2 = R2 + 1 ELSE LET R1 = R1 + 1
210  .
```

Method 2—Use of the IF-THEN *statement*

```
        .
        .
200  IF R$ = "Y" THEN 230
210     LET R1 = R1 + 1
220  GOTO 240
230     LET R2 = R2 + 1
240  .
```

Figure 5.8 **Implementation of an If-Then-Else structure with alternative processing for the true and false cases.**

In the second method shown in Figure 5.8, an IF-THEN and a GOTO combine to implement the structure. Line 200 compares R$ to "Y." If R$ is equal to "Y," control transfers to line 230 and R2 is incremented by 1. If R$ does not equal "Y," control passes to line 210 and R1 is incremented by 1. Following execution of line 210, the GOTO 240 in line 220 transfers control to the structure terminator.

Although both methods satisfy the If-Then-Else structure, the first method is more straightforward, involves fewer lines of code and does not use the GOTO statement. Therefore, this method is usually recommended. In this second method, the alternative tasks (lines 210 and 230) are indented by 3 positions for readability. We shall use this style of indentation when alternative tasks are listed on separate lines.

As shown in Figures 5.9, 5.10 and 5.11, the If-Then-Else structure can take on a variety of appearances. In Figure 5.9, there is a task only if the condition is true.

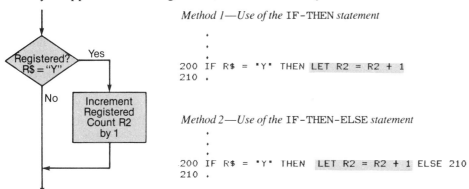

Method 1—Use of the IF-THEN *statement*

```
        •
        •
        •
200 IF R$ = "Y" THEN LET R2 = R2 + 1
210 •
```

Method 2—Use of the IF-THEN-ELSE *statement*

```
        •
        •
        •
200 IF R$ = "Y" THEN  LET R2 = R2 + 1 ELSE 210
210 •
```

Figure 5.9 **Implementation of an If-Then-Else structure with alternative processing for the true case.**

In Figure 5.9, both methods of implementation of the If-Then-Else structure involve one line of code. The first method is preferred over the second, since the IF-THEN automatically passes control to the next higher line number following execution of the statement after the keyword THEN.

The If-Then-Else structure in Figure 5.10 illustrates the incrementation of a counter R1 when the condition is false. Included in Figure 5.10 are three methods that may be used to implement the logic.

In method 1, the relation in the condition found in the partial flowchart has been negated. The condition R$ = "Y" has been modified to read R$ < > "Y" in the BASIC code. Since we often develop algorithms using positive thought patterns, negating relations in IF statements is a common and necessary practice and should always be considered when there is alternative processing for only one of the two cases.

In method 2, an IF-THEN-ELSE statement is used to implement the structure. If R$ is equal to "Y," then control transfers to line 210. If R$ does not equal "Y," the system executes the statement following the keyword ELSE and then passes control to line 210.

The third method of implementing the If-Then-Else structure in Figure 5.10 is the least preferred, since it involves a branch forward around a statement and an additional line of code. If R$ is equal to "Y," control transfers to line 220. If R$ does not equal "Y," then control passes to line 210 and R1 is incremented by 1 before passing control to the structure terminator, line 220.

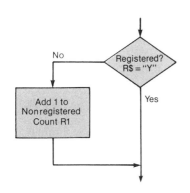

Method 1—Use of the IF-THEN *statement with the relation negated.*

```
200 IF R$ <> "Y" THEN LET R1 = R1 + 1
210 •
```

Method 2—Use of the IF-THEN-ELSE *statement.*

```
200 IF R$ = "Y" THEN 210 ELSE LET R1 = R1 + 1
210 •
```

Method 3—Use of the IF-THEN *statement.*

```
200 IF R$ = "Y" THEN 220
210    LET R1 = R1 + 1
220 •
```

Figure 5.10 **Implementation of an If-Then-Else structure with alternative processing for the false case.**

The If-Then-Else structure in Figure 5.11 includes alternative tasks for both the true and false cases. Each task is made up of multiple statements.

In method 1 of Figure 5.11, the IF-THEN-ELSE statement is used to implement the structure. If the condition R$ = "Y" is true, control transfers to line 210 and the true task (lines 210 and 220) is executed. The GOTO statement in line 230 transfers control to line 260, thereby branching forward past the false task (lines 240 and 250). If the condition is false, control transfers to line 240 and the false task is executed.

The second method in Figure 5.11 is similar to the first, except that an IF-THEN statement has replaced the IF-THEN-ELSE statement of method 1, and the false task is positioned just below the decision statement. As illustrated in both methods of solution, when alternative tasks include multiple statements, each statement is placed on a separate line and indented three positions. The GOTO that divides the two tasks is not indented. Method 1 is preferred over method 2 in Figure 5.11 primarily because the IF-THEN-ELSE statement allows you to position the true task immediately below the decision statement. This style helps make the program easier to read.

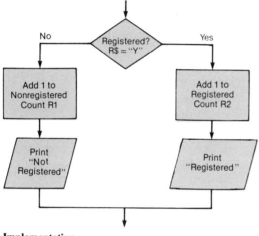

Figure 5.11 Implementation of an If-Then-Else structure with multiple statements for both the true and false cases.

Method 1—Use of the IF-THEN-ELSE *statement.*

```
        200 IF R$ = "Y" THEN 210 ELSE 240
True  { 210    LET R2 = R2 + 1
task  { 220    PRINT "REGISTERED"
        230 GOTO 260
False { 240    LET R1 = R1 + 1
task  { 250    PRINT "NOT REGISTERED"
        260 .
```

Method 2—Use of the IF-THEN *statement.*

```
        200 IF R$ = "Y" THEN 240
False { 210    LET R1 = R1 + 1
task  { 220    PRINT "NOT REGISTERED"
        230 GOTO 260
True  { 240    LET R2 = R2 + 1
Task  { 250    PRINT "REGISTERED"
        260 .
```

In summary, the following may be stated regarding the implementation of simple If-Then-Else structures in BASIC:

1. Use the IF-THEN-ELSE statement when there are alternative tasks for both cases.
2. Use the IF-THEN statement when there is an alternative task for only one of the two cases.
3. If there are multiple statements in a task, place each statement on a separate line. Indent each statement by three positions. If there are alternative tasks for both cases, divide the two tasks with a GOTO statement that is not indented. The GOTO statement should reference the line designated as the structure terminator.

The program flowcharts presented thus far in this chapter are common to so many applications which require the generation of information in the form of reports that there is a standard form for organizing the program. This standard form is a sequence of programming steps:

1. Initialize
   a. Display report titles and column headings.
   b. Set accumulators (counters and running totals) to a predetermined value.
2. Read first record
3. Test for end-of-file
   a. Test for the sentinel value.
   b. If the sentinel value is detected, proceed to the Finalization step (7); otherwise, continue to the next step (4).
4. Process
   a. Complete all computations.
   b. Increment all counters and running totals.
5. Output
   a. Display any intermediate detailed results.
6. Read next record
   a. Return to step 3 to test for end-of-file.
7. Finalize
   a. Compute summaries.
   b. Display final totals.
   c. Terminate processing.

The GOTO statement is defined as an **unconditional** GOTO statement because each time such a statement is executed, control is always transferred to the line number following the keyword GOTO, regardless of any conditions existing in the program.

On the other hand, the ON–GOTO statement is called a **conditional** GOTO statement. Depending on the current value of the numeric expression associated with this statement, control will be transferred to one of two or more different lines.

The ON–GOTO statement can be used to implement an extension of the If-Then-Else structure in which execution of one of many alternatives is to be selected based on an integer test. This extended version of the If-Then-Else structure is called the Case structure; it is illustrated in Figure 5.12.

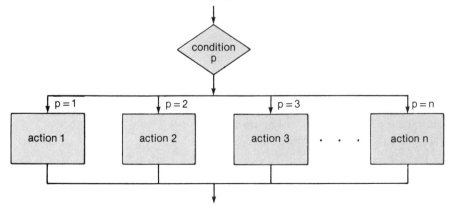

Figure 5.12 **The Case structure.**

The condition in the ON-GOTO statement may be a numeric variable or a numeric expression. The condition is placed between the keywords ON and GOTO. Depending on the value of the condition, control transfers to one of several line numbers appearing in a list following the keyword GOTO. Commas are mandatory punctuation in the list of line numbers in the ON-GOTO statement. It is also mandatory that the variables for the expression be defined in the program before the ON-GOTO is executed. The general form of the ON-GOTO statement is given in Table 5.6.

TABLE 5.6   The ON-GOTO Statement

General Form:	ON numeric expression GOTO $k_1, k_2, \ldots, k_n$
Purpose:	Causes control to be transferred to a selected line number k_i, where i is the current value of the numeric expression.
Examples:	300 ON Y GOTO 400, 100, 600
	500 ON K/10 + 1 GOTO 600, 1200, 3300, 100
	750 ON A + B*C/D GOTO 850, 650, 1400, 5000, 650

Execution of the ON-GOTO Statement

When the ON-GOTO statement is executed, control transfers to one of the line numbers in the list following the keyword GOTO. The system reads the line numbers in the ON-GOTO statement from left to right, beginning with the first one in the list. If the value of the condition is 1, then control is transferred to the first line number in the list; if 2, then the second, and so on. Consider the following example:

```
200 ON X GOTO 300, 300, 300, 400, 400, 500, 300, 600
```

Condition   List of line numbers to which control is transferred depending on the value of the condition.

If the value of X is 1 at the instant of the execution of line 200, control will be transferred to line number 300 and the statement with this indicated line number will be the next statement executed after the ON-GOTO statement. The same thing will take place whenever X has the integer value of 2, 3 or 7. When X has the integer value of 4 or 5, control will pass to line number 400. When X has the value of 6, control will pass to line number 500. Finally, when X has the value of 8, control will be transferred to line number 600. The number of line numbers that can follow the keyword GOTO is limited only by the length of the line.

On most BASIC systems, the numeric expression in an ON-GOTO statement is evaluated and any decimal portion is rounded to obtain an integer whose value is then used to select a line number from the list following the keyword GOTO. Consider the following example:

```
300 ON A * B - C/D + E GOTO 400, 600, 800
```

If the value of the expression A * B − C/D + E is 2.64, it will be rounded to an integer value of 3 and control will be transferred to line number 800, the third line number in the list following the GOTO.

Restrictions with the ON-GOTO Statement

In a BASIC program, you must never permit the value of an expression in an ON-GOTO statement to be negative or zero, or to attain a value that is larger than the total number of line numbers in the list of the ON-GOTO statement. A value that is too large, zero or negative cannot be used to select a line number from the list. An IF-THEN statement may be used to prevent an error condition like this from happening by validating the value of the expression just before the ON-GOTO statement is executed. Thus, the following portion of a program can be used to test for all of the non-permissible values of X:

```
200 INPUT "ENTER A ONE DIGIT JOB CODE BETWEEN 1 AND 8"; X
210 IF X < 1 THEN 230
220 IF X <= 8 THEN 250
230     PRINT "JOB CODE "; X; "IS INVALID"
240     GOTO 200
250 ON X GOTO 260, 300, 350, 400, 450, 500, 550, 600
```

In this program, each such non-permissible value of X will cause a diagnostic message to be displayed before control is transferred back to line 200, which requests a valid value for X.

The restrictions on the value of the expression in an ON-GOTO may be summarized as:

> ON-GOTO **Rule 1:** At the instant of execution of the ON-GOTO statement, the integer obtained as the value of the expression must never be negative, zero, or greater than the total number of line numbers in the list of the statement.

Programs are often characterized as being batch or interactive in mode. A **batch program** is one that generates information based on data that has been collected over a period of time. The data is placed in DATA statements or into a file and made available to the program via READ statements. The majority of programs presented in Chapter 4 and thus far in Chapter 5 can be classified as batch programs. An **interactive program** is one that generates information based on data as it occurs; the data is usually entered into the program by the operator via INPUT statements in response to questions. Most of the programs presented in Chapters 2 and 3 were of the interactive type.

BASIC at Work

A Menu-Driven Program

It is not at all uncommon for interactive programs to have multiple functions. A **menu**, a list of the functions that a program can perform, is often used to guide an operator through a multi-function interactive program. When a menu-driven program is first executed, it displays a menu of functions like the one illustrated in Figure 5.13. The operator can then choose the desired function from the list by entering a

```
MENU FOR COMPUTING AREAS
-----------------------------

CODE       FUNCTION
----       --------
  1   -    COMPUTE AREA OF A SQUARE
  2   -    COMPUTE AREA OF A RECTANGLE
  3   -    COMPUTE AREA OF A PARALLELOGRAM
  4   -    COMPUTE AREA OF A CIRCLE
  5   -    COMPUTE AREA OF A TRAPEZOID
  6   -    COMPUTE AREA OF A TRIANGLE
  7   -    END PROGRAM

ENTER A CODE 1 THROUGH 7?
```

Figure 5.13   **A menu of program functions.**

corresponding code. Once the request is satisfied, the program again displays the menu. As illustrated in Figure 5.13, one of the codes (in this case 7) terminates execution of the program.

The following problem uses the menu illustrated in Figure 5.13. An analysis of the problem and a program solution follow.

Problem

A menu-driven program is to compute the area of a square, rectangle, parallelogram, circle, trapezoid and triangle. The program should display the menu shown in

Figure 5.13. Once a code is entered, the program must validate it to ensure that the code corresponds to one of the menu functions. After the selection of the proper function, the program should prompt the operator for the necessary data, compute the area, and display it accordingly. The displayed results are to remain on the screen until the Enter key on the keyboard is pressed. After that, the program should display the menu again.

Use the following formulas for the areas:

1. Area of a square:

$$A = S * S$$

where S is the length of a side of the square.
2. Area of a rectangle:

$$A = L * W$$

where L is the length and W is the width of the rectangle.
3. Area of a parallelogram:

$$A = B * H$$

where B is the length of the base and H is the height of the parallelogram.
4. Area of a circle:

$$A = 3.14159 * R * R$$

where R is the radius of the circle.
5. Area of a trapezoid:

$$A = \frac{H(B1 + B2)}{2}$$

where H is the height, B1 is the length of the primary base, and B2 is the length of the secondary base of the trapezoid.
6. Area of a triangle:

$$A = \frac{B * H}{2}$$

where B is the base and H is the height of the triangle.

Program Tasks

1. Clear the screen and display the menu shown in Figure 5.13.
2. Request the operator to enter a code.
3. Validate the code. If the code is invalid, display an appropriate diagnostic message and again request the operator to select a function.
4. When a valid code is entered, clear the screen and use an ON-GOTO statement to transfer control to that portion of the program that carries out the requested function.
5. Request the data using one or more INPUT statements.
6. Compute the area and display the results.
7. Use the following prompt message to re-display the menu:

PRESS ENTER KEY TO RETURN TO THE MENU

8. Repeat steps 1 through 7 as necessary.
9. Enter a code of 7 to terminate the program.

When Program 5.5 is first executed, line 140 clears the screen, and lines 150 through 290 display the menu as illustrated in Figure 5.13. Assume function 3 is selected. When the Enter key is pressed, lines 300 and 310 validate the code and control transfers to line 340.

```
100 REM PROGRAM 5.5
110 REM A MENU-DRIVEN PROGRAM
120 REM C = FUNCTION CODE      A = AREA
130 REM ************************************************
140 CLS
150 PRINT
160 PRINT "          MENU FOR COMPUTING AREAS"
170 PRINT "          ------------------------"
180 PRINT
190 PRINT "    CODE     FUNCTION"
200 PRINT "    ----     --------"
210 PRINT "     1  -  COMPUTE AREA OF A SQUARE"
220 PRINT "     2  -  COMPUTE AREA OF A RECTANGLE"
230 PRINT "     3  -  COMPUTE AREA OF A PARALLELOGRAM"
240 PRINT "     4  -  COMPUTE AREA OF A CIRCLE"
250 PRINT "     5  -  COMPUTE AREA OF A TRAPEZOID"
260 PRINT "     6  -  COMPUTE AREA OF A TRIANGLE"
270 PRINT "     7  -  END PROGRAM"
280 PRINT
290 INPUT "    ENTER A CODE 1 THROUGH 7"; C
300 IF C < 1 THEN 320
310 IF C <= 7 THEN 340
320    PRINT "   CODE OUT OF RANGE, PLEASE"
330    GOTO 290
340 CLS
350 ON C GOTO 370, 420, 480, 540, 590, 660, 750
360 REM ***********COMPUTE AREA OF A SQUARE**************
370 INPUT "LENGTH OF SIDE OF SQUARE"; S
380 LET A = S * S
390 PRINT "AREA OF SQUARE IS"; A; "SQUARE UNITS"
400 GOTO 710
410 REM **********COMPUTE AREA OF A RECTANGLE************
420 INPUT "LENGTH OF RECTANGLE"; L
430 INPUT "WIDTH OF RECTANGLE"; W
440 LET A = L * W
450 PRINT "AREA OF RECTANGLE IS"; A; "SQUARE UNITS"
460 GOTO 710
470 REM **********COMPUTE AREA OF A PARALLELOGRAM*********
480 INPUT "BASE OF PARALLELOGRAM"; B
490 INPUT "HEIGHT OF PARALLELOGRAM"; H
500 LET A = B * H
510 PRINT "AREA OF PARALLELOGRAM IS"; A; "SQUARE UNITS"
520 GOTO 710
530 REM ***********COMPUTE AREA OF A CIRCLE**************
540 INPUT "RADIUS OF CIRCLE"; R
550 LET A = 3.14159 * R * R
560 PRINT "AREA OF CIRCLE IS"; A; "SQUARE UNITS"
570 GOTO 710
580 REM **********COMPUTE AREA OF A TRAPEZOID************
590 INPUT "PRIMARY BASE OF TRAPEZOID"; B1
600 INPUT "SECONDARY BASE OF TRAPEZOID"; B2
610 INPUT "HEIGHT OF TRAPEZOID"; H
620 LET A = H * (B1 + B2)/2
630 PRINT "AREA OF TRAPEZOID IS"; A; "SQUARE UNITS"
640 GOTO 710
650 REM **********COMPUTE AREA OF A TRIANGLE************
660 INPUT "BASE OF TRIANGLE"; B
670 INPUT "HEIGHT OF TRIANGLE"; H
680 LET A = B * H/2
690 PRINT "AREA OF TRIANGLE IS"; A; "SQUARE UNITS"
700 REM ****************RETURN TO MENU****************
710 PRINT
720 INPUT "PRESS ENTER KEY TO RETURN TO THE MENU"; A$
730 GOTO 140
740 REM ****************EOF ROUTINE*******************
750 PRINT
760 PRINT "END OF PROGRAM"
770 END
```

Program 5.5

Line 340 clears the screen of the menu, and line 350, the ON-GOTO statement, transfers control to line 480. Figure 5.14, for example, shows a base of 10 units and a height of 4 units to have been entered, which results in an area of 40 square units for the parallelogram. After line 520 transfers control to line 710, the last line is displayed in Figure 5.14. Once the Enter key is pressed, control returns to line 140, the screen is cleared, and the menu is again displayed.

Figure 5.15 shows an out-of-range code generating a diagnostic message. The diagnostic message is displayed by line 320. Line 330 transfers control back to line 290 so that another code may be entered. After a valid code is entered (see the last line of Figure 5.15), the screen is again cleared and the ON-GOTO statement in line 350 transfers control to that portion of the program (lines 590 through 640) that computes the area of a trapezoid.

Figure 5.16 shows that for a trapezoid with primary base 18, secondary base 9, and height 5, the area is 67.5 square units.

To terminate execution of Program 5.5, a code of 7 is entered. The ON-GOTO statement in line 350 transfers control to line 750 and the end of program message is displayed.

The preceding problem could have been solved by replacing the ON-GOTO statement with a series of consecutive IF statements. Usually, however, when a series of three or more integer tests is to be performed in succession, the ON-GOTO statement is the better alternative.

Figure 5.14 The display from the selection of code 3 (compute area of a parallelogram).

```
BASE OF PARALLELOGRAM? 10
HEIGHT OF PARALLELOGRAM? 4
AREA OF PARALLELOGRAM IS 40 SQUARE UNITS

PRESS ENTER KEY TO RETURN TO THE MENU?
```

```
        MENU FOR COMPUTING AREAS
        ------------------------

    CODE      FUNCTION
    ----      --------
     1    -   COMPUTE AREA OF A SQUARE
     2    -   COMPUTE AREA OF A RECTANGLE
     3    -   COMPUTE AREA OF A PARALLELOGRAM
     4    -   COMPUTE AREA OF A CIRCLE
     5    -   COMPUTE AREA OF A TRAPEZOID
     6    -   COMPUTE AREA OF A TRIANGLE
     7    -   END PROGRAM

ENTER A CODE 1 THROUGH 7? 9
CODE OUT OF RANGE, PLEASE
ENTER A CODE 1 THROUGH 7? 5
```

Figure 5.15 Diagnostic message displayed by line 320 due to the invalid code 9.

```
PRIMARY BASE OF TRAPEZOID? 18
SECONDARY BASE OF TRAPEZOID? 9
HEIGHT OF TRAPEZOID? 5
AREA OF TRAPEZOID IS 67.5 SQUARE UNITS

PRESS ENTER KEY TO RETURN TO THE MENU?
```

Figure 5.16 The display from the selection of code 5 (compute area of a trapezoid).

Many menu-driven programs call for logic that is similar to Program 5.5. That is, the same general pattern can be found in most menu-driven programs. These steps will handle most problems requiring a menu-driven program:

1. Clear the screen.
2. Display a menu.
3. In a friendly manner, prompt the operator to enter a response code.
4. Validate the response.
5. If the response is valid, transfer control to the appropriate function or to another menu.
6. If the response is invalid, in a clear and courteous manner notify the operator of the incorrect response and request the operator to enter a new response code.
7. Perform the function chosen.
   a. If the function is another menu, repeat steps 1 through 6.
   b. If the function is interactive, input the data and execute the function accordingly. When the function is completed, prompt the operator to enter a response to the code for:
      i. The main menu
      ii. Another menu
   c. If the function is batch, follow the general logic pattern in Section 5.6. Steps 8 and 9 below may not apply in this case.
8. Repeat steps 1 through 7 as necessary.
9. Enter a response to terminate the program.

**5.8
A STANDARD
FORM OF
PROGRAM
ORGANIZATION
FOR A
MENU-DRIVEN
PROGRAM**

**5.9
BASIC SELF-TEST
EXERCISES**

1. Consider the valid programs listed below. What is displayed if each each is executed?

a.
```
100 REM EXERCISE 5.1A
110 READ A
120 IF A = -1 THEN 170
130    LET A1 = 0.2 * A
140    PRINT A, A1
150    READ A
160 GOTO 120
170 PRINT "END OF REPORT"
180 DATA -20, 20, 500.3
190 DATA 500.6, 1.9, 3.8, -1
200 END
```

b.
```
100 REM EXERCISE 5.1B
110 READ A, C
120 WHILE A <> -999999
130    IF A >= C THEN LET B = 1 ELSE LET B = 0
140    PRINT A, C, B
150    READ A, C
160 WEND
170 PRINT "END OF REPORT"
180 DATA 1, 4, 8, 6, 5, 5, -999999, 0
190 END
```

c.
```
100 REM EXERCISE 5.1C
110 READ A, B, C
120 IF A = 0 THEN 230
130    LET D = B^2 - 4 * A * C
140    IF D > 0 THEN 180
150       IF D = 0 THEN 200
160          PRINT A, B, C, "NO REAL ROOTS EXIST"
170          GOTO 210
180       PRINT A, B, C, "TWO REAL ROOTS EXIST"
190       GOTO 210
200          PRINT A, B, C, "ONE REAL ROOT EXISTS"
210    READ A, B, C
220 GOTO 120
230 PRINT "END OF REPORT"
240 DATA 1, 0, 0, 3, 5, 2
250 DATA 4, 3, 3, 0, 0, 0
260 END
```

d.
```
100 REM EXERCISE 5.1D
110 LET A = 1
120 PRINT A
130 IF A - 2 < 0 THEN 250
140    IF A - 2 = 0 THEN 230
150       IF A - 4 < 0 THEN 210
160          IF A - 4 = 0 THEN 190
170             LET A = 1
180          GOTO 260
190             LET A = 5
200          GOTO 260
210       LET A = 4
220       GOTO 260
230    LET A = 3
240    GOTO 260
250 LET A = 2
260 PRINT A
270 GOTO 130
280 END
```

2. Write a BASIC statement that will initialize X to 0 and another that will initialize T to 10. Also, write additional BASIC statements that will consecutively increment these variables by:

    a. 1   b. 7   c. 2   d. double each value   e. minus 1

3. Write an IF statement which will perform the test and branch operations indicated below for each example:

    a.   b.

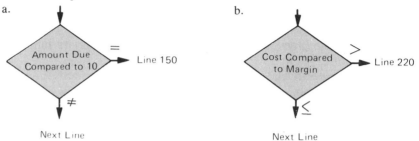

4. Determine the value of Q that will cause the condition in the IF-THEN statements below to be true.

    a. 100 IF Q > 8 THEN LET Z = Z/10
    b. 110 IF Q + 10 >= 7 THEN PRINT "THE ANSWER IS"; A
    c. 120 IF Q/3 < 9 THEN 300
    d. 130 IF Q<> 3 THEN LET S = S + A

5. Write a series of statements to perform the test and branching operations indicated below:

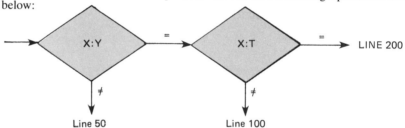

6. Construct partial programs for each of the logic structures found below. Do not use any GOTO statements.

    a.   b.

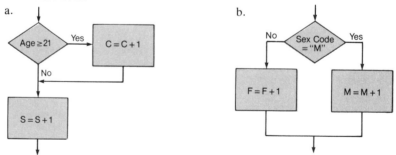

7. Given two positive valued variables A and B, write a sequence of statements to assign the variable with the larger value to G and the variable with the smaller value to S. If A and B are equal, assign either to E. After completion, go to line number 150.

8. The values of three variables U, V and W are positive and not equal to each other. Using IF statements, determine which has the smallest value and assign this value to S. After completion, go to line number 270.

9. The symbol N! represents the product of the first N positive integers: N! = N * (N − 1) * (N − 2) * . . . * 1. When a result is defined in terms of itself, we call it a **recursive definition**. Construct a program that will accept from the keyboard a positive integer and

compute its factorial. The recursive definition is as follows: If $N = 1$, then $N! = 1$; otherwise $N! = N(N - 1)!$.

10. Consider the following program:

```
100 REM EXERCISE 5.10
110 LET C = 0
120 LET S = 0
130 READ X, Y, Z
140 WHILE X > 0
150     IF X < Y + 2 THEN 160 ELSE 180
160         LET C = C - 1
170     GOTO 240
180         IF X < Z + 1 THEN 190 ELSE 210
190             LET C = C - 2
200         GOTO 240
210             LET S = S + X * Y * Z
220             LET C = C + 1
230             PRINT X, Y, Z, C, S
240     READ X, Y, Z
250 WEND
260 PRINT S, C
270 PRINT "END OF REPORT"
280 DATA 4, 1, 3, 12, 7, 1, 8, 4, 7
290 DATA 6, 2, 3, 3, 7, 2, -1, 0, 0
300 END
```

a. Which variable is used to test for end-of-file?

b. What are the values of C and S just prior to the third time line 240 is executed?

c. How many lines are displayed by the program?

d. What is the maximum value of S displayed?

e. What is the maximum value of C displayed?

11. The sequence of Fibonacci numbers begins with 1, 1 and continues endlessly, each number being the sum of the preceding two:

$1, 1, 2, 3, 5, 8, 13, 21, 34, \ldots$

Construct a program to compute the first X numbers of the sequence where the value of X is entered in response to an INPUT statement.

12. Write a partial program to set $A = -1$ if C and D are both zero, set $A = -2$ if neither C nor D is zero and set $A = -3$ if either, but not both, C or D is zero. After completion go to line number 150.

13. The WESAVU NATIONAL BANK computes its monthly service charge on checking accounts by adding 25¢ to a value computed from the following:

$0.09 per check for the first ten checks

$0.08 per check for the next ten checks

$0.07 per check for the next ten checks

$0.06 per check for all the rest of the checks

Write a sequence of statements that includes an ON-GOTO statement and a PRINT statement to display the account number A, the number of checks cashed C, and the computed monthly charge B. Assume the account number and the number of checks cashed are entered via an INPUT statement prior to the execution of the ON-GOTO statement.

Purpose: To illustrate the concepts of counter and running total initialization, counter and running total incrementation, looping, and testing for the last value in a set of data.

Problem: Construct a program to read, count records, accumulate salaries, and display a sequence of data consisting of employee numbers and salaries for various employees in a payroll file. After the sentinel value ("EOF") is processed, display the total number of employees and the average yearly salary of all the employees processed.

**5.10
BASIC
PROGRAMMING
PROBLEMS**

**1:
Employee Average
Yearly Salary**

Input Data: Prepare and use the following sample data:

Employee Number	Employee Salary
123	$16,000
148	8,126
184	14,800
196	17,400
201	18,950
EOF	0

Output Results: The following results are displayed:

```
EMPLOYEE   EMPLOYEE
NUMBER     SALARY
--------   --------
   123     16,000.00
   148      8,126.00
   184     14,800.00
   196     17,400.00
   201     18,950.00

THE NUMBER OF EMPLOYEES IS   5
THE AVERAGE SALARY IS $15,055.20
```

**2:
Stockbroker's
Commission**

Purpose: To become familiar with the If-Then-Else structure and methods used to determine a stockbroker's commission.

Problem: Write a program that will read a stock transaction and determine the stockbroker's commission. Each transaction includes the following data: the stock name, price per share, number of shares involved and the stockbroker's name.

The stockbroker's commission is computed in the following manner: if price per share P is less than or equal to $40.00 the commission rate is 15¢ per share; if P is greater than $40.00 the commission rate is 25¢ per share. If the number of shares sold is less than 125, the commission is 1.5 times the rate per share.

Each line of output is to include the stock transaction data set and the commission paid the stock broker. Test the stock name for the EOF. Display the total commission earned.

Input Data: Prepare and use the following sample data:

Stock Name	Price per Share	Number of Shares	Stockbroker Name
CRANE	$32.50	200	Baker, G.
FSTPA	17.50	100	Smith, J.
GENDYN	56.25	300	Smith, A.
HARRIS	40.00	125	Lucas, M.
BELLCD	48.00	160	Soley, K.
BELLHOW	22.00	300	Jones, D.

Output Results: The following results are displayed:

```
STOCK        PRICE        NUMBER       STOCKBROKER
NAME         PER SHARE    OF SHARES    NAME            COMMISSION
-----        ---------    ---------    -----------     ----------
CRANE        32.50        200          BAKER, G.       30.00
FSTPA        17.50        100          SMITH, J.       22.50
GENDYN       56.25        300          SMITH, A.       75.00
HARRIS       40.00        125          LUCAS, M.       18.75
BELLCD       48.00        160          SOLEY, K.       40.00
BELLHOW      22.00        300          JONES, D.       45.00

TOTAL COMMISSION EARNED IS   $231.25

END OF REPORT
```

Purpose: To become familiar with a multi-function program and the use of a menu.

Problem: Write a menu-driven program to compute the volume of a box, cylinder, cone, and sphere. The program should display the menu which is shown under Output Results. Once a code is entered, it must be validated. After the selection of the proper function, the program should prompt the operator for the necessary data, compute the volume, and display it accordingly. The displayed results are to remain on the screen until the Enter key on the keyboard is pressed. After that the program should re-display the menu.

3:
A Menu-Driven Program with Multi-Functions

Use the following formulas for the volumes V:

1. Volume of a box: $V = L * W * H$ where L is the length, W is the width, and H is the height of the box.
2. Volume of a cylinder: $V = \pi * R * R * H$ where π equals 3.14159, R is the radius, and H is the height of the cylinder.
3. Volume of a cone: $V = (\pi * R * R * H)/3$ where π equals 3.14159, R is the radius of the base, and H is the height of the cone.
4. Volume of a sphere: $V = 4 * \pi * R * R * R$ where π equals 3.14159, and R is the radius of the sphere.

Input Data: Use the following sample data:

Code = 3, Radius = 7, Height = 9
Code = 4, Radius = 10
Code = 1, Length = 4.5, Width = 6.7, Height = 12
Code = 2, Radius = 8, Height = 15
Code = 7 (This code should return a diagnostic message.)

Output Results: The following menu is displayed:

```
        MENU FOR COMPUTING VOLUMES
        -----------------------------

   CODE      FUNCTION
   ----      --------
     1    -  COMPUTE VOLUME OF A BOX
     2    -  COMPUTE VOLUME OF A CYLINDER
     3    -  COMPUTE VOLUME OF A CONE
     4    -  COMPUTE VOLUME OF A SPHERE
     5    -  END PROGRAM

   ENTER A CODE 1 THROUGH 5?
```

Purpose: To become familiar with decision-making and some payroll concepts.

Problem: Modify Payroll Problem III in Chapter 4, Problem 4, to include the following conditions:

4:
Payroll Problem IV— Weekly Payroll Computations with Time-and-One-Half for Overtime

1. Overtime (hours worked > 80) is paid at 1.5 times the hourly rate.
2. Federal withholding tax is determined in the same manner as indicated in Payroll Problem III. However, assign a value of $0.00 if the gross pay less the product of the number of dependents and $38.46 is not positive.
3. After processing the employee records, display the total gross pay, federal withholding tax and net pay.

Input Data: Use the sample data found in Payroll Problem II in Problem 3 of Chapter 3. Modify the DATA statement representing employee 126 so that the number of dependents equals 9.

Output Results: The following results are displayed:

EMPLOYEE NUMBER	GROSS PAY	FED. TAX	NET PAY
--------	---------	--------	-------
123	1,000.00	184.62	815.38
124	880.00	168.31	711.69
125	1,040.00	200.31	839.69
126	90.00	0.00	90.00

```
TOTAL GROSS PAY=========>    3,010.00
TOTAL WITHHOLDING TAX===>      553.24
TOTAL NET PAY===========>    2,456.76

JOB COMPLETE
```

MORE ON LOOPING, DECISION-MAKING AND PROGRAM CONSTRUCTION

In Chapter 5, loops were implemented (coded) using the IF-THEN and GOTO statements or the WHILE and WEND statements. In this chapter, loops will be implemented using a third method of controlling loops, FOR and NEXT statements. This chapter also presents internal **subroutines**, which can be an effective tool for designing and implementing algorithms.

Up to now, we have been working with relational operators, like >, < and =, and relational expressions, or conditions. **Logical operators**, like AND, OR and NOT, may also be used to combine conditions. Logical operators reduce the number of IF statements required to implement certain If-Then-Else structures.

6.1 LOGICAL OPERATORS

There are many instances in which a decision to execute one alternative or another is based upon two or more conditions. In previous examples that involved two or more conditions, we tested each condition in a separate decision statement. In this section, we will discuss combining conditions within one decision statement using the logical operators AND and OR. When two or more conditions are combined by logical operators, the expression is called a **compound condition**. The logical operator NOT allows you to write a condition in which the truth value is **complemented**, or reversed.

The AND Logical Operator

The AND operator requires that both conditions be true for the compound condition to be true. Consider the following IF-THEN statement:

```
200 IF S$ = "M" AND A > 20 THEN 210 ELSE 400
210 .
```

If S$ is equal to "M" *and* A is greater than 20, then control transfers to line 210. If either one of the two conditions is false, the compound condition is false and control passes to line 400.

Like a single condition, a compound condition can only be true or false. To determine the truth value of the compound condition, the system must evaluate and assign a truth value to each individual condition. Then the truth value is determined for the compound condition, which contains a logical operator like AND.

For example, if X equals 4 and Y equals 0, the system evaluates the following compound condition like this:

```
300 IF X = 3 AND Y = 0 THEN 310 ELSE 400
```

```
       1. false    2. true
```

```
              3. false
```

The system first determines the truth value for each condition, then it concludes that the compound condition is false because of the AND operation.

The following rule summarizes the use of the logical operator AND:

Logical Operator Rule 1: The logical operator AND requires that all conditions be true for the compound condition to be true.

The OR Logical Operator

The OR operator requires that only one of the two conditions be true for the compound condition to be true. If both conditions are true, the compound condition is also true. The use of the OR operator is illustrated below.

```
500 IF W = 4 OR Q < 5 THEN 510 ELSE 530
510     LET S = S + 1
520     PRINT "W = 4 OR Q < 5"
530 .
```

In line 500, if either W equals 4 *or* Q is less than 5, control transfers to line 510. If both conditions are true, control also transfers to line 510. If both conditions are false, control passes to line 530.

The following rule summarizes the use of the logical operator OR:

Logical Operator Rule 2: The logical operator OR requires that *only one* of the conditions be true for the compound condition to be true. If both conditions are true, the compound condition is also true.

The NOT Logical Operator

A relational expression preceded by the logical operator NOT forms a condition which is false when the relational expression is true. If the relational expression is false, then the condition is true. Consider the following IF-THEN-ELSE statement:

```
700 IF NOT A > B THEN 710 ELSE 800
710 .
```

If A is greater than B (if the relational expression is true), then the condition NOT A > B is false. If A is less than or equal to B (if the relational expression is false), then the condition is true.

Because the logical operator NOT can increase the complexity of the decision statement significantly, use it sparingly.

The following rule summarizes the use of the logical operator NOT:

Logical Operator Rule 3: The logical operator NOT requires that the relational expression be false for the condition to be true. If the relational expression is true, then the condition is false.

Combining Logical Operators AND, OR **and** NOT

The logical operators AND, OR and NOT can be combined in a decision statement to form a compound condition.

The order of evaluation is a part of what are sometimes called the **rules of precedence**. Just as we have rules of precedence for arithmetic operations (see Section 3.4), we also have rules of precedence for logical operations.

> **Precedence Rule 3:** Unless parentheses dictate otherwise, reading from left to right, conditions containing relational operators are evaluated first, then those containing NOT operators, then those containing AND operators, and finally those conditions containing OR operators.

Consider the compound condition that follows. Assume that D = 3, H = 3, R = 2, T = 5, X = 3 and Y = 2:

```
X > Y  OR  T = D  AND  H < 3  OR  NOT  Y = R
1. true    2. false   3. false       4. true
                 6. false         5. false
           7. true
                    8. true
```

The Effect of Parentheses in the Evaluation of Compound Conditions

Parentheses may be used to change the order of precedence. In BASIC, parentheses are normally used to avoid ambiguity and to group conditions with a desired logical operator. When there are parentheses in a compound condition, the system evaluates that part of the compound condition within the parentheses first and then continues to evaluate the remaining compound condition according to the rules of precedence. Consider the previous example, if parentheses surround the latter two conditions:

```
X > Y  OR  T = D  AND  (H < 3  OR  NOT  Y = R)
5. true   6. false   1. false      2. true
                              3. false
                       4. false
                  7. false
          8. true
```

The FOR and NEXT statements make it possible in BASIC to execute a section of a program repeatedly, with automatic changes in the value of a variable between repetitions.

In Chapter 5, the WHILE and WEND statements were used to implement a loop structure that executed a section of a program repeatedly. A **counter-controlled loop**

**6.2
THE** FOR **AND** NEXT **STATEMENTS**

executes a specified number of times. Whenever a While loop is developed to execute a counter-controlled loop, the coding requires statements for initializing, incrementing and testing of a counter. Any While loop involving this type of coding may be rewritten as a **For loop** using the FOR and NEXT statements and still perform the same tasks. The FOR and NEXT statements provide for the construction of counter-controlled loops.

The While Loop Versus the For Loop

To illustrate the similarity between the While loop and For loop, consider Programs 6.1 and 6.2. Both programs compute the sum of the integers from 1 to 10.

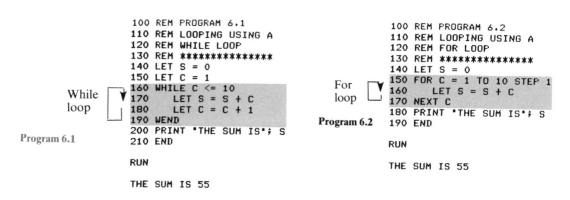

```
100 REM PROGRAM 6.1
110 REM LOOPING USING A
120 REM WHILE LOOP
130 REM ***************
140 LET S = 0
150 LET C = 1
160 WHILE C <= 10
170    LET S = S + C
180    LET C = C + 1
190 WEND
200 PRINT "THE SUM IS"; S
210 END

RUN

THE SUM IS 55
```

While loop

Program 6.1

```
100 REM PROGRAM 6.2
110 REM LOOPING USING A
120 REM FOR LOOP
130 REM ***************
140 LET S = 0
150 FOR C = 1 TO 10 STEP 1
160    LET S = S + C
170 NEXT C
180 PRINT "THE SUM IS"; S
190 END

RUN

THE SUM IS 55
```

For loop

Program 6.2

Program 6.2 incorporates the FOR and NEXT statements to define the For loop (lines 150 through 170). Read through Program 6.2 carefully and note how compact it is and how superior it is to Program 6.1. Using a single FOR statement, as in line 150 of Program 6.2, we can delete two statements (lines 150 and 180) in Program 6.1.

The statements in the For loop, except for the first and last, should be indented by three spaces for the purposes of readability (see line 160). This style allows you to scan a For loop quickly, and it simplifies the debugging effort.

The Execution of a For Loop

When the FOR statement in Program 6.2 is executed for the first time, the For loop becomes "active" and C is set equal to 1. The statements in the For loop, in this case line 160, are executed. Control returns to the FOR statement where the value of C is incremented by a value of 1 following the keyword STEP. If the value of C is less than or equal to 10, execution of the For loop continues. If the value of C is greater than 10, control transfers to the statement (line 180) following the NEXT C statement.

The general forms of the FOR and NEXT statements are given in Tables 6.1 and 6.2.

TABLE 6.1   **The FOR Statement**

General Form:	FOR k = initial value TO limit value STEP increment value *or* FOR k = initial value TO limit value where k is a simple numeric variable called the **control variable**, and initial, limit and increment values are each numeric expressions. In the absence of the keyword STEP, the value of the increment is 1.
Purpose:	Causes the statements between the FOR and NEXT statements to be executed repeatedly until the value of k exceeds the limit. When k exceeds the limit, control transfers to the line just after the corresponding NEXT statement.

Examples:	```250 FOR X = 1 TO 20```
	```350 FOR A = 5 TO 15 STEP 2```
	```400 FOR C = 10 TO -5 STEP -3```
	```450 FOR Y = 1 TO 10 STEP 0.1```
	```500 FOR T = A TO B STEP C```
	```550 FOR S = A + 5 TO C/D STEP F * B```

TABLE 6.2   **The NEXT Statement**

General Form:	NEXT k where k is the same variable as the control variable in the corresponding FOR statement.
Purpose:	Identifies the end of a For loop.
Examples:	```300 NEXT X``` ```380 NEXT A```

The terminology used to describe the FOR statement is shown below:

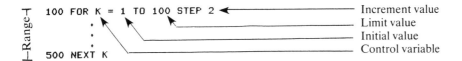

The **range** of a For loop is the set of repeatedly executed statements beginning with the FOR statement and continuing up to and including the NEXT statement with the same control variable.

Flowchart Representation of a For Loop

The flowchart representation for a For loop corresponds to a Do-While structure (see Figure 6.1 on page 100). In the first process symbol, the control variable k is assigned the initial value. If the condition is true, the loop is terminated and control transfers to the statement following the Do-While structure.

   If the condition is false, control passes into the body of the For loop. After the statements in the For loop are executed, the control variable k is incremented by the imcrement value, and control transfers back up to the decision symbol again to test if the control variable k exceeds the limit value. Figure 6.2 illustrates a flowchart that corresponds to Program 6.2.

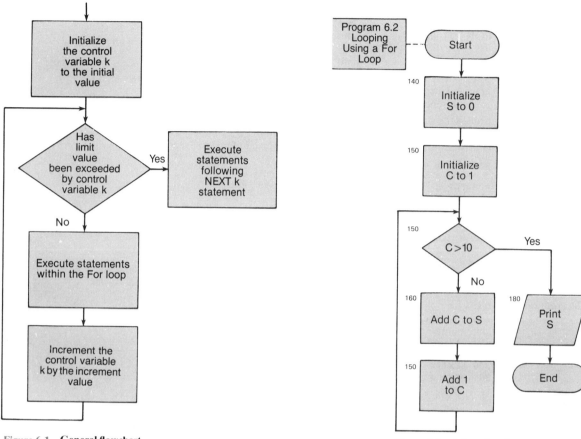

Figure 6.1   **General flowchart representation for a For loop.**

Figure 6.2   **A flowchart for Program 6.2.**

Nested For Loops

When the statements of one For loop lie within the range of another For loop, the loops are said to be **nested** or embedded. The outer For loop may be nested in the range of still another For loop, which may be nested in the range of still another, and so on.

When one For loop is nested within another, the name of the control variable for each For loop must be different.

Program 6.3 generates the multiplication table. Each time the control variable in the outer For loop (lines 160 through 220) is assigned a new value, the inner For loop (lines 180 through 200) computes and displays one row of the table. The PRINT USING statements in lines 170 and 190 end with the semicolon separator. Recall from Chapter 4 that when a PRINT statement ends with a semicolon, the cursor remains on that same line. Each time the inner loop is satisfied, the PRINT statement in line 210 prints blanks and moves the cursor to the beginning of the next line.

The usefulness of the FOR and NEXT statements for looping purposes should be apparent from the examples and illustrations presented thus far. However, you will see an even greater use for them in applications involving the manipulation of arrays, which are discussed in the next chapter. The material in this section can be summarized in the following rules:

```
100 REM PROGRAM 6.3
110 REM GENERATING THE MULTIPLICATION TABLE
120 REM ************************************
130 CLS
140 PRINT "  X !   0   1   2   3   4   5   6   7   8   9  10  11  12"
150 PRINT "-----+--------------------------------------------------"
160 FOR R = 0 TO 12
170    PRINT USING "###  !"; R;
180    FOR C = 0 TO 12
190       PRINT USING "####"; R * C;
200    NEXT C
210    PRINT
220 NEXT R
230 PRINT
240 PRINT "END OF MULTIPLICATION TABLE"
250 END
```

Program 6.3

```
RUN

  X !   0   1   2   3   4   5   6   7   8   9  10  11  12
-----+--------------------------------------------------
  0 !   0   0   0   0   0   0   0   0   0   0   0   0   0
  1 !   0   1   2   3   4   5   6   7   8   9  10  11  12
  2 !   0   2   4   6   8  10  12  14  16  18  20  22  24
  3 !   0   3   6   9  12  15  18  21  24  27  30  33  36
  4 !   0   4   8  12  16  20  24  28  32  36  40  44  48
  5 !   0   5  10  15  20  25  30  35  40  45  50  55  60
  6 !   0   6  12  18  24  30  36  42  48  54  60  66  72
  7 !   0   7  14  21  28  35  42  49  56  63  70  77  84
  8 !   0   8  16  24  32  40  48  56  64  72  80  88  96
  9 !   0   9  18  27  36  45  54  63  72  81  90  99 108
 10 !   0  10  20  30  40  50  60  70  80  90 100 110 120
 11 !   0  11  22  33  44  55  66  77  88  99 110 121 132
 12 !   0  12  24  36  48  60  72  84  96 108 120 132 144

END OF MULTIPLICATION TABLE
```

NEXT **Rule 1:** The NEXT statement must have a higher line number than its corresponding FOR statement.

FOR **Rule 1:** The FOR statement may be located anywhere before the corresponding NEXT statement.

FOR **Rule 2:** The value of the increment value must not be zero.

FOR **Rule 3:** If the range of a For loop includes another For loop, all statements in the range of the inner For loop must also be within the range of the outer For loop.

FOR **Rule 4:** When one For loop is within another, the name of the control variable for each For loop must be different.

In this section, internal **subroutines** are presented. A subroutine is a *group of statements* within a BASIC program associated with a single programming task. Internal subroutines, or **modules**, as they can also be called, are useful in solving large, complex problems, because they allow a problem to be subdivided into smaller and more manageable subproblems, which can then be solved with appropriate subroutines.

6.3 INTERNAL SUBROUTINES (MODULES)

An internal subroutine is executed only if referenced, **called**, by an explicit instruction from some other part of the program, as illustrated in Figure 6.3 on page 102. Following execution of the internal subroutine, control passes back to the statement immediately following the instruction that activated the subroutine.

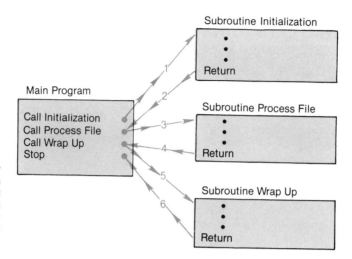

Figure 6.3   **A conceptual view of control transferring to an internal subroutine and eventually returning to the statement that immediately follows the instruction that activated the subroutine.**

The GOSUB, ON–GOSUB and RETURN Statements

A subroutine may be called by either a GOSUB or an ON–GOSUB statement. The GOSUB statement is similar to the GOTO statement in that the keyword GOSUB is immediately followed by a line number to which control is transferred. The ON–GOSUB statement is similar to the ON–GOTO in that a series of line numbers follow the keyword GOSUB, and the system selects which line to transfer control based on the integer value of the numeric expression between the keywords ON and GOSUB. Hence, the GOSUB and RETURN statements allow for subroutine calls, and the ON–GOSUB and RETURN statements allow for *selected* subroutine calls. The last statement executed in a subroutine must be the RETURN statement. A subroutine, therefore, can only exit through a RETURN statement.

The major difference between a GOSUB and a GOTO statement, or between an ON–GOSUB and an ON–GOTO statement, lies in the execution of a subroutine. For a GOSUB or ON–GOSUB,

1. The Main program calls or transfers control to the subroutine.
2. The called subroutine executes and performs a particular or recurring task for the Main program.
3. The RETURN statement of the subroutine transfers control back to the statement immediately following the GOSUB or ON–GOSUB which referenced the subroutine.

The general forms for the GOSUB, ON–GOSUB and RETURN statements are shown in Tables 6.3, 6.4 and 6.5.

TABLE 6.3   The GOSUB Statement

General Form:	GOSUB line number where the line number represents the first line of a subroutine.
Purpose:	Causes control to transfer to the subroutine represented by the specified line number. Causes also the line number of the next statement following the GOSUB to be retained.
Examples:	250 GOSUB 600 900 GOSUB 2000

TABLE 6.4   The ON-GOSUB **Statement**

General Form:	ON numeric expression GOSUB k_1, k_2, . . . , k_n where k, the line number, represents the first line of a subroutine, and where k_1, k_2, . . . , k_n collectively represent a list of line numbers of one or more subroutines.
Purpose:	Causes control to transfer to the subroutine represented by the selected line number k_i, where i is the current value of the numeric expression. Causes also the line number of the next statement following the ON-GOSUB to be retained.
Examples:	300 ON X GOSUB 400, 500, 600, 700 800 ON F - D/Y GOSUB 850, 900, 1000, 900

TABLE 6.5   The RETURN **Statement**

General Form:	RETURN
Purpose:	Causes control to transfer from the subroutine back to the statement immediately following the corresponding GOSUB or ON-GOSUB statement.
Examples:	700 RETURN 900 RETURN

A subroutine does not have a unique *initial* statement to differentiate it from other subroutines or from the Main program, sometimes called the **Main module**. In order to highlight the beginning of a subroutine, a remark or comment line is often used before the first executable statement of a subroutine (see lines 500, 510 and 520 of Figure 6.4 on page 104). This boxed-in remark should define the purpose of the subroutine and indicate to the reader that a subroutine follows.

The last statement of a subroutine should always be the RETURN statement. Any attempt to execute a RETURN statement without executing a prior corresponding GOSUB or ON-GOSUB statement results in the display of a diagnostic message and the termination of the program. This can be summarized by the following rule:

> RETURN **Rule 1:** The execution of a RETURN statement must be preceded by the execution of a corresponding GOSUB or ON-GOSUB statement.

In the partial program in Figure 6.4, lines 100 through 120 highlight the Main module and lines 500 to 520 highlight the subroutine defined as the Display Menu module. When the RUN command is issued, the Main module (lines 100 to 490) executes and calls the subroutine (lines 500 to 720) from lines 410 and 450. Line 440 refers to the location of other subroutines not shown in Figure 6.4.

So that subroutines can be located easily, for debugging purposes, they should be placed near the end of the program but before any DATA statements and the END line. Assigning distinctive line numbers, like 1000, 1100, 1200, and so on, to subroutines would also be helpful.

Figure 6.4 also illustrates the flow of control from the Main module of the program to the subroutine and the eventual transfer from the subroutine back to the line immediately following the corresponding GOSUB or ON-GOSUB statement.

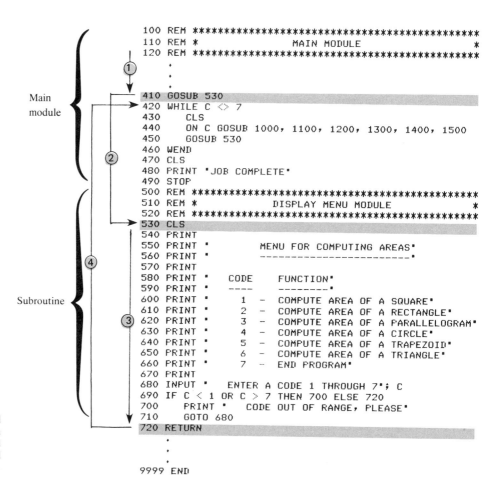

```
100 REM ************************************************
110 REM *                   MAIN MODULE                *
120 REM ************************************************
      .
      .
      .
410 GOSUB 530
420 WHILE C <> 7
430    CLS
440    ON C GOSUB 1000, 1100, 1200, 1300, 1400, 1500
450    GOSUB 530
460 WEND
470 CLS
480 PRINT "JOB COMPLETE"
490 STOP
500 REM ************************************************
510 REM *                DISPLAY MENU MODULE           *
520 REM ************************************************
530 CLS
540 PRINT
550 PRINT "          MENU FOR COMPUTING AREAS"
560 PRINT "          -------------------------"
570 PRINT
580 PRINT "     CODE      FUNCTION"
590 PRINT "     ----      --------"
600 PRINT "      1   -   COMPUTE AREA OF A SQUARE"
610 PRINT "      2   -   COMPUTE AREA OF A RECTANGLE"
620 PRINT "      3   -   COMPUTE AREA OF A PARALLELOGRAM"
630 PRINT "      4   -   COMPUTE AREA OF A CIRCLE"
640 PRINT "      5   -   COMPUTE AREA OF A TRAPEZOID"
650 PRINT "      6   -   COMPUTE AREA OF A TRIANGLE"
660 PRINT "      7   -   END PROGRAM"
670 PRINT
680 INPUT "    ENTER A CODE 1 THROUGH 7"; C
690 IF C < 1 OR C > 7 THEN 700 ELSE 720
700    PRINT "    CODE OUT OF RANGE, PLEASE"
710    GOTO 680
720 RETURN
      .
      .
      .
9999 END
```

Figure 6.4 The flow of control from the Main module of a program to a subroutine and the eventual return of control to the Main module.

When line 410 transfers control to line 530 of the subroutine, the subroutine displays a menu and requests a code to be entered. Once the code is entered and verified, the RETURN statement in line 720 causes control to transfer back to line 420.

As long as the code C is not 7, control enters the While loop. Line 430 clears the screen, and the ON-GOSUB in line 440 selects to transfer control to one of six subroutines, depending upon the value of C. Any one of the subroutines selected by line 440 eventually transfers control back to line 450, which again displays the menu. The While loop (lines 420 to 460) continues to execute until C is assigned a value of 7 in line 680 of the subroutine.

The STOP Statement

The STOP statement halts the execution of the program. The STOP statement also causes the following or an equivalent message to be displayed:

```
BREAK IN 490
```

In Figure 6.4, line 490, the STOP statement is the last statement executed and it causes the program to halt. Note that by placing the STOP statement at line 490, we prevent the Display Menu module from being executed again, as a part of the end-of-job routine. The general form of the STOP statement is shown in Table 6.6.

TABLE 6.6   The STOP **Statement**

General Form:	STOP
Purpose:	Causes termination of execution of the program after displaying the message BREAK IN k, where k represents the line number of the STOP statement.
Examples:	500 STOP 700 STOP
Note:	The STOP statement differs from the END statement in that it halts or suspends execution of the program, rather than terminating it. Execution of the program will resume if the system command CONT is entered.

Flowchart Representation of GOSUB, ON-GOSUB, RETURN and Referenced Subroutine

The program flowchart representation of the GOSUB statement and the referenced subroutine are shown in Figure 6.5. The GOSUB statement, which calls the subroutine, is represented by the **predefined process symbol**, which was defined in Table 1.2 (p. 8). The predefined process symbol consists of a set of vertical lines in the left and right sides of a rectangle and indicates that the program steps of the subroutine are specified elsewhere. In Figure 6.5, the subroutine is represented by the flowchart to the right of the Main module and the RETURN statement is represented by the terminal symbol.

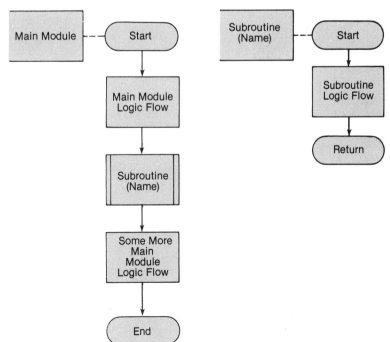

Figure 6.5   **General flowchart representation of the** GOSUB **statement and the referenced subroutine.**

The ON-GOSUB statement is represented by the decision symbol and each case is illustrated by a predefined process symbol

Nested Subroutines

Just as there are nested For loops, there are nested subroutines. In a nest of subroutines, one subroutine may call another subroutine, which may in turn call another, and so on. However, each subroutine must terminate with a RETURN statement. Figure 6.6 illustrates the flow of control from the Main module to the nested subroutines. The lines and circled numbers represent the flow of control.

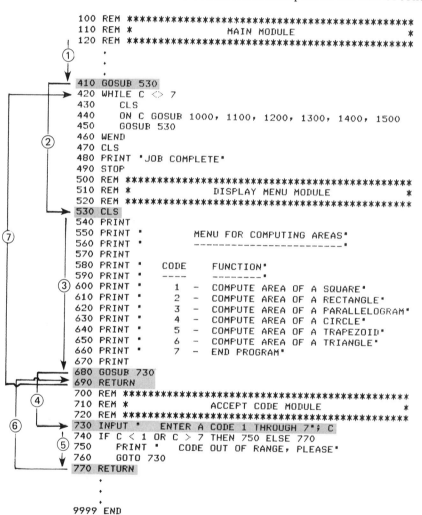

Figure 6.6 **The flow of control in a program with nested subroutines.**

```
100 REM ************************************************
110 REM *                    MAIN MODULE                *
120 REM ************************************************
       .
       .
       .
410 GOSUB 530
420 WHILE C <> 7
430     CLS
440     ON C GOSUB 1000, 1100, 1200, 1300, 1400, 1500
450     GOSUB 530
460 WEND
470 CLS
480 PRINT "JOB COMPLETE"
490 STOP
500 REM ************************************************
510 REM *              DISPLAY MENU MODULE              *
520 REM ************************************************
530 CLS
540 PRINT
550 PRINT "              MENU FOR COMPUTING AREAS"
560 PRINT "              --------------------------"
570 PRINT
580 PRINT "    CODE      FUNCTION"
590 PRINT "    ----      --------"
600 PRINT "     1   -   COMPUTE AREA OF A SQUARE"
610 PRINT "     2   -   COMPUTE AREA OF A RECTANGLE"
620 PRINT "     3   -   COMPUTE AREA OF A PARALLELOGRAM"
630 PRINT "     4   -   COMPUTE AREA OF A CIRCLE"
640 PRINT "     5   -   COMPUTE AREA OF A TRAPEZOID"
650 PRINT "     6   -   COMPUTE AREA OF A TRIANGLE"
660 PRINT "     7   -   END PROGRAM"
670 PRINT
680 GOSUB 730
690 RETURN
700 REM ************************************************
710 REM *               ACCEPT CODE MODULE              *
720 REM ************************************************
730 INPUT "    ENTER A CODE 1 THROUGH 7"; C
740 IF C < 1 OR C > 7 THEN 750 ELSE 770
750     PRINT "   CODE OUT OF RANGE, PLEASE"
760     GOTO 730
770 RETURN
       .
       .
       .
9999 END
```

6.4
BASIC
SELF-TEST
EXERCISES

1. Consider the valid programs listed below. What is displayed if each is executed?

```
a. 100 REM EXERCISE 6.1A
   110 READ X, Y
   120 WHILE X >= 0
   130     IF X = Y AND Y >= 10 THEN PRINT Y ELSE PRINT X, Y
   140     IF X = Y OR Y >= 10 THEN PRINT 2 * Y ELSE PRINT X, 2 * Y
   150     READ X, Y
   160 WEND
   170 PRINT "END OF JOB"
   180 DATA 3, 5, 8, 10, 15, 15, 4, 4, -1, 0
   190 END
```

b.   Assume that the following data items are entered in sequence as requested: 15, 8, 17, −999999.

```
100 REM EXERCISE 6.1B
110 INPUT "INVENTORY NUMBER"; I1
120 WHILE I1 <> -999999
130    LET C = 0
140    WHILE C = 0
150       READ I2, P
160       IF I2 <> 0 THEN 200
170          PRINT "INVENTORY ITEM NOT FOUND"
180          LET C = 1
190          GOTO 230
200       IF I1 <> I2 THEN 230
210          PRINT "THE PRICE IS"; P
220          LET C = 1
230    WEND
240    RESTORE
250    INPUT "INVENTORY NUMBER"; I1
260 WEND
270 PRINT "JOB COMPLETE"
280 DATA 6, 4.54, 8, 12.96, 15, 14.98, 22, 4.96, 0, 0
290 END
```

2.   Given the following:

Employee number E = 500
Salary S = $700
Job code J = 1
Tax T = $60
Insurance deduction I = $40

Determine the truth value of the following compound conditions.

a.   E < 400 OR J = 1   e.   NOT J < 0
b.   S = 700 AND T = 50   f.   NOT S > 500 AND NOT T > 80
c.   S − T = 640 AND J = 1   g.   NOT (J = 1 OR T = 60)
d.   T + I = S − 500 OR J = 0   h.   S < 300 AND (I < 50 OR J = 2)

3.   Assume P and Q are simple conditions. The following logical equivalences are known as **DeMorgan's Laws:**

> NOT (P OR Q) is equivalent to NOT P AND NOT Q
> NOT (P AND Q) is equivalent to NOT P OR NOT Q

Use DeMorgan's Laws to find a logical equivalent for each of the following:

a.   NOT (P OR (NOT Q))   c.   NOT (NOT P AND Q)
b.   NOT ((NOT P) OR Q)   d.   NOT ((NOT P) AND (NOT Q))

4.   Construct a partial flowchart for each of the following:

a.   NOT S = Q AND (X > 1 OR C < 3)
b.   (K = 9 AND Q = 2) OR (NOT Z = 3 OR T = 0)

5.   Write a *single* IF-THEN-ELSE statement for each of the following partial flowcharts. When appropriate, use logical operators.

a.

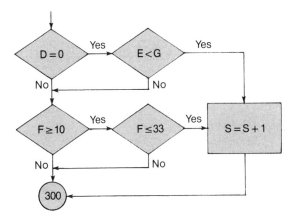

b.

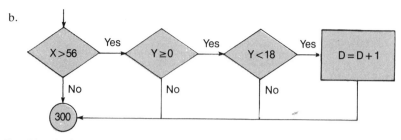

6. Consider the following program:

```
100 REM EXERCISE 6.6
110 LET F = 0
120 FOR I = 1 TO 3
130    LET G = 0
140    LET F = F + 1
150    FOR J = 1 TO 4
160       LET G = G + F
170       PRINT F, G
180    NEXT J
190 NEXT I
200 END
```

    a. How many lines are displayed?
    b. What is the maximum value of F?
    c. What is the maximum value of G?

7. Write a program for each of the following expressions and display the result.

    a. $2 \times 4 \times 6 \times 8 \times \cdots \times 40$ b. $1 + \dfrac{1}{2} + \dfrac{1}{4} + \dfrac{1}{8} + \cdots + \dfrac{1}{2^{10}}$

    c. $1^1 + 2^2 + 3^3 + 4^4 + 5^5$

6.5 BASIC PROGRAMMING PROBLEMS

1: Sum of a Series of Numbers

Purpose: To become familiar with counter-controlled loops.

Problem: Write four programs, one for each part.

Part A: Construct a program to compute and display the sum of the following series: $1 + 2 + 3 + \cdots + 100$. Use a For loop to create these integers and sum them.

Part B: Same as in Part A, but instead sum all the even numbers from 2 to 100 inclusive.

Part C: Same as in Part A, but instead input the lower and upper limits.

Part D: Same as in Part A and C, but instead include a variable step.

Input Data: For Parts A and B there is no input. For C, input a lower limit of 15 and an upper limit of 42. For Part D, input a lower limit of 20, an upper limit of 75 and a step of 5.

Output Results: For Part A, the sum is 5050.   For Part C, the sum is 798.
                          For Part B, the sum is 2550.   For Part D, the sum is 570.

2: Solution of an Equation

Purpose: To become familiar with techniques for writing efficient code and avoiding repetitive evaluation of expressions.

Problem: Construct an efficient program to solve for the roots of the quadratic equation $ax^2 + bx + c = 0$ where $a \neq 0$, using the quadratic formula

$$x = \frac{-b \pm \sqrt{b^2 - 4ac}}{2a}$$

Read three values of the coefficients a, b, c, respectively. Print the values of the coefficients and the roots on one line. If the roots are equal, print only one root. Assume the coefficient *a* does not have a value of zero and that complex roots do not exist (that is, that 4ac is always less than or equal to b^2).

Input Data: Prepare and use the following sample values for the coefficients.

A	B	C
3	−5	−2
1	−4	2
1	6	9
4	−20	2.5
8	0	0
1	80	1

Output Results: The following results are displayed:

A	B	C	ROOT 1	ROOT 2
3.00	−5.00	−2.00	2.000	−0.333
1.00	−4.00	2.00	3.414	0.586
1.00	6.00	9.00	−3.000	
4.00	−20.00	2.50	4.872	0.128
8.00	0.00	0.00	0.000	
1.00	80.00	1.00	−0.013	−79.987

```
END OF REPORT
```

3:
Aging Accounts:

Purpose: To become familiar with the concepts of aging accounts receivable using Julian Calendar dates (i.e., using a number between 1 and 365 to signify a date).

Problem: Write a program to compute the total amount due and percentage of the total amount of receivables that are:

1.   Less than 30 days past due (accounts due < 30 days)
2.   Past due between 30 and 60 days ($30 \leq$ accounts due ≤ 60)
3.   Past due over 60 days (accounts due > 60)

Include in the output the number of accounts in each category. The first input value will be today's Julian date. However, the account number, amount due and the date due for each customer shall be stored in one or more DATA statements.

Input Data: Prepare and use the following sample data. Assume today's Julian date is 155 (i.e., 155th day of the year).

Account Number	Amount Due	Date Due
1168	1495.67	145
2196	3211.16	15
3485	1468.12	130
3612	1896.45	98
7184	5.48	126
8621	965.10	75
9142	613.50	105

Output Results: The following results are displayed:

```
WHAT IS THE JULIAN DATE? 155
```

ACCOUNTS PAST DUE	NUMBER OF ACCOUNTS	TOTAL AMOUNT DUE	PERCENT OF TOTAL AMOUNT
LESS THAN 30 DAYS	3	2,969.27	30.7522
30 TO 60 DAYS	2	2,509.95	25.9951
OVER 60 DAYS	2	4,176.26	43.2528

```
JOB COMPLETE
```

4:
Payroll Problem V—
Social Security
Computations

Purpose: To become familiar with the use of subroutines and program modifications.

Problem: Modify Payroll Problem IV in Chapter 5, Problem 4, to determine the social security deduction. The social security deduction is equal to 6.70% of the gross pay to a maximum of $2,579.50 (6.70% of $38,500) for the year. Modify the solution to Payroll Problem IV by adding this additional computation as a subroutine. Round the social security tax to the nearest cent. Use the formula INT(S * 100 + .5)/100 to round the computed social security deduction S. See Chapter 9 for a discussion of the function INT.

Input Data: Use the sample data found in Payroll Problem IV and add the following year-to-date social security deductions to the corresponding DATA statements.

Employee Number	Year-to-Date Social Security
123	$ 725.15
124	2,579.50
125	2,573.32
126	100.00

Output Results: The following results are displayed:

```
EMPLOYEE                                                       YEAR-TO-DATE
NUMBER     GROSS PAY    FED. TAX    SOC. SEC.   NET PAY    SOC. SEC.
--------   ---------    --------    ---------   -------    ------------
  123      1,000.00      184.62       67.00     748.38          792.15
  124        880.00      168.31        0.00     711.69        2,579.50
  125      1,040.00      200.31        6.18     833.51        2,579.50
  126         90.00        0.00        6.03      83.97          106.03

TOTAL GROSS PAY==============>    3,010.00
TOTAL WITHHOLDING TAX=======>       553.24
TOTAL SOCIAL SECURITY=======>        79.21
TOTAL NET PAY===============>     2,377.55

JOB COMPLETE
```

ARRAYS, SORTING AND TABLE PROCESSING

In the previous chapters, the programs used simple variables like A, B1 and X$ to store and access data. Each variable was assigned a single value in an INPUT, LET or READ statement. Another technique which can make a program shorter, easier to code, and more general is the use of arrays. In this chapter we will discuss the advantages of grouping similar data into an array.

An **array** is an ordered set of string or numeric data defined in terms of 1 or more dimensions. In mathematics, an array is sometimes called a **matrix** or a **table**.

In BASIC, an **array** is a variable allocated a specified number of storage locations, each of which can be assigned a unique value. Each member of an array is called an **array element.** An array allows a programmer to store more than one value under the same variable name. Arrays are commonly used for sorting and table processing.

Arrays versus Simple Variables

Arrays permit a programmer to represent many values with one variable name. The variable name assigned to represent an array is called the **array name**. The elements in the array are distinguished from one another by **subscripts.** The subscript is written inside a set of parentheses immediately to the right of the array name.

Consider the problem of writing a program that is to manipulate the 12 monthly sales for a company and generate a year-end report. Figure 7.1 on page 112 illustrates the difference between using an array to store the 12 monthly sales and using simple variables.

The monthly sales stored in an array require the same memory allocation that the sales represented as independent variables do. The difference lies in the programming techniques which can access the different values. For example, the programmer may assign the values of simple variables in a READ statement, like this:

```
150 READ J1, F, M1, A1, M2, J2, J3, A2, S, O, N, D
```

Each simple variable must explicitly appear in a LET or PRINT statement if the monthly sales are to be summed or displayed. Not only is the programming time-consuming, but the variables *must* be properly placed in the program.

The same function can be accomplished by entering all 12 values into array S:

```
140 FOR M = 1 TO 12
150     READ S(M)
160 NEXT M
```

In line 140, the value of M is initialized to 1, and the first value in the data holding area is assigned to S(1) (read "S sub 1"). Then M is incremented to 2, and the next

111

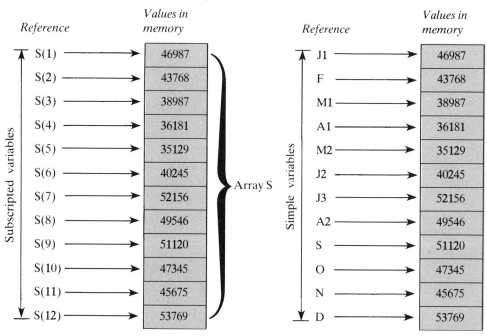

Figure 7.1 **Utilizing an array versus simple variables.**

Storing monthly sales in an array S.

Storing monthly sales in **12** simple variables.

value is assigned to S(**2**). This continues until S(**12**) is assigned the **12**th value in the data holding area.

S2 and S(**2**) are different from each other. S2 is a simple variable, no different from K, Y, X or G. On the other hand, S(**2**) is the second element in array S, and it is called upon in a program in a different fashion than a simple variable is.

7.2
DECLARING
ARRAYS

Before arrays can be used, the amount of memory to reserve for them must be declared in the program. This is the purpose of the DIM statement. The keyword DIM is an abbreviation of **dimension**. The DIM statement also declares the **upper bound value** of the subscript.

The DIM Statement

The main function of the DIM statement is to declare to the system the necessary information regarding the allocation of storage locations for arrays used in a program. Good programming practice dictates that every program that utilizes array elements should have a DIM statement that properly defines the arrays.

The general form of the DIM statement is given in Table 7.1. Note that commas are required punctuation between the declared array elements.

To ensure the proper placement of DIM statements, most programmers put them at the beginning of the program.

> DIM **Rule 1:** The DIM statement may be located anywhere before the first use of an array element in a program.

In Table 7.1, line 100 reserves memory for a one-dimensional array B consisting of 5 elements or storage locations. These elements—B(**0**), B(**1**), B(**2**), B(**3**) and

TABLE 7.1 The DIM **Statement**

General Form:	DIM array name (size), . . . , array name (size)
	where **array name** represents a numeric or string variable name, and where **size** represents the upper bound value of each array. The size may be an integer or simple variable for one-dimensional arrays. The size may be a series of integers or a series of simple variables separated by commas for multi-dimensional arrays.
Purpose:	To reserve storage locations for arrays.

Examples:	``100 DIM B(4)``
	``200 DIM M(6), J$(200), L(N), T(20, 20)``
	``300 DIM X(50), F(10, 45), K$(X, Y, Z), D(2, 25, 7)``

B(4)—can be used in a program much as a simple variable can. For this DIM statement, elements B(5) or B(6) are considered invalid.

Line 200 declares 3 one-dimensional arrays M, J$ and L, and two-dimensional array T. Line 200 reserves space for 7 elements for array M, 201 elements for array J$, N + 1 elements for array L and 441 elements for array T.

BASIC allocates the zero element for each one-dimensional array. For two-dimensional arrays an extra row, the zero row, and an extra column, the zero column, are reserved. The additional element, row or column is the **lower bound** of that array.

Line 300 in Table 7.1 declares 4 arrays. The first array, X, is a one-dimensional array. The second array, F, is a two-dimensional array. The last two, K$ and D, are three-dimensional arrays.

In this section several sample programs that manipulate the elements of arrays will be discussed. Before the programs are presented, however, it is important that you understand the syntax and limitations of subscripts.

7.3 MANIPULATING ARRAYS

Subscripts

As indicated in Section 7.1, the elements of an array are referenced by assigning a subscript to the array name. The subscript may be any valid non-negative number, variable or numeric expression within the **range** of the array. The lower and upper bounds of an array should never be exceeded. For example, if an array G is declared as follows:

```
100 DIM G(50)
```

it is invalid to reference G(−3), G(51) or any others that are outside the lower and upper bounds of the array.

Summing the Elements of an Array

Many applications call for summing the elements of an array. In Program 7.1 on page 114, the monthly sales are summed, an average is computed and the sales are displayed, four to a line.

In program 7.1, line 170 is used to sum the values of the array of elements. For example, when line 150 activates the For loop, M is assigned the value of 1. Line 160

```
100 REM PROGRAM 7.1
110 REM MONTHLY SALES ANALYSIS II
120 REM **************************
130 DIM S(12)
140 LET T = 0
150 FOR M = 1 TO 12
160     READ S(M)
170     LET T = T + S(M)
180 NEXT M
190 LET A = T/12
200 PRINT USING "THE AVERAGE MONTHLY SALES IS ###,###.##", A
210 PRINT
220 FOR M = 1 TO 12 STEP 4
230     PRINT S(M), S(M + 1), S(M + 2), S(M + 3)
240 NEXT M
250 PRINT
260 PRINT "JOB COMPLETE"
270 REM ***************DATA FOLLOWS****************
280 DATA 46987, 43768, 38987, 36181, 35129, 40245
290 DATA 52156, 49546, 51120, 47345, 45675, 53769
300 END
```

Program 7.1

```
RUN

THE AVERAGE MONTHLY SALES IS   45,075.60

    46987         43768         38987         36181
    35129         40245         52156         49546
    51120         47345         45675         53769

JOB COMPLETE
```

reads the first data item, 46987, and assigns it to S(1). Line 170 increments the running total T by S(1), and line 180 returns control to the FOR statement in line 140, where M is incremented to 2.

After the READ statement, T is assigned the sum of T and S(2). This process continues until the 12th element is added to the sum of the first 11 elements of the array S. Line 190 computes the average, and line 200 displays it.

The For loop found in lines 220 through 240 displays the monthly sales four to a line. The first time through the loop, M is equal to 1, and S(1), S(2), S(3) and S(4) display on one line. The next time through the loop, M is equal to 5 and S(5), S(6), S(7) and S(8) display on the next line. Finally, M is set equal to 9 and S(9), S(10), S(11) and S(12) display on the third line. The subscripts in line 230 are in the form of numeric expressions.

BASIC at Work

Daily Sales Report by Department

The following problem and program solution incorporate arrays and other concepts discussed in this chapter.

Problem

The Twin City retail store has ten departments that submit their daily sales to the store manager. Management has asked the data processing department to generate a daily report that includes the department number, daily sales and percent of the total sales each department contributes. Management also wants the total company sales displayed at the end of the report. A sample set of sales for the ten departments follows.

Department Number	Daily Sales
1	$ 800
2	2,250
3	1,450
4	1,280
5	1,690
6	2,460
7	3,880
8	4,690
9	2,250
10	1,360

An analysis of the problem, a flowchart, and a program solution follow.

Program Tasks

The flowchart is shown on page 116. The following points should be noted concerning Program 7.2:

1. Sum the department daily sales to determine the total sales T.
2. Since the percent P of total sales for each department cannot be computed until after the total sales for the store have been determined, store the department's daily sales into an array S.
3. Determine the percent of total sales from the following formula:

$$P = \frac{100 \times S(I)}{T}$$

   where P = the percent of total sales per department
         T = total sales
       S(I) = sales of the Ith department
4. Use a For loop to read the department sales into array S and sum the department sales.
5. Use a For loop to determine the percent of total sales and display the results for each department.
6. Display the total sales T prior to termination of the program.

The flowchart is shown on page 116. The following points should be noted concerning Program 7.2:

1. The DIM statement in line 140 sets aside 11 storage locations for array S, as illustrated:

0	0	0	0	0	0	0
S(0)	S(1)	S(2)	S(3)	S(4)	S(9)	S(10)

2. The For loop, lines 230 through 260, loads the array S beginning with S(1), as shown below, and accumulates the sum of the sales of the ten departments.

0	800	2250	1450	1280	2250	1360
S(0)	S(1)	S(2)	S(3)	S(4)	S(9)	S(10)

3. The second For loop, lines 280 through 310, computes the various departments' percent of total sales and displays a line each time through the loop.

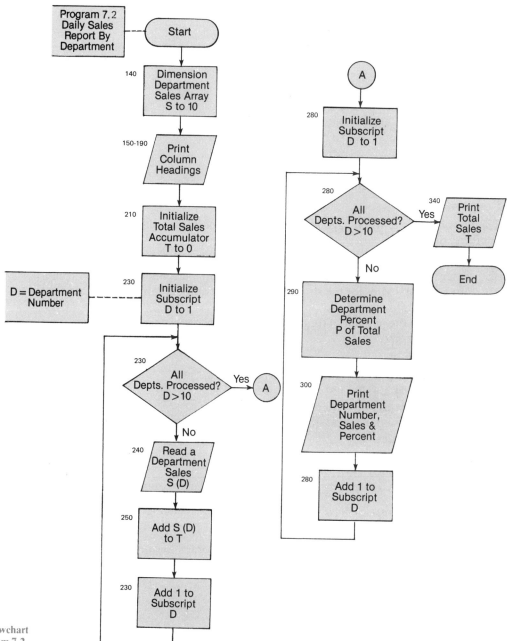

Figure 7.2 Flowchart for Program 7.2.

Dynamic Allocation of Arrays

Some applications call for arrays to have their upper bounds assigned **dynamically**. For example, a program may manipulate 60 elements of an array during one run, 100 elements the next time, and so on. Rather than modify the value of the size of a DIM statement each time the number of elements changes, BASIC systems permit the size of an array in a DIM statement to be written as a simple variable, as in:

```
140 DIM S(N)
```

```
100 REM PROGRAM 7.2
110 REM DAILY SALES REPORT BY DEPARTMENT
120 REM ********************************
130 REM *****DECLARE DEPARTMENT SALES ARRAY S*****
140 DIM S(10)
150 PRINT     "   DAILY SALES REPORT BY DEPARTMENT"
160 PRINT
170 PRINT     "DEPARTMENT     DAILY           % OF"
180 PRINT     "NUMBER         SALES       TOTAL SALES"
190 PRINT     "----------     -----       -----------"
200 LET A$ = "    ##       ##,###.##          ###.##"
210 LET T = 0
220 REM *****READ SALES INTO ARRAY S AND SUM ARRAY*****
230 FOR D = 1 TO 10
240    READ S(D)
250    LET T = T + S(D)
260 NEXT D
270 REM *****DETERMINE DEPT. % OF TOTAL SALES*****
280 FOR D = 1 TO 10
290    LET P = 100 * S(D)/T
300    PRINT USING A$; D, S(D), P
310 NEXT D
320 REM *****DISPLAY TOTAL SALES*****
330 PRINT
340 PRINT USING "TOTAL      ###,###.##"; T
350 REM **********DATA FOLLOWS**********
360 DATA  800, 2250, 1450, 1280, 1690
370 DATA 2460, 3880, 4690, 2250, 1360
380 END
```

Program 7.2

```
RUN

    DAILY SALES REPORT BY DEPARTMENT

DEPARTMENT     DAILY           % OF
NUMBER         SALES       TOTAL SALES
----------     -----       -----------
    1         800.00           3.62
    2       2,250.00          10.18
    3       1,450.00           6.56
    4       1,280.00           5.79
    5       1,690.00           7.64
    6       2,460.00          11.13
    7       3,880.00          17.55
    8       4,690.00          21.21
    9       2,250.00          10.18
   10       1,360.00           6.15

TOTAL      22,110.00
```

This DIM statement reserves a variable number of elements for the one-dimensional array S.

Usually an INPUT or READ statement is used before the DIM statement to assign a value to the variable N. Once N is assigned a value, the DIM statement allocates the actual number of elements to array S. Any FOR statements involved in the manipulation of the array must contain as their limit values the same simple variable N.

Program 7.3 on page 118 is nearly identical to Program 7.2 except for the addition of lines 123 and 126, the modification of the DIM statement to 140 DIM S(N) to permit dynamic allocation of arrays, and the modification of the FOR statements to include the simple variable N as their limit values.

Program 7.3 generates the same type of report that Program 7.2 does. By changing the value of the size of the array in the DATA statement in line 360, the system can process any number of departments.

```
100 REM PROGRAM 7.3
110 REM DAILY SALES REPORT BY DEPARTMENT
120 REM ********************************
123 REM *****READ THE NUMBER OF DEPARTMENTS TO PROCESS*****
126 READ N
130 REM *****DECLARE DEPARTMENT SALES ARRAY S*****
140 DIM S(N)
150 PRINT     "    DAILY SALES REPORT BY DEPARTMENT"
160 PRINT
170 PRINT     "DEPARTMENT      DAILY            % OF"
180 PRINT     "NUMBER          SALES         TOTAL SALES"
190 PRINT     "----------      -----         -----------"
200 LET A$ = "      ##        ##,###.##          ###.##"
210 LET T = 0
220 REM *****READ SALES INTO ARRAY S AND SUM ARRAY*****
230 FOR D = 1 TO N
240     READ S(D)
250     LET T = T + S(D)
260 NEXT D
270 REM *****DETERMINE DEPT. % OF TOTAL SALES*****
280 FOR D = 1 TO N
290     LET P = 100 * S(D)/T
300     PRINT USING A$; D, S(D), P
310 NEXT D
320 REM *****DISPLAY TOTAL SALES*****
330 PRINT
340 PRINT USING "TOTAL      ###,###.##"; T
350 REM ***********DATA FOLLOWS***********
360 DATA 6
370 DATA 800, 2250, 1450, 1280, 1690, 2460
380 END

RUN
```

Program 7.3

```
        DAILY SALES REPORT BY DEPARTMENT

    DEPARTMENT      DAILY           % OF
    NUMBER          SALES        TOTAL SALES
    ----------      -----        -----------
         1         800.00           8.06
         2       2,250.00          22.66
         3       1,450.00          14.60
         4       1,280.00          12.89
         5       1,690.00          17.02
         6       2,460.00          24.77

    TOTAL       9,930.00
```

In line 126, N is assigned the value of 6. Line 140 then allocates 6 elements to array S. Both For loops are processed 6 times, since N is also the limit value for each FOR statement.

7.4 TWO-DIMENSIONAL ARRAYS

The dimension of an array is the number of subscripts required to reference an element in an array. Up to now, all the arrays were one-dimensional, and an element was referenced by an integer, variable or single expression in the parentheses following the array name. The maximum number of dimensions that an array may have varies among BASIC systems. Some BASIC systems allow only a maximum of two dimensions, while others allow arrays to have up to 255 dimensions. One and two-dimensional arrays are the most common arrays used.

As illustrated in Table 7.1, the number of dimensions is declared in the DIM statement. For example,

```
140 DIM C(2, 5)
```

declares an array to be two-dimensional. A two-dimensional array usually takes the form of a table. The first subscript tells how many rows there are and the second subscript tells how many columns. Figure 7.3 shows a 2×5 array (read "2 by 5 array"). C(1, 1)—read "C sub one one"—references the element found in the first row and first column. C(2, 3)—read "C sub two three"—references the element found in the second row and third column. Ignoring the zeroth row and column of array C, let us assume that the elements are assigned values as shown in Figure 7.4.

Columns

	1	2	3	4	5
Rows 1	C(1, 1)	C(1, 2)	C(1, 3)	C(1, 4)	C(1, 5)
2	C(2, 1)	C(2, 2)	C(2, 3)	C(2, 4)	C(2, 5)

Figure 7.3 Conceptual view of the storage locations reserved for a 2×5 two-dimensional array called C, with the name of each element specified.

Columns

	1	2	3	4	5
Rows 1	6	12	−52	3.14	0.56
2	8	2	5	6	2

Figure 7.4 A 2×5 array with each element assigned a value.

If the name of the array in Figure 7.4 is C, then the following statements are true:

C(1, 2) is equal to 12
C(2, 4) is equal to 6
C(3, 5) is outside the range of the array; it does not exist
C(−2, −5) is outside the range of the array; it does not exist

Excluding the zeroth row and column, you may write the following code to initialize to zero, row by row, all the elements in a 4×3 array called A:

```
200 DIM A(4, 3)
210 FOR R = 1 TO 4
220    FOR C = 1 TO 3
230       LET A(R, C) = 0
240    NEXT C
250 NEXT R
```

To initialize to one all elements on the main diagonal of a 5×5 array called B, you may write the following:

```
300 DIM B(5, 5)
310 FOR R = 1 TO 5
320    LET B(R, R) = 1
330 NEXT R
```

As a result, elements B(1, 1), B(2, 2), B(3, 3), B(4, 4), and B(5, 5) are assigned the value of 1.

Given the following 6×5 array called M:

Columns

		1	2	3	4	5	6
	1	13	30	5	17	12	45
	2	23	12	13	16	0	20
Rows	*3*	45	12	28	16	10	13
	4	21	16	15	22	19	26
	5	23	50	17	43	15	18

To sum all the elements in row 4 into a counter called S4 and to sum all the elements in column 2 into a counter called S2, you may write the following:

```
500 DIM M(5, 6)
510 LET S2 = 0
520 LET S4 = 0
530 FOR R = 1 TO 5
540    LET S2 = S2 + M(R, 2)
550 NEXT R
560 FOR C = 1 TO 6
570    LET S4 = S4 + M(4, C)
580 NEXT C
```

These short partial programs should give you an idea how to handle elements appearing in various rows and columns of two-dimensional arrays.

**7.5
SORTING**

The need to sort data into alphabetical or numerical order is one of the more frequent operations carried out in a business data processing environment. It is also a time-consuming operation, especially when there are large amounts of data involved. Computer scientists have spent a great deal of time developing algorithms to speed up the sorting process. Usually, the faster the process, the more complex the algorithm. In this section we will discuss one of the more common sort algorithms: the bubble sort. Figure 7.5 illustrates the difference between unsorted data and the same data in ascending and descending sequence. Data that is in sequence from lowest to highest in value is in **ascending sequence**. Data that is in sequence from highest to lowest in value is in **descending sequence**.

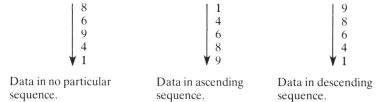

Figure 7.5   **Data in various sequences.**

Data in no particular sequence.   Data in ascending sequence.   Data in descending sequence.

The Bubble Sort

The bubble sort is a straightforward method of sorting data items that have been placed in an array. To illustrate the logic of a bubble sort we will sort the data found in Figure 7.5 into ascending sequence. Assume that the data has been assigned to array B, as illustrated below:

B(1)   8

B(2)   6

B(3)   9   Original order of unsorted data in array B.

B(4)   4

B(5)   1

The bubble sort involves comparing adjacent elements and **swapping** the values of those elements when they are out of order. For example, B(1) is compared to B(2). If

B(1) is less than or equal to B(2), no swap occurs. If B(1) is greater than B(2), the values of the 2 elements are swapped. B(2) is then compared to B(3), and so on until B(4) is compared to B(5). One complete time through the array is called a **pass**. At the end of the first pass, the largest value is in the last element of array B, as illustrated in Figure 7.6. Its box has been shaded to show that it is in its final position and will not move again.

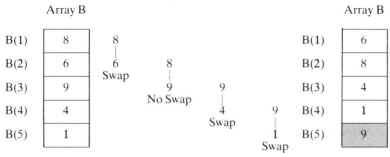

Figure 7.6 **First pass through array B.**

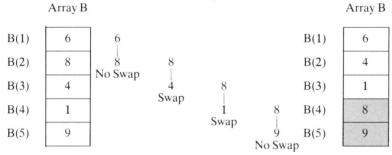

Figure 7.7 **Second pass through array B.**

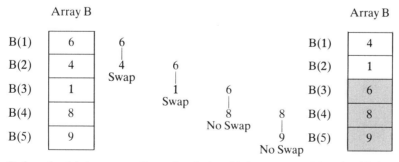

Figure 7.8 **Third pass through array B.**

The maximum number of passes necessary to sort the elements in an array is equal to the number of elements in the array less 1. Since array B has 5 elements, a maximum of four passes are made on the array. Figures 7.7, 7.8 and 7.9 illustrate the second, third and fourth passes made on array B. On the fifth pass no elements are swapped. The swapping pushes the larger values down in the illustrations, and as a side effect, the smaller numbers "bubble" up to the top of the array.

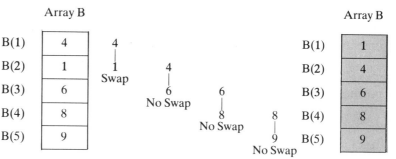

Figure 7.9 **Fourth pass through array B, which is now in ascending sequence.**

Before the fourth pass.   Swapping during fourth pass.   After the fourth pass.

The SWAP statement allows you to write one statement that will exchange the values of two storage locations. It will exchange two variables or two elements of an array. The general form of the SWAP statement is illustrated in Table 7.2.

TABLE 7.2   The SWAP Statement

General form:	SWAP A, B
	where A and B are variables or elements of an array
Purpose:	To exchange the values of two variables or two elements of an array.
Examples:	100 SWAP B(I), B(I + 1)
	200 SWAP A, B
	300 SWAP C$(I, I), D$(I, I)
Caution:	Not available on all BASIC systems.

Not all BASIC systems have the SWAP statement. If it is available on your BASIC system, then this partial program sorts array B of Figure 7.5:

```
210 LET S = 0
220 WHILE S = 0
230     LET S = 1
240     FOR I = 1 TO 4
250         IF B(I) <= B(I + 1) THEN 280
260             SWAP B(I), B(I + 1)
270             LET S = 0
280     NEXT I
290 WEND
300 .
```

The variable S controls whether another pass will be done on the array. Line 210 assigns S a value of zero. Since S equals zero, line 220 passes control into the body of the While loop. Line 230 assigns S a value of 1. If S is not modified later in the loop (line 270), the values in the array are in sequence and the next time line 220 is executed, control transfers to line 300.

The FOR statement in line 240 initializes I to 1. The first element B(1) is then compared to B(2). If B(1) is less than or equal to B(2), no swap occurs. If B(1) is greater than B(2), line 260 swaps the values of the two elements and line 270 assigns S a value of zero. Next, B(2) is compared to B(3) and so on. The number of comparisons per pass is equal to the number of elements to compare minus 1. Since the number of data items to sort is 5, the limit value in the FOR statement is set to 4.

In programming, the variable S is called a **switch**, or **flag**, or **indicator**, a variable that usually takes on two values during the duration of a program. When S is

0, the switch is "on," and the loop is executed. When S is 1, the switch is "off," and the loop in lines 220 through 290 is not executed.

If your BASIC system does not have the SWAP statement, then you must use a temporary storage location to complete the swap. The temporary storage location is necessary, since without the SWAP statement two values cannot be switched simultaneously. The following partial program will swap two values on systems that do not have the SWAP statement:

```
210 LET S= 0
220 WHILE S = 0
230    LET S = 1
240    FOR I = 1 TO 4
250       IF B(I) <= B(I + 1) THEN 300
260          LET T = B(I)
270          LET B(I) = B(I + 1)
280          LET B(I + 1) = T
290          LET S = 0
300    NEXT I
310 WEND
320 .
```

Program 7.4 incorporates the logic found in this partial program to sort 8, 6, 9, 4 and 1. Line 130 reserves storage for array B. The For loop made up of lines 150 through 180 loads and displays the unsorted elements of the array. Lines 210 through 310 sort the numeric array without the SWAP statement. Lines 330 through 350 display the elements after the array has been sorted.

```
100 REM PROGRAM 7.4
110 REM SORTING NUMERIC DATA USING THE
115 REM BUBBLE SORT TECHNIQUE
120 REM ******************************
130 DIM B(5)
140 PRINT "UNSORTED -";
150 FOR I = 1 TO 5
160    READ B(I)
170    PRINT B(I);
180 NEXT I
190 PRINT
200 REM *****SORT ROUTINE*****
210 LET S= 0
220 WHILE S = 0
230    LET S = 1
240    FOR I = 1 TO 4
250       IF B(I) <= B(I + 1) THEN 300
260          LET T = B(I)
270          LET B(I) = B(I + 1)
280          LET B(I + 1) = T
290          LET S = 0
300    NEXT I
310 WEND
320 PRINT "SORTED    -";
330 FOR I = 1 TO 5
340    PRINT B(I);
350 NEXT I
360 REM ***DATA FOLLOWS***
370 DATA 8, 6, 9, 4, 1
380 END

RUN

UNSORTED - 8  6  9  4  1
SORTED   - 1  4  6  8  9
```

Program 7.4

```
100 REM PROGRAM 7.5
110 REM SORTING STRING DATA USING THE
115 REM BUBBLE SORT TECHNIQUE
120 REM ******************************
125 READ D
130 DIM N$(D)
140 PRINT "UNSORTED - ";
150 FOR I = 1 TO D
160    READ N$(I)
170    PRINT N$(I); " ";
180 NEXT I
190 PRINT
200 REM *****SORT ROUTINE*****
210 LET S= 0
220 WHILE S = 0
230    LET S = 1
240    FOR I = 1 TO D - 1
250       IF N$(I) <= N$(I + 1) THEN 300
260          LET T$ = N$(I)
270          LET N$(I) = N$(I + 1)
280          LET N$(I + 1) = T$
290          LET S = 0
300    NEXT I
310 WEND
320 PRINT "SORTED   - ";
330 FOR I = 1 TO D
340    PRINT N$(I); " ";
350 NEXT I
360 REM ****DATA FOLLOWS******
370 DATA 8
380 DATA JIM, JOHN, LOUIS, FRAN
390 DATA TOM, ANDY, LOU, MARK
400 END

RUN

UNSORTED - JIM JOHN LOUIS FRAN TOM ANDY LOU MARK
SORTED   - ANDY FRAN JIM JOHN LOU LOUIS MARK TOM
```

Program 7.5

Changing the relation in line 250 from "less than or equal to" to "greater than or equal to" causes Program 7.4 to sort the data into descending rather than ascending sequence.

To make the sort algorithm more general, a variable for the size of the array and a variable number of elements can be used. This generalization is illustrated in Program 7.5, which uses the same techniques as Program 7.4 to sort string data items.

In Program 7.5 the string array N$ is dimensioned to D elements. Line 125 assigns the variable D the number of data items to be sorted. The limit value in each of the FOR statements in Program 7.4 (lines 150, 240 and 330) is changed from 5, 4, 5 to D, D − 1 and D in Program 7.5. Program 7.5 can sort from 1 to D data items, depending on the value assigned to the variable D.

7.6 TABLE PROCESSING

Many applications call for the use of data that is arranged in tabular form. Rates of pay, tax brackets, parts cost and insurance rates are examples of tables that contain systematically arranged data. Arrays make it easier to write programs for applications involving tables.

Table Organization

Tables are organized based on how the data (also called **table functions**) is to be referenced. Table functions can be accessed by their position in the table in **positionally organized tables**. In **argument organized tables**, table functions are accessed by the value that corresponds to the desired table function.

Positionally Organized Tables

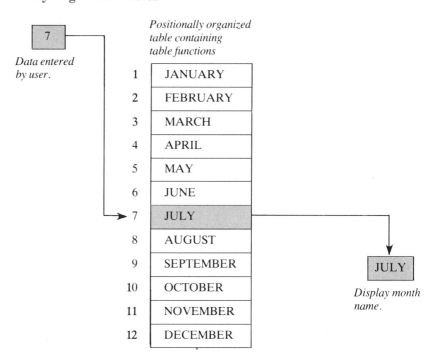

Figure 7.10 **Accessing a table function in a positionally organized table.**

To illustrate a positionally organized table, a program can be written that displays the name of the month in response to a month number, 1 through 12. Figure 7.10 shows the basic concept behind accessing a table function in a positionally organized table.

In Figure 7.10, the month name is selected from the table based on its location. A value of 1, entered by the user, equates to January, 2 to February, and so on. To write a program that uses table processing techniques, you must:

1. Define the table by declaring an array.
2. Load the table functions into the array, normally by using a For loop.
3. Write statements to access the table entries.

Program 7.6 illustrates how to declare, load and access the table of month names described in Figure 7.10. Line 140 declares the table by declaring array M$ to

```
100 REM PROGRAM 7.6
110 REM ACCESSING FUNCTIONS IN A POSITIONALLY
115 REM ORGANIZED TABLE
120 REM **************************************
130 REM *****DECLARE THE TABLE*****
140 DIM M$(12)
150 REM *****LOAD THE TABLE*****
160 FOR I = 1 TO 12
170    READ M$(I)
180 NEXT I
190 LET A$ = "Y"
200 WHILE A$ = "Y"
210    INPUT "MONTH NUMBER"; N
220    IF N >= 1 AND N <= 12 THEN 260
230       PRINT "MONTH NUMBER INVALID, PLEASE RE-ENTER"
240       GOTO 210
250    REM *****ACCESS THE TABLE FUNCTION*****
260       PRINT "THE MONTH NAME IS "; M$(N)
270    PRINT
280    INPUT "ANOTHER MONTH NUMBER (Y OR N)"; A$
290    PRINT
300 WEND
310 PRINT
320 PRINT "JOB COMPLETE"
330 REM ***********TABLE ENTRIES***************
340 DATA JANUARY, FEBRUARY, MARCH, APRIL
350 DATA MAY, JUNE, JULY, AUGUST
360 DATA SEPTEMBER, OCTOBER, NOVEMBER, DECEMBER
370 END
```

Program 7.6

```
RUN

MONTH NUMBER? 2
THE MONTH NAME IS FEBRUARY

ANOTHER MONTH NUMBER (Y OR N)? Y

MONTH NUMBER? 14
MONTH NUMBER INVALID, PLEASE RE-ENTER
MONTH NUMBER? 8
THE MONTH NAME IS AUGUST

ANOTHER MONTH NUMBER (Y OR N)? Y

MONTH NUMBER? 12
THE MONTH NAME IS DECEMBER

ANOTHER MONTH NUMBER (Y OR N)? N

JOB COMPLETE
```

12. Lines 160 through 180 load the table functions—in this case, the month names—into the array. Line 260 accesses the desired table function.

The routine to access the table function in Program 7.6 is rather straightforward. The user enters a value for N and line 260 references the Nth element of the array containing the table functions.

Positionally organized tables are not difficult to understand. Unfortunately, few tables can be constructed based on the relative positions of the table functions. Month name, day of the week name and job class tables are examples of systematic data that can be organized into positional tables.

Argument Organized Tables

In most applications, tables are characterized by entries made up of multiple functions. Multiple function entries are accessed by means of a **search argument**. The search argument is entered by the user, much as the month number was in Program 7.6. The search argument is compared to the **table argument**, a table entry, to retrieve the corresponding table function. Figure 7.11 illustrates the composition of a table that is organized by arguments.

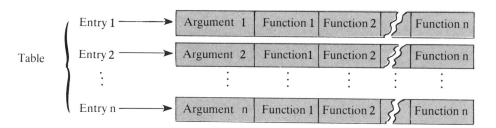

Figure 7.11   Conceptual view of an argument organized table.

The table argument is assigned to a one-dimensional array. Functions are assigned to parallel arrays. Unlike a positionally organized table, in which the value entered is used to obtain the table function, an argument organized table must be searched until the search argument agrees with one of the table arguments. This search is a **table search** or a **table look-up**.

Serial Search

A **serial search** is a procedure that all of us use in everyday life. Suppose, for example, you have a parts list that contains the part numbers and corresponding part descriptions and part costs. If you have a part number, one method of finding the part description and cost is to read through the part number list until you find the part number you are searching for. You can then read off the description and cost that correspond to the part number. Figure 7.12 illustrates the basic concept of a serial search.

The search argument is tested against each of the table arguments, beginning with the first, until a **hit** is made. At that point, the part description and part cost that correspond to the table argument can be selected from the table.

A program that completes the serial search illustrated in Figure 7.12 first needs to have the table defined. Since each entry is made up of a search argument and two

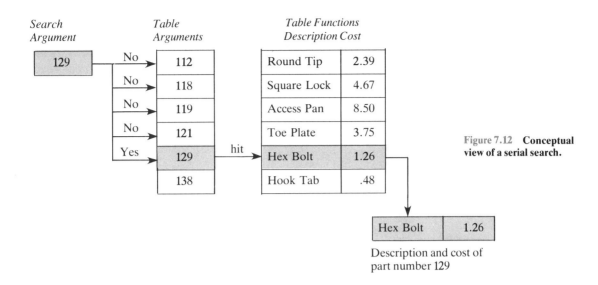

Figure 7.12 **Conceptual view of a serial search.**

```
150 REM *****DECLARE THE TABLE*****
160 READ R
170 DIM N(R), D$(R), C(R)
```

functions, we can declare three parallel arrays—N, D$ and C, as shown above. The variable R will be assigned the number of parts in the parts list.

Array N can be assigned the part numbers, array D$ the part descriptions and array C the part costs. A For loop is used to load the table, as follows:

```
180 REM ****LOAD THE TABLE*****
190 FOR I = 1 TO R
200    READ N(I), D$(I), C(I)
210 NEXT I
```

Each time the READ statement is executed, one entry is loaded into each of the arrays. Each entry consists of an argument and two functions. A For loop can be used to implement the serial search algorithm. Within the loop, an IF statement compares the part number entered by the user against the part numbers in the table. When the two are equal, the IF statement causes a branch to a statement outside the loop. If the For loop runs through the entire list of arguments without finding a table argument that is equal to the search argument, a diagnostic message will be displayed. The following statements search the table, cause the part description and cost to be displayed or cause a diagnostic message to be displayed.

```
250 REM *****SEARCH THE TABLE*****
260 FOR I = 1 TO R
270    IF P = N(I) THEN 310
280 NEXT I
290 PRINT "**ERROR**"; P; "IS AN INVALID PART NUMBER"
300 GOTO 330
310 PRINT "THE DESCRIPTION IS "; D$(I)
320 PRINT USING "THE COST IS ###.##"; C(I)
330 .
```

The complete program follows.

```
100 REM PROGRAM 7.7
110 REM SERIAL SEARCH OF AN ARGUMENT ORGANIZED TABLE
120 REM N = PART NUMBER ARGUMENTS   D$ = PART DESCRIPTION FUNCTIONS
130 REM C = PART COST FUNCTIONS     R = NUMBER OF TABLE ENTRIES
140 REM ******************************************************
150 REM *****DECLARE THE TABLE*****
160 READ R
170 DIM N(R), D$(R), C(R)
180 REM *****LOAD THE TABLE*****
190 FOR I = 1 TO R
200    READ N(I), D$(I), C(I)
210 NEXT I
220 LET A$ = "Y"
230 WHILE A$ = "Y"
240    INPUT "ENTER THE PART NUMBER"; P
250    REM *****SEARCH THE TABLE*****
260    FOR I = 1 TO R
270       IF P = N(I) THEN 310
280    NEXT I
290    PRINT "**ERROR**"; P; "IS AN INVALID PART NUMBER"
300    GOTO 330
310    PRINT "THE DESCRIPTION IS "; D$(I)
320    PRINT USING "THE COST IS ###.##; C(I)
330    PRINT
340    INPUT "ANOTHER PART NUMBER (Y OR N)"; A$
350 WEND
360 PRINT
370 PRINT "JOB COMPLETE"
380 REM ****************TABLE ENTRIES****************
390 DATA 6
400 DATA 112, ROUND TIP, 2.39, 118, SQUARE LOCK, 4.67
410 DATA 119, ACCESS PAN, 8.50, 121, TOE PLATE, 3.75
420 DATA 129, HEX BOLT, 1.26, 138, HOOK TAB, 0.48
430 END
```

Program 7.7

```
RUN

ENTER THE PART NUMBER? 129
THE DESCRIPTION IS HEX BOLT
THE COST IS    1.26

ANOTHER PART NUMBER (Y OR N)? Y
ENTER THE PART NUMBER? 119
THE DESCRIPTION IS ACCESS PAN
THE COST IS    8.50

ANOTHER PART NUMBER (Y OR N)? Y
ENTER THE PART NUMBER? 122
**ERROR** 122 IS AN INVALID PART NUMBER

ANOTHER PART NUMBER (Y OR N)? Y
ENTER THE PART NUMBER? 138
THE DESCRIPTION IS HOOK TAB
THE COST IS    0.48

ANOTHER PART NUMBER (Y OR N)? N

JOB COMPLETE
```

7.7
BASIC
SELF-TEST
EXERCISES

1. What is displayed if these valid programs are executed?

a.
```
100 REM EXERCISE 7.1A
110 DIM B$(7)
120 LET A$ = "PROGRAM"
130 FOR I = 1 TO 7
140    LET B$(I) = MID$(A$, I, 1)
150    PRINT B$(I)
160 NEXT I
170 END
```

b.
```
100 REM EXERCISE 7.1B
110 DIM A$(26)
120 FOR I = 1 TO 26
130     READ A$(I)
140 NEXT I
150 LET S = 0
160 IF S <> 0 THEN 260
170     LET S = 1
180     FOR I = 1 TO 25
190         IF A$(I) <= A$(I + 1) THEN 240
200             LET T$ = A$(I)
210             LET A$(I) = A$(I + 1)
220             LET A$(I + 1) = T$
230             LET S = 0
240     NEXT I
250 GOTO 160
260 FOR I = 1 TO 26
270     PRINT " "; A$(I);
280 NEXT I
290 REM ********DATA FOLLOWS*********
300 DATA L, J, A, C, X, Z, N, Q, B, E
310 DATA D, H, O, T, W, Y, F, R, V, I
320 DATA K, M, G, U, S, P
330 END
```

2. Assume array L is declared to have 5 rows and 5 columns and the elements of array L are assigned the following values:

ARRAY L

2	5	14	30	50
7	12	21	70	10
5	15	70	60	0
19	20	30	10	20
22	45	20	40	50

Write the subscripted variable name that references the following values found in array L.

a. 12   b. 70   c. 15   d. 45   e. 60   f. 7   g. 14   h. 22

3. Assume array A has 4 rows and 4 columns and the elements of array A are assigned the following values:

ARRAY A

1	2	3	4
5	6	7	8
9	10	11	12
13	14	15	16

What will be the final arrangement of array A after the following partial program is executed? Select from the choices below.

```
100 REM EXERCISE 7.3
110 FOR I = 1 TO 4
120     FOR J = 1 TO 4
130         LET A(I, J) = A(J, I)
140     NEXT J
150 NEXT I
```

a.

1	2	3	4
5	6	7	8
9	10	11	12
13	14	15	16

b.

16	15	14	13
12	11	10	9
8	7	6	5
4	3	2	1

c.

1	2	2	4
5	6	6	8
9	10	10	12
13	14	14	16

d.

1	5	9	13
5	6	10	14
9	10	11	15
13	14	15	16

e. None of these.

4. Refer to the initial array A given in Exercise 3. What will be the final arrangement of array A after each of the following partial programs is executed? Select your answer from the choices given in Exercise 3.

a.
```
100 REM EXERCISE 7.4A
110 FOR I = 1 TO 4
120     LET A(I, 3) = A(I, 2)
130 NEXT I
```

c.
```
100 REM EXERCISE 7.4C
110 FOR I = 1 TO 4
120     LET A(I, I) = A(I - 2, I + 2)
130 NEXT I
```

b.
```
100 REM EXERCISE 7.4B
110 LET J = 2
120 FOR I = 1 TO 4
130     LET A(I, J + 1) = A(I, J)
140 NEXT I
```

d.
```
100 REM EXERCISE 7.4D
110 FOR I = 1 TO 4
120     FOR J = 1 TO 4
130         LET A(I, J) = A(I, J)
140     NEXT J
150 NEXT I
```

5. Given array F declared to have 100 elements, assume each element of array F has been assigned a value. Write a partial program to shift all the values up one location. That is, assign the value of F_1 to F_2, F_2 to F_3 and F_{100} to F_1. Do not use any array other than array F. Be careful not to destroy a value before it is shifted.

6. Given three arrays A, B and C, each declared to 50 elements, assume the elements of arrays A and B have been assigned values. Write a partial program that compares each element of array A to its corresponding element in array B. Assign a 1, 0 or −1 to the corresponding element in array C, as follows:

      1 if A is greater than B
      0 if A is equal to B
     −1 if A is less than B

7. Identify the error(s), if any, in each of the following partial programs:

a.
```
100 REM EXERCISE 7.7A
110 DIM X(300)
120 FOR I = 1 TO 500
130     READ X(I)
140 NEXT I
```

b.
```
100 REM EXERCISE 7.7B
110 DIM X(700)
120 FOR K = 700 TO 1 STEP −1
130     READ X(K)
140 NEXT K
```

8. Identify the error(s), if any, in each of the following variables and their subscripts.

a. F3(8)
b. A(6 − 8)
c. A(K)
d. F(I(K))
e. X(3.7)
f. D(5, 6, 7)
g. Q(K, A)
h. M1$(3)
i. L$(6, 9)
j. Y(I * 3/J, K + M ∧ P)

9. Write a program to generate the first 6 rows of Pascal's Triangle. Each entry in a given row of the triangle is generated by adding the two adjacent entries in the immediately preceding row. For example, the third entry in row 4 is the sum of the second and third entries in row 3. The first 6 rows of Pascal's Triangle are as follows:

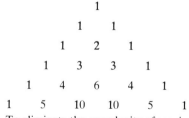

To eliminate the complexity of spacing, display each row starting in column 1.

7.8
BASIC
PROGRAMMING
PROBLEMS

Purpose: To become familiar with declaring, loading and searching a table.

Problem: Write a program that will accept a 6-digit credit card number and verify that this number is in a table. If the credit card number is in the table, display the message "Credit Card Number Is Valid." If the credit card number is not in the table, display the message "Credit Card Number Invalid—Alert Your Manager." Declare the credit card number table to N elements. Use the following table of 15 credit card numbers:

131416	238967	384512	583214
172319	345610	410001	672354
194567	351098	518912	691265
210201	372198	562982	

Input Data: Use the following sample data:

```
372198
518912
102002
672354
210200
```

Output Results: The following partial results are shown:

```
CREDIT CARD NUMBER? 372198
CREDIT CARD NUMBER IS VALID

ANOTHER CREDIT CARD NUMBER (Y OR N)? Y
        .
        .
        .
CREDIT CARD NUMBER? 210200
CREDIT CARD NUMBER INVALID - ALERT YOUR MANAGER

ANOTHER CREDIT CARD NUMBER (Y OR N)? N

JOB COMPLETE
```

Purpose: To become familiar with the use of arrays for determining totals.

Problem: Businesses are usually subdivided into smaller units for the purpose of better organization. The Tri-Quality retail store is subdivided into four departments. Each department submits its daily receipts at the end of the day to the store manager. Write a program, using an array consisting of 5 rows and 6 columns, that is assigned the daily sales. Use the 5th row and 6th column to accumulate the totals. After accumulating the totals, display the entire array.

Input Data: Use the following sample data:

Dept.	Monday	Tuesday	Wednesday	Thursday	Friday
1	$2,146	$6,848	$8,132	$8,912	$5,165
2	8,123	9,125	6,159	5,618	9,176
3	4,156	5,612	4,128	4,812	3,685
4	1,288	1,492	1,926	1,225	2,015

Output Results: The following results are displayed:

```
           WEEK ENDING STORE RECEIPTS

DEPT  MONDAY   TUESDAY WEDNESDAY  THURSDAY    FRIDAY       TOTAL
-----------------------------------------------------------------
 1   2,146.00  6,848.00  8,132.00  8,912.00  5,165.00 31,203.00
 2   8,123.00  9,125.00  6,159.00  5,618.00  9,176.00 38,201.00
 3   4,156.00  5,612.00  4,128.00  4,812.00  3,685.00 22,393.00
 4   1,288.00  1,492.00  1,926.00  1,225.00  2,015.00  7,946.00
 T  15,713.00 23,077.00 20,345.00 20,567.00 20,041.00 99,743.00
JOB COMPLETE
```

3:

Determining the Mean, Variance and Standard Deviation

Purpose: To apply the concepts of array elements to a statistical problem.

Problem: Construct a program to find the mean (average), variance and standard deviation of a variable number of student grades. Use the following relationships:

for the mean:
$$M = \frac{\sum_{j=1}^{n} X_j}{n}$$

for the variance:
$$V = \sum_{j=1}^{n} \frac{(X_j - M)^2}{n-1}$$

for the standard deviation: $SD = \sqrt{V}$

where n is the total number of grades, to be read in first, followed by the student grades, represented by X_j.

Input Data: Enter the following sample data via the INPUT statement:

Number of students: 10
Grades: 97, 90, 87, 93, 96, 88, 78, 95, 96, 87

Output Results: The following partial results are shown:

```
THE MEAN IS 90.7
THE VARIANCE IS 35.1222
THE STANDARD DEVIATION IS 5.9264
```

4:

Property Tax Rate Table Look-Up

Purpose: To become familiar with argument organized tables.

Problem: Construct a program that requests the assessed value, searches a table for the tax rate and computes the property tax. The property tax is determined by multiplying the assessed value times the rate. Use the following table to construct the program table. Use the upper limit of each category for the argument. The tax rate will be the corresponding function.

Assessed Value	Tax Rate
$15,000.00 or less	2%
$15,000.01–$25,000.00	2.5%
$25,000.01–$40,000.00	3%
$40,000.01–$50,000.00	3.5%
$50,000.01–$70,000.00	4%
above $70,000.00	4.5%

Input Data: Input the following sample data:

Assessed Value

$27,400.00
32,500.00
46,800.00
90,000.00
14,600.00

Output Results: The following results are displayed:

```
WHAT IS THE ASSESSED VALUE? 27400
THE TAX CHARGE IS     822.00
     .
     .
     .
WHAT IS THE ASSESSED VALUE? 14600
THE TAX CHARGE IS     292.00

WHAT IS THE ASSESSED VALUE? -1
END OF REPORT
```

Purpose: To become familiar with sorting data into ascending or descending sequence.

**5:
Sorting Customer
Numbers**

Problem: Write a program which requests the selection from a menu of functions for sorting customer numbers into either ascending or descending sequence.

Input Data: Prepare and use the following sample data:

Input File	Input File Continued	Input File Continued
03000	03035	03067
03012	03039	03068
03013	03042	03079
03015	03043	03077
03014	03043	03076
03016	03043	03076
03017	03042	03075
03018	03043	03078
03018	03044	03080
03019	03063	03081
03020	03062	03094
03034	03064	03096
03038	03065	03095
03037	03066	
03036	03066	

Output Results: The following partial results are shown for the ascending sort of the customer numbers:

```
DO YOU WANT THE CUSTOMER NUMBERS SORTED IN:

        1. ASCENDING SEQUENCE
        2. DESCENDING SEQUENCE
        3. EXIT THE PROGRAM

ENTER A 1 OR 2 OR 3? 1

CUSTOMER NUMBERS
 3000
 3012
   .
   .
   .
 3095
 3096

JOB COMPLETE
```

FILE PROCESSING 8

8.1
FILES

In previous exercises, the INPUT statement or the READ and DATA statements were used to enter data into the system. A more efficient and convenient method of organizing data is to store it on an auxiliary storage device, like a floppy diskette, tape or disk, and keep it separate from the programs that will process the data. Data stored in this fashion is a **file**, a group of related records. Each record within the file contains related data items. The number of records making up a file may range from a few to thousands or millions.

Nearly all dialects of BASIC include a set of file handling statements that allow a user to:

1. Create data files
2. Define the data files to be used by a program
3. Open a data file
4. Read data from a data file
5. Write data to a data file
6. Test for the end of the data file
7. Close a data file

Unfortunately, the format of these file handling statements varies from one dialect of BASIC to another. In this book the Microsoft version of these statements is used. Microsoft BASIC, or MBASIC, is the most popular BASIC system; it is used with personal computers like the DEC Rainbow, IBM PC, Macintosh and TRS-80.

8.2
FILE
ORGANIZATION

File organization is a method for arranging records on an auxiliary storage device. BASIC systems allow for two types of file organization:

1. Sequential
2. Random

The choice of organization is made during the early stages of development of an application. The type of file organization depends on how the records within the file are to be processed by other programs.

Sequential Files

The records of a **sequential file** can only be processed in the order in which they are placed in the file. Such a file is organized sequentially, and it is limited to sequential processing. Conceptually, using DATA statements within a BASIC program is identical to using a sequential file. For example, the 14th record in a sequential file cannot be processed until after the previous 13 records are processed. Similarly, the 14th data item in a DATA statement of a BASIC program cannot be processed until after the previous 13 data items are processed.

Sequential organization may also be used to write reports to auxiliary storage instead of an external device, like a video display device. Once the report is in auxiliary storage, it may be displayed at any time and as often as needed. Writing reports to auxiliary storage is a common practice, especially with programs that generate multiple reports. In such programs, each report is written to a separate file.

Random Files

A file organized randomly is a **random file**. The sequence of processing a random file has no relationship to the sequence in which the records are stored in it. If the 10th record in a file is required by a program, the record can be directly accessed without processing the previous 9 records. However, the program must indicate to the system the location of the record relative to the beginning of the file. For example, to access the 10th record instead of the 3rd or 4th record, the program must explicitly indicate to the system that the 10th record is requested for processing.

Indexed Files

A type of file organized by an index, known as an **indexed file**, is also widely used in data processing. An indexed file is organized around a specified data item, the **key**, which is common to every record. In an airline reservation file, the key may be the flight number. In an inventory file, the key may be the part number or a part description.

Indexed files have one advantage over random files: the program need only supply the key of the record to be accessed instead of the record's relative location. Indexed files are not available with most BASIC systems.

A **filename** identifies a file on auxiliary storage. A filename consists of a name, from one to eight characters, followed by a period and an **extension**. The extension may be from one to three characters in length. Most personal computers also use a **device name** that identifies the device upon which the file is located. The device name and filename are separated by a colon, as shown:

8.3 FILENAMES

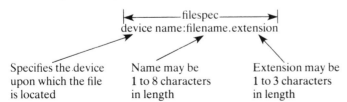

Collectively, the device name, filename and extension are the **file specification**, or **filespec**. If an extension is used, a period precedes it.

In the selection of a name and extension, the letters of the alphabet, the digits 0 through 9 and certain special characters may be used. Check the specifications of your BASIC system in the user's manual to determine which special characters may be used. Names that are meaningful should be selected. For a payroll file, for example, the name PAYROLL better describes the contents of the file than the names A or Z or R234.

Extensions are used to classify files. The following extensions are used by most programmers:

Extension	Represents a
BAS	— BASIC program
TXT	— Text or word processing file
LIS	— File containing a report
DAT	— Data file
TBL	— File containing tables
SAV	— Backup copy of a file or program

Table 8.1 illustrates several examples of valid filenames.

TABLE 8.1   Valid Filenames

Filename	Comment
B:PARTS.DAT	
A:REPORT1.LIS	
FLIGHT.DAT	BASIC assumes the file is on disk drive A of a personal computer.
ACCOUNTS	BASIC assumes the file is on disk drive A. The period and extension are optional on some BASIC systems.

**8.4
SEQUENTIAL FILE
PROCESSING**

This section presents the file handling statements required to create and process sequential files. Also, sample programs are presented to illustrate how:

1. Reports can be written to auxiliary storage instead of a video display device.
2. Data files which other programs can process can be created.
3. Reports from data located in data files can be generated.

Opening and Closing Sequential Files

Before any file can be read from or written to, it must be opened by the OPEN statement. When a program finishes reading from or writing to a file, it must close the file using the CLOSE statement.

When executed, the OPEN statement carries out the following five basic functions:

1. It requests the system to allocate a **buffer**, a part of main memory through which data is passed between the program and auxiliary storage.
2. It identifies by name the file to be processed.
3. It indicates whether the file is to be read from or written to.
4. It assigns the file a filenumber.
5. It sets the "pointer" to the beginning of the file.

The CLOSE statement terminates the association between the file and the filenumber assigned in the OPEN statement and de-allocates the part of main memory assigned to the buffer. If a file is being written to, the CLOSE statement ensures that the last record is transferred from the buffer in main memory to auxiliary storage.

TABLE 8.2   The OPEN **Statement for Sequential Files**

General Form:	OPEN mode, #filenumber, filespec
	where **mode** is a string expression equal to one of the following:
	    "I" specifies sequential input mode.
	    "O" specifies sequential output mode.
	    filenumber is a numeric expression whose value is between 1 and 15 and is associated with the file (**filespec**) for as long as it is open. The file-number may be used by other file handling statements to refer to the specific file.

Purpose:	Allows a program to read records from a sequential file or write records to a sequential file.
Examples:	``` 100 OPEN "O", #1, "PAYROLL.DAT" 200 OPEN "I", #F, "B:EMPLOYEE.DAT" 300 OPEN M$, #3, "ACCOUNTS" 400 OPEN "I", #1, N$ ```

The general forms of the OPEN and CLOSE statements are shown in Tables 8.2 and 8.3.

As illustrated in Table 8.2, a sequential file may be opened for input or output.

If a file is opened for input, the progam can only read records from the file. For example, the following statement

```
500 OPEN "I", #2, "CLASS.DAT"
```

opens the file CLASS.DAT so that the program can only read records. An attempt to write a record to CLASS.DAT results in a diagnostic message. The system also displays a diagnostic message if you try to open a file for input that does not exist.

If a file is opened for output, as shown below in line 600, then the program can only write records to the file.

```
600 OPEN "O", #1, "STUDENT.DAT"
```

Opening a file for output always creates a new file. If, for example, STUDENT. DAT already exists, then the file is deleted before it is opened.

TABLE 8.3   The CLOSE **Statement**

General Form:	CLOSE #filenumber$_1$, . . . , #filenumber$_n$
Purpose:	Terminates the association between a filenumber and file. If the file is opened for output, the CLOSE statement ensures that the last record is transferred from main memory to auxiliary storage. A CLOSE statement with no filenumbers closes all open files.
Examples:	``` 600 CLOSE #1, #2, #3 700 CLOSE #1 800 CLOSE #2, #1 900 CLOSE ```

The CLOSE statement terminates access to a file. For example,

```
600 CLOSE #2, #3
```

causes the files assigned to filenumbers 2 and 3 to be closed. Any other files previously opened by the program remain open.

Following the close of a specified file, the filenumber may be assigned again to the same or a different file by an OPEN statement. For example, the following partial program is valid.

```
150 OPEN 'I', #1, 'INVEN.DAT'
      .
      .
      .
500 CLOSE #1
510 OPEN 'I', #1, 'INVEN.DAT'
      .
      .
      .
700 CLOSE #1
710 END
```

Line 150 opens INVEN.DAT for input as filenumber 1. Line 500 closes INVEN.DAT. Line 510 reopens INVEN.DAT for input as filenumber 1. Opening and closing a file more than once in a program is quite common.

The following rules summarize the OPEN and CLOSE statements:

CLOSE **Rule 1:** A file must be opened before it can be closed.

OPEN **Rule 1:** A file must be opened before it can be read from or written to.

OPEN **Rule 2:** If a file is opened for input, it must already exist on auxiliary storage.

OPEN **Rule 3:** If a file is opened for output and it exists on auxiliary storage, it is deleted before it is opened.

OPEN **Rule 4:** A filenumber cannot be assigned to more than one file at a time.

Writing Data to a Sequential File

The PRINT #n and PRINT #n, USING statements write data or information to sequential files. The PRINT #n and PRINT #n, USING statements are similar in format to the PRINT and PRINT USING statements from Chapter 4, except that the data or information is written to a file instead of to an external device like a video display device. The general form of the PRINT #n and PRINT #n, USING statements are shown in Tables 8.4 and 8.5

TABLE 8.4   **The** PRINT #n **Statement**

General Form:	PRINT #n, item pm item pm . . . pm item
	where n is a filenumber assigned to a file defined in an OPEN statement and where each item is a constant, variable, expression, function reference or null and where each punctuation mark pm is a comma or semicolon.
Purpose:	Provides for the generation of labeled and unlabeled output or of output in a consistent tabular format from the program to a sequential file in auxiliary storage.
| *Examples:* | ```
100 PRINT #1,
200 PRINT #2, A, B; C
300 PRINT #1, TAB(10); 'THE ANSWER IS'; A
400 PRINT #2, X + Y/4, C * B
500 PRINT #3, A; ','; B; ','; C$; ','; D
600 PRINT #2, S;
``` |
```

TABLE 8.5 **The** PRINT #n, USING **Statement**

General Form:	PRINT #n, USING string expression; list where n is a filenumber assigned to a file defined in an OPEN statement and where string expression is either a string constant or a string variable and where list is a list of items to be written to the file in auxiliary storage.
Purpose:	Provides for controlling exactly the format of the record written to a sequential file in auxiliary storage.
| *Examples:* | ```
150 PRINT #1, USING "THE AVERAGE IS #,###.##"; A
190 PRINT #2, USING "## IS THE SUM OF # AND #"; S, S1, S2

200 LET A$ = "\        \       ##       ##.##"
210 PRINT #3, USING A$; S$, D, B
``` |

The statement

```
500 PRINT #1, A, B, C
```

creates and transmits a record image to the sequential file, assigned to filenumber 1, with the values of A, B and C beginning in zones 1, 2 and 3 of the record.

The following partial program illustrates how an image may be displayed on a video display device and transmitted to a file called REPORT.LIS.

Displays the values of P, M1 and M2 →
Writes a record with the values of P, M1, and M2 to the file REPORT.LIS →

```
150 OPEN "O", #3, "REPORT.LIS"
        .
        .
        .
400 PRINT USING "## IS THE PRODUCT OF # AND #"; P, M1, M2
410 PRINT #3, USING "## IS THE PRODUCT OF # AND #"; P, M1, M2
```

Line 400 displays the results on a video display device. Line 410 writes a record that is identical to the line displayed by line 400 to the file REPORT.LIS.

The PRINT #n statement is used to write data to a file that may later be read by another program. The statement used in BASIC to read data from a file is the INPUT #n statement, and it will be discussed shortly. The format requirement is similar to that of the READ and DATA statements—all data items must be separated by commas.

The following PRINT #n statement writes records containing data items that are in a format required by the INPUT #n statement.

```
500 PRINT #2, A; ","; B; ","; C; ","; D$
```

The technique used in line 500 places a comma between the values of A and B, B and C, and C and D$. The semicolon separator following A, B, C and each of the commas, which are string constants, compresses the data. The result is that the record looks the same as data separated by commas in a DATA statement. If the list within a PRINT #n or PRINT #n, USING statement does not end with a comma or semicolon, then a carriage return is appended to the last data item written to form a record.

Some versions of Microsoft BASIC have the WRITE #n statement available to write records to a file in the format required by the INPUT #n statement. The WRITE #n statement automatically writes data in the following format:

```
500 WRITE #2, A, B, C, D$
```
```

1. Data items are separated by commas.
2. String data items are surrounded by quotation marks.
3. All leading and trailing spaces are omitted.

Check the specifications on your BASIC system in the user's manual to determine if the WRITE #n statement may be used to write records to a file in the format required by the INPUT #n statement. It is recommended that the WRITE #n statement be used, if it is available, to build files that will be processed at a later date using the INPUT statement. Since the PRINT #n statement works on nearly all BASIC systems, the PRINT #n statement will be used in this chapter.

The following rule summarizes the use of the PRINT #n and PRINT #n USING statements:

> OUTPUT **Rule 2:**   Before the PRINT #n or PRINT #n USING statement is executed in a program, the filenumber n must be assigned to a file that has been opened for output.

BASIC at Work

In Chapter 5 the Weekly Payroll and Summary Report was introduced. In the solution of Program 5.4 on page 79, the PRINT and PRINT USING statements displayed the report on an external device like a video display device.

Writing the Weekly Payroll and Summary Report to Auxiliary Storage

```
100 REM PROGRAM 8.1
110 REM WRITING THE WEEKLY PAYROLL AND SUMMARY REPORT
115 REM TO AUXILIARY STORAGE
120 REM C  = EMPLOYEE COUNT     T = TOTAL GROSS PAY
130 REM E$ = EMPLOYEE NUMBER    H = HOURS WORKED
140 REM R  = RATE OF PAY        B = HOURS GREATER THAN 40
150 REM G  = GROSS PAY          A = AVERAGE GROSS PAY
155 REM REPORT FILE NAME = REPORT.LIS
160 REM ***********************************************
165 OPEN 'O', #1, 'REPORT.LIS'
170 PRINT #1, TAB(12); 'WEEKLY PAYROLL REPORT'
180 PRINT #1,
190 PRINT #1, 'EMPLOYEE NO.     HOURS      RATE      GROSS PAY'
200 PRINT #1, '-------------    -----      ----      ---------'
210 LET A$ = '     \   \            ###.#     ##.##     ##,###.##'
220 LET C = 0
230 LET T = 0
240 READ E$, H, R
250 REM ****************PROCESS A RECORD***************
260 WHILE E$ <> 'EOF'
270    LET C = C + 1
280    LET B = H - 40
290    IF B <= 0 THEN LET G = H*R ELSE LET G = H*R +0.5*B*R
300    LET T = T + G
310    PRINT #1, USING A$; E$, H, R, G
320    READ E$, H, R
330 WEND
340 REM *****************EOF ROUTINE******************
350 LET A = T/C
360 PRINT #1,
370 PRINT #1, USING 'THE TOTAL GROSS PAY IS $$#,###.##'; T
380 PRINT #1, USING 'THE TOTAL NUMBER OF EMPLOYEES IS ###'; C
390 PRINT #1, USING 'THE AVERAGE GROSS PAY IS $$#,###.##'; A
395 CLOSE #1
397 PRINT 'REPORT COMPLETE AND STORED UNDER FILENAME REPORT.LIS'
400 REM *****************DATA FOLLOWS*****************
410 DATA 124, 40, 5.60
420 DATA 126, 56, 5.90
430 DATA 128, 38, 4.60
440 DATA 129, 48.5, 6.10
450 DATA EOF, 0, 0
460 END

RUN

REPORT COMPLETE AND STORED UNDER FILENAME REPORT.LIS
```

Program 8.1

Program 8.1 is identical to Program 5.4 except for the inclusion of:

1. Additional comments (lines 115 and 155)
2. An OPEN statement (line 165) and a CLOSE statement (line 395)
3. The filenumber 1 in each PRINT and PRINT USING statement
4. An additional PRINT statement (line 397)

Program 8.1 writes the report, illustrated in Figure 8.1, to auxiliary storage under the filename REPORT.LIS.

```
               WEEKLY PAYROLL REPORT

EMPLOYEE NO.    HOURS     RATE    GROSS PAY
------------    -----     ----    ---------
    124         40.0      5.60      224.00
    126         56.0      5.90      377.60
    128         38.0      4.60      174.80
    129         48.5      6.10      321.77

THE TOTAL GROSS PAY IS   $1,098.17
THE TOTAL NUMBER OF EMPLOYEES IS    4
THE AVERAGE GROSS PAY IS    $274.54
```

Figure 8.1 Results of Program 8.1 written to auxiliary storage under the filename REPORT. LIS.

When the RUN command is issued for Program 8.1, line 165 opens the sequential file REPORT.LIS for output as filenumber 1. Lines 170 through 200 write the report title and column headings to REPORT.LIS. Line 310 writes a detail record to REPORT.LIS for each employee record read. When the trailer record is read, control transfers to line 360 and the total lines are written to REPORT.LIS. Line 395 closes REPORT.LIS and line 397 displays the message

REPORT COMPLETE AND STORED UNDER FILENAME REPORT. LIS.

Following the execution of Program 8.1, the report may be displayed on a video display device or printed on a line printer as often as needed. To view the report on a video display device, use the system command that lists a file, TYPE REPORT. LIS. To print the report on a line printer, use the system command that prints a file, PRINT REPORT. LIS.

The following problem requests the creation of a sequential file.

Problem

Company PUC has requested that a sequential file be created from the inventory data listed below. Commas must be included between the data items in each record so that they may be read and processed by other programs using the INPUT #n statement.

BASIC at Work

Creating a Sequential File

In the following inventory data, each line represents an inventory record.

Stock Number	Warehouse Location	Description	Unit Cost	Selling Price	Quantity on Hand
C101	1	Roadhandler	97.56	125.11	25
C204	3	Whitewalls	37.14	99.95	140
C502	2	Tripod	32.50	38.99	10
S209	1	Maxidrill	88.76	109.99	6
S416	2	Normalsaw	152.55	179.40	1
S812	2	Router	48.47	61.15	8
S942	4	Radialsaw	376.04	419.89	3
T615	4	Oxford-Style	26.43	31.50	28
T713	2	Moc-Boot	24.99	29.99	30
T814	2	Work-Boot	22.99	27.99	56

INPUT statements are to be used to request the operator to enter the 6 data items found in each record. A sentinel value of EOF for the stock number S$ indicates all records have been entered.

The end-of-job routine includes the following:

1. Write a trailer record with a stock number of EOF so it may be used by other programs to determine end-of-file.
2. Close the file.
3. Display a message indicating that file creation is complete.
4. Display the number of records written to the file (do not count the trailer record in the final total).

When Program 8.2 is executed, line 150 opens INVNTORY.DAT for output as filenumber 1. Line 160 and lines 180 through 220 request the operator to enter the data items for the first record. Line 230 writes the record to INVNTORY.DAT in a format that is consistent with the INPUT #n statement. Line 260 requests the stock

```
100 REM PROGRAM 8.2
110 REM CREATING A SEQUENTIAL FILE
120 REM FILE CREATED BY THIS PROGRAM - INVNTORY.DAT
130 REM ********************************************
140 LET R = 0
150 OPEN "O", #1, "INVNTORY.DAT"
160 INPUT "STOCK NUMBER"; S$
170 WHILE S$ <> "EOF"
180     INPUT "WAREHOUSE LOCATION"; L
190     INPUT "DESCRIPTION"; D$
200     INPUT "UNIT COST"; C
210     INPUT "SELLING PRICE"; P
220     INPUT "QUANTITY ON HAND"; Q
230     PRINT #1, S$; ","; L; ","; D$; ","; C; ","; P; ","; Q
240     LET R = R + 1
250     PRINT
260     INPUT "STOCK NUMBER"; S$
270 WEND
280 PRINT #1, S$; ","; O; ","; S$; ","; O; ","; O; ","; O
290 CLOSE #1
300 PRINT
310 PRINT "CREATION OF SEQUENTIAL FILE INVNTORY.DAT IS COMPLETE."
320 PRINT
330 PRINT "TOTAL NUMBER OF RECORDS IN INVNTORY.DAT IS"; R; "."
340 END

RUN
```

Program 8.2

```
STOCK NUMBER? C101
WAREHOUSE LOCATION? 1
DESCRIPTION? ROADHANDLER
UNIT COST? 97.56
SELLING PRICE? 125.11
QUANTITY ON HAND? 25
                 .
                 .
                 .
STOCK NUMBER? T814
WAREHOUSE LOCATION? 2
DESCRIPTION? WORK-BOOT
UNIT COST? 22.99
SELLING PRICE? 27.99
QUANTITY ON HAND? 56

STOCK NUMBER? EOF

CREATION OF SEQUENTIAL FILE INVNTORY.DAT IS COMPLETE.

TOTAL NUMBER OF RECORDS IN INVNTORY.DAT IS 10 .
```

Record 1

Record 10

number of the next record. If S$ is assigned a value of EOF, then line 170 transfers control to the end-of-job routine (lines 280 through 330). If S$ is not assigned the value EOF in line 260, then the While loop continues execution and the remaining data for the next record is requested and written to the file.

As part of the end-of-job routine, line 280 writes the trailer record to INVNTORY.DAT. When line 280 is executed, S$ is set equal to EOF. The variable S$ is also used to assign a description value of EOF to the trailer record.

Figure 8.2 shows the contents of INVNTORY.DAT after Program 8.2 has been executed.

```
C101, 1 ,ROADHANDLER, 97.56 , 125.11 , 25
C204, 3 ,WHITEWALLS, 37.14 , 99.95 , 140
C502, 2 ,TRIPOD, 32.5 , 38.99 , 10
S209, 1 ,MAXIDRILL, 88.76 , 109.99 , 6
S416, 2 ,NORMALSAW, 152.55 , 179.4 , 1
S812, 2 ,ROUTER, 48.47 , 61.15 , 8
S942, 4 ,RADIALSAW, 376.04 , 419.89 , 3
T615, 4 ,OXFORD-STYLE, 26.43 , 31.5 , 28
T713, 2 ,MOC-BOOT, 24.99 , 29.99 , 30
T814, 2 ,WORK-BOOT, 22.99 , 27.99 , 56
EOF, 0 ,EOF, 0, 0, 0
```

Figure 8.2 A listing of INVENTORY.DAT created by Program 8.2.

The INPUT#n Statement

The INPUT #n statement is used to read data from a sequential file and is similar to the READ statement, except that it reads data from a file instead of from DATA statements. Line 250 in the following partial program

```
240 OPEN "I", #3, "INVNTORY.DAT"
250 INPUT #3, S$, L, D$, C, P, Q
```

reads six data items from the file INVNTORY. DAT.

For data to be read from a file, the following must be true:

1. The file must already exist.
2. The file must be opened for input.
3. The data items in the file must be separated by a comma or carriage return character.

The general form of the INPUT #n statement is shown in Table 8.6.

TABLE 8.6 The INPUT #n Statement

General Form:	INPUT #n, list of variables
	where n is a filenumber assigned to an existing file that is opened for input.
Purpose:	Reads data items from a sequential file in auxiliary storage and assigns them to variables.
Examples:	300 INPUT #1, S, F, D$, P
	400 INPUT #3, A$
	500 INPUT #2, A(I), G, B(4), C(1, 4, T)

The INPUT #n statement causes the variables in its list to be assigned specific values, in order, from the data sequence found in the file assigned to filenumber n. In order to visualize the relationship between the INPUT #n statement and the associated file, you may think of a pointer associated with the data items. When the OPEN statement is executed, this pointer references the first data item in the data sequence. Each time an INPUT #n statement is executed, the variables in the "list" are assigned values from the data sequence beginning with the data item indicated by the pointer, and the pointer is advanced, one value per variable. Hence, the pointer points to the next data item to be assigned when the INPUT #n statement is executed.

The following rules summarize the material discussed in this section:

> INPUT **Rule 4:** Before the INPUT #n statement is executed, the file-number n must be assigned to a sequential file that is opened for input.

> INPUT **Rule 5:** The INPUT #n statement requires the data items be separated by commas within a sequential file.

BASIC at Work

Processing a Sequential File

The following problem requires data to be read and processed from the sequential file created by Program 8.2.

Problem

INVNTORY.DAT was created by Program 8.2; the contents of the data file are shown in Figure 8.2 on the previous page.

For each record in INVNTORY.DAT, the following is to be displayed:

1. Stock number
2. Description
3. Unit cost
4. Selling price
5. Quantity on hand
6. Total item cost of a stock item (unit cost times quantity on hand)
7. Total selling price of a stock item (selling price times quantity on hand)

The total inventory cost and total inventory selling price are also displayed.

An analysis of the problem, and program solution follow.

Program Tasks

1. Initialize total inventory cost S1 and total inventory selling price S2 to zero.
2. Open the sequential file INVNTORY.DAT for input as filenumber 1.
4. Display report and column headings.
4. Read an inventory record. For purposes of consistency, use the same variable names in the list of the INPUT #1 statement as used in the PRINT #1 statement of Program 8.2.
5. Use a While loop to process the records in the file until the trailer record is read. In the While loop, do the following:
   a. Compute T1, the total item cost of a stock item, and T2, the total selling price of a stock item.
   b. Increment the running totals: total inventory cost S1 by T1 and total inventory selling price S2 by T2.
   c. Display the detail record as specified in the problem definition.
   d. Read the next inventory record.
6. Display the running totals S1 and S2, close the file INVNTORY.DAT and display an end-of-job message when the trailer record is read.

```
100 REM PROGRAM 8.3
110 REM PROCESSING A SEQUENTIAL FILE
120 REM S$ = STOCK NUMBER           L  = WAREHOUSE NUMBER
130 REM D$ = DESCRIPTION            C  = UNIT COST
140 REM P  = SELLING PRICE          Q  = QUANTITY ON HAND
150 REM T1 = TOTAL ITEM COST        T2 = TOTAL SELLING PRICE
160 REM S1 = TOTAL INVENTORY COST   S2 = TOTAL INVENTORY SELLING PRICE
170 REM FILE PROCESSED BY THIS PROGRAM - INVNTORY.DAT
180 REM *********************************************************
190 LET S1 = 0
200 LET S2 = 0
210 OPEN 'I', #1, 'INVNTORY.DAT'
220 PRINT TAB(21); 'INVENTORY ANALYSIS'
230 PRINT TAB(21); '------------------'
240 PRINT
250 PRINT TAB(57); 'TOTAL'
260 PRINT     'STOCK                  UNIT SELLING QUANTITY TOTAL        SELLING'
270 PRINT     'NO.   DESCRIPTION      COST PRICE   ON HAND  ITEM COST    PRICE'
280 PRINT     '----- -----------      ---- ------- -------- ----------   -------'
290 LET A$ = '\   \   \             \ ###.## ####.##      #### ##,###.##  ##,###.##'
300 LET B$ = 'TOTALS                                       ###,###.## ###,###.##'
310 REM *****PROCESS FILE INVNTORY.DAT*****
320 INPUT #1, S$, L, D$, C, P, Q
330 WHILE S$ <> 'EOF'
340     LET T1 = C*Q
350     LET T2 = P*Q
360     LET S1 = S1 + T1
370     LET S2 = S2 + T2
380     PRINT USING A$; S$, D$, C, P, Q, T1, T2
390     INPUT #1, S$, L, D$, C, P, Q
400 WEND
410 REM *********************END OF FILE ROUTINE*******************
420 PRINT
430 PRINT USING B$; S1, S2
440 CLOSE #1
470 PRINT 'JOB COMPLETE'
480 END
```

Program 8.3

```
RUN

                    INVENTORY ANALYSIS
                    ------------------

                                                       TOTAL
STOCK                   UNIT SELLING QUANTITY TOTAL    SELLING
NO.   DESCRIPTION       COST PRICE   ON HAND  ITEM COST PRICE
----- -----------       ---- ------- -------- --------- -------
C101  ROADHANDLER       97.56  125.11      25  2,439.00  3,127.75
C204  WHITEWALLS        37.14   99.95     140  5,199.60 13,993.00
C502  TRIPOD            32.50   38.99      10    325.00    389.90
S209  MAXIDRILL         88.76  109.99       6    532.56    659.94
S416  NORMALSAW        152.55  179.40       1    152.55    179.40
S812  ROUTER            48.47   61.15       8    387.76    489.20
S942  RADIALSAW        376.04  419.89       3  1,128.12  1,259.67
T615  OXFORD-STYLE      26.43   31.50      28    740.04    882.00
T713  MOC-BOOT          24.99   29.99      30    749.70    899.70
T814  WORK-BOOT         22.99   27.99      56  1,287.44  1,567.44

TOTALS                                       12,941.77 23,448.00
JOB COMPLETE
```

The following points should be noted concerning the program solution represented by Program 8.3:

1. In line 210, the OPEN statement opens INVNTORY.DAT for input as filenumber 1. The remaining file handling statements, lines 320, 390 and 440, reference INVNTORY.DAT by specifying the filenumber 1.
2. The While loop, lines 330 through 400, continues to process records until the trailer record in INVNTORY.DAT is read and S$ is assigned the value EOF.

3. Even though the warehouse location is not manipulated or displayed by Program 8.3, it is necessary to include a variable L representing the warehouse location in the list of the INPUT #n statement, since the data item is part of the record. You cannot be selective and input from a sequential data file only those data items you plan to manipulate or display. All data items within the record must be assigned to variables in the INPUT #n statement as shown in lines 320 and 390.
4. The same variable names used in the INPUT #n statement of Program 8.3 were used in the PRINT #n statement of Program 8.2. Such consistency among programs referencing the same file is good programming practice.

Alternative Methods for Detecting End-of-File

Up to this point, a trailer record has been added to the end of a sequential data file to indicate the physical end-of-file. When programs process the file, a test has been made to determine when to branch to an end-of-job routine. It is not necessary to write a trailer record. Each time a CLOSE statement is executed for a sequential file opened for output, the system automatically writes an **end-of-file mark** after the last record.

The method used to test for the end-of-file mark varies between the dialects of BASIC. Since most BASIC systems treat reading past the end-of-file as an error, this error can be trapped and control passed to an end-of-job routine through the use of the ON ERROR GOTO statement. An alternative method, supported by Microsoft BASIC, is to use the function EOF(n) to test for the end-of-file mark. In this section we will discuss the ON ERROR GOTO statement and, later, the use of the function EOF(n).

The ON ERROR GOTO Statement

The ON ERROR GOTO statement enables error trapping and specifies a line number to branch to when an error occurs. The line number may be the beginning of an end-of-job routine. Once the ON ERROR GOTO statement is executed, *all* errors detected cause the system to branch to the specified line number. The user's manual will list the various errors that the ON ERROR GOTO statement can trap.

Most BASIC systems include two special variables named ERR and ERL. When an error is trapped, ERR is assigned an error code. ERL is assigned the line number of the statement that caused the error. Following the branch to the end-of-job routine,

TABLE 8.7 **The ON ERROR GOTO Statement**

General Form:	ON ERROR GOTO line number
Purpose:	Enables error trapping and specifies a line number to branch to when an error occurs. The special variables ERR and ERL may be used to test for the type of error and line number of the statement that caused the error. The statement ON ERROR GOTO 0 may be used to terminate execution of the program if the error is not of the type that can be handled by the routine.
Examples:	100 ON ERROR GOTO 500 200 ON ERROR GOTO 0

the value of ERR can be tested to determine if the error was caused by reading past end-of-file. If ERR is equal to the correct code (62 with Microsoft BASIC), then execution of the end-of-job routine can continue. If ERR does not equal the proper code, then the program should be terminated. The system can be instructed to terminate execution through the use of the statement ON ERROR GOTO 0. When this statement is executed, the system terminates the program.

The general form of the ON ERROR GOTO statement is shown in Table 8.7.

The ON ERROR GOTO statement must be placed in a program in such a way that it is executed prior to the lines in which errors are to be trapped. In order to trap an out-of-data error, the ON ERROR GOTO statement must be executed before the INPUT #n statement. The following partial program illustrates the correct placement of the ON ERROR GOTO statement and the use of the special variable ERR.

```
       100 REM USE OF THE ON ERROR GOTO STATEMENT AND VARIABLE ERR
       110 REM TO TRANSFER CONTROL TO AN END-OF-JOB ROUTINE.
       120 REM ***********************************************
       130 ON ERROR GOTO 310
       140 OPEN "I", #1, "INVNTORY.DAT"
     ▶ 150 INPUT #1, S$, L, D$, C, P, Q
                .
Loop            .
                .
       290 GOTO 150
       300 REM *****END-OF-JOB ROUTINE*****
       310 IF ERR = 62 THEN 320 ELSE ON ERROR GOTO 0
       320 .
                .
                .
       390 CLOSE #1
       400 END
```

Line 130 enables error trapping. Line 150 reads the first record. If the file INVNTORY.DAT is empty, then control transfers to line 310. If the file is not empty, the record is processed, line 290 transfers control back to line 150, and the next record is read and processed. The loop continues until there are no more records left in INVNTORY.DAT.

When line 150 attempts to read past end-of-file, control automatically transfers to line 310, which compares ERR to the error code 62. If ERR is equal to 62, then the end-of-job routine is executed. If ERR does not equal 62, then another type of error caused the system to branch to line 310 and the ON ERROR GOTO 0 causes the system to display an appropriate diagnostic message and terminate the program.

Another statement that can be used along with the ON ERROR GOTO statement is the RESUME statement. The RESUME statement instructs the system to continue execution at any line number in the program following an error. For example, always closing a file is good programming practice. In the previous partial program, line 310 can be changed to the following to ensure that the file INVNTORY.DAT is closed even if an error other than out-of-data occurs:

```
310 IF ERR = 62 THEN 320 ELSE RESUME 390
```

The following rule summarizes the placement of the ON ERROR GOTO statement in a program.

ON ERROR GOTO **Rule 1:** The ON ERROR GOTO statement should be executed prior to the lines in which errors are to be trapped.

The Function EOF(n)

The function EOF(n), where n represents the filenumber, tests for end-of-file. Unfortunately, this function is not available on all BASIC systems. If the function EOF is available, it is preferable to the ON ERROR GOTO statement.

When referenced in a program, the function EOF returns a value of 0 (false) if it is not end-of-file. The function EOF returns a value of −1 (true), when end-of-file has been reached.

The following partial program illustrates how this function may be used to control a loop that reads and processes data found in a file until the end-of-file is detected:

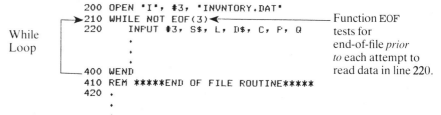

Line 210 tests for the end-of-file mark *prior to* the execution of the INPUT #n statement in line 220. If INVNTORY.DAT is empty, line 210 transfers control to the end-of-file routine and the statements within the While loop are not executed. If INVNTORY.DAT is not empty, control passes to line 220 and the first record is read and then processed. Before each succeeding pass, the function EOF(3) in line 210 returns a value of 0 (false) or −1 (true). If the function returns a 0, indicating it is not end-of-file, then the loop continues. If the function returns a −1, indicating it is end-of-file, then control transfers to the end-of-file routine beginning at line 420.

---

1. Consider the valid program listed below. Explain the function of this program. Assume the following values are entered in response to the INPUT statements.

Stock Item	Selling Price	Discount Code
138	$ 78.56	2
421	123.58	3
617	475.65	2
812	23.58	1
917	754.56	4
EOF		

```
100 REM EXERCISE 8.1
110 OPEN 'O', #1, 'SALES.DAT'
120 INPUT 'STOCK ITEM'; S$
130 WHILE S$ <> 'EOF'
140    INPUT 'SELLING PRICE'; S
150    INPUT 'DISCOUNT CODE'; C
160    PRINT #1, S$; ','; S; ','; C
170    INPUT 'STOCK ITEM'; S$
180 WEND
190 PRINT #1, 'EOF'; ','; 0; ','; 0
200 CLOSE #1
210 PRINT 'JOB COMPLETE'
220 END
```

2. Write a program that lists in columns the contents of the sequential file created by the program in Exercise 1. A program that lists the contents of a file is often called a **file list program**. As part of the end-of-job routine, display the total number of records and average selling price.

3. List the three methods described in this chapter for determining end-of-file.

4. State the purpose of the ON ERROR GOTO 0 statement and the RESUME statement.

5. State the purpose of the special variables ERR and ERL. What error code corresponds to reading past the end-of-file on *your* BASIC system?

6. A program is required to read records from one of three sequential files, SALES1.DAT, SALES2.DAT and SALES3.DAT. Write an INPUT statement and OPEN statement that allow the program to open any of the three sequential files. Use filenumber 1.

7. Construct a PRINT #n statement that writes the values of A, B, C$ and D to a sequential file in the format required by the INPUT #n statement. Use filenumber 1.

8. Is the following sequence of INPUT #n statements valid for reading data from the sequential file created through the use of the PRINT #n statement in Exercise 7?

```
300 INPUT #1, A
310 INPUT #1, B
320 INPUT #1, C$
330 INPUT #1, D
```

9. Fill in the following:
   a. A sequential file must be _____ for _____ before a corresponding PRINT #n statement is executed.
   b. A sequential file must be _____ for _____ before a corresponding INPUT #n statement is executed.
   c. A file may be opened as often as required provided it is _____ before each subsequent open.

10. Which of the following are invalid file handling statements? Why?
```
a. 100 OPEN "FILE1.DAT", "I", #1        f. 600 INPUT #2, A,
b. 200 OPEN M, #N, N$                   g. 700 CLOSE "FILE1.DAT"
c. 300 PRINT #1,                        h. 800 ON ERROR GOTO 800
d. 400 PRINT #1, A,                     i. 900 WHILE EOF(#3)
e. 500 PRINT #1 USING "####.##"; A
```

Purpose: To become familiar with creating a sequential file that is consistent with the format required by the INPUT #n statement.

Problem: Construct a program to create a sequential file named PAYMAST.DAT that represents the payroll master file for company PUC. Each record in the file describes an employee, including the year-to-date (YTD) payroll information, as shown under the Input Data.

Write the data to the file in the format required by the INPUT #n statement. If you do not plan to use the ON ERROR GOTO statement or the function EOF in the later exercises of this chapter, then write a trailer record as the last record to identify end-of-file. As part of the end-of-job routine, display a message indicating the file was created and the total number of records written to the file.

After the program creates the file properly, modify the program to validate the marital status and numeric values. The marital status should be M or S and the numeric values should be non-negative. Select your own data to test the validation routines.

8.6
BASIC
PROGRAMMING
PROBLEMS

1:
Creating a Master File

Input Data: Prepare and use the following sample data:

Employee Number	Employee Name	Dependents	Marital Status	Rate of Pay	Gross Pay	Federal With. Tax	Social Security
						Year-to-Date	
123	Cole Jim	2	M	$12.50	5,345.23	$1,256.34	$725.15
124	Fiel Don	1	S	18.00	5,910.45	1,546.45	791.90
125	Dit Bill	1	S	13.00	4,115.23	1,035.78	585.72
126	Snow Joe	9	M	4.50	1,510.05	354.34	100.00
134	Hi Frank	0	M	8.75	9,298.65	2,678.25	576.23
167	Brink Ed	3	S	10.40	190.45	17.50	16.76
210	Liss Ted	6	M	8.85	7,098.04	2,120.55	825.35
234	Son Fred	2	M	6.75	0.00	0.00	0.00

Output Results: The sequential file PAYMAST.DAT is created in auxiliary storage. The following partial results are shown:

```
EMPLOYEE NUMBER? 123
EMPLOYEE NAME? COLE JIM
NUMBER OF DEPENDENTS? 2
MARITAL STATUS? M
RATE OF PAY? 12.50
YEAR-TO-DATE GROSS PAY? 5345.23
YEAR-TO-DATE WITHHOLDING TAX? 1256.34
YEAR-TO-DATE SOCIAL SECURITY? 725.15
     .
     .
     .
EMPLOYEE NUMBER? EOF

CREATION OF SEQUENTIAL FILE PAYMAST.DAT IS COMPLETE.
TOTAL NUMBER OF RECORDS WRITTEN TO PAYMAST.DAT IS 8.
JOB COMPLETE
```

2:
Master File List

Purpose: To become familiar with reading and displaying records in a sequential data file.

Problem: Write a program that displays the data items found in each employee record of the sequential file PAYMAST.DAT created in Programming Problem 1. As part of the end-of-job routine, display the following totals: employee-record count, YTD gross pay, YTD federal withholding tax, and YTD social security tax.

Input Data: Use the sequential file PAYMAST.DAT created in Programming Problem 1.

Output Results: The following results are displayed.

```
                    PAYROLL MASTER FILE LIST
                    ------------------------

EMPLOYEE             MARITAL RATE OF  <-------YEAR-TO-DATE-------->
NO. NAME        DEP. STATUS  PAY      GROSS PAY WITH. TAX SOC. SEC.
--- --------    ---- ------- -------  --------- --------- ---------
123 COLE JIM     2     M       12.50   5,345.23  1,256.34    725.15
124 FIEL DON     1     S       18.00   5,910.45  1,546.45    791.90
125 DIT BILL     1     S       13.00   4,115.23  1,035.78    585.72
126 SNOW JOE     9     M        4.50   1,510.05    354.34    100.00
134 HI FRANK     0     M        8.75   9,298.65  2,678.25    576.23
167 BRINK ED     3     S       10.40     190.45     17.50     16.76
210 LISS TED     6     M        8.85   7,098.04  2,120.55    825.35
234 SON FRED     2     M        6.75       0.00      0.00      0.00

TOTAL NUMBER OF RECORDS=====================>        8
TOTAL YEAR-TO-DATE GROSS PAY===============> 33,468.10
TOTAL YEAR-TO-DATE WITHHOLDING TAX=========>  9,009.21
TOTAL YEAR-TO-DATE SOCIAL SECURITY TAX=====>  3,621.11

JOB COMPLETE
```

3:
Writing a Report to Auxiliary Storage

Purpose: To become familiar with writing a report to a sequential file.

Problem: Same as BASIC Programming Problem 2, except write the report to the sequential file REPORT.DAT.

Input Data: Use the sequential file PAYMAST.DAT created in BASIC Programming Problem 1.

Output Results: The sequential file REPORT.DAT is created in auxiliary storage. The following results are displayed:

```
REPORT COMPLETE AND STORED UNDER THE FILENAME REPORT.DAT.
JOB COMPLETE
```

MORE ON STRINGS AND FUNCTIONS

9

Computers were originally built to perform mathematical calculations. Today, they are still used for that purpose. However, more and more applications require computers to process string data as well. Section 3.4 briefly introduced four string functions, LEFT\$, MID\$, RIGHT\$ and LEN. As you shall see in this chapter, BASIC includes several additional string functions and string statements that place it among the better programming languages for manipulating letters, numbers, words and phrases.

BASIC also includes numeric functions to handle common mathematical calculations. For example, it is often necessary in programming to obtain the square root or the logarithm of a number. In this chapter we will discuss the two numeric functions that handle these two calculations as well as ten others that are frequently found with BASIC systems.

A second type of function that will be discussed in this chapter is the **user-defined function**. With a function that is defined by the user, numeric or string functions can be created to perform an often needed task.

Table 9.1 on page 152 shows a list of some common string functions discussed in this chapter and their availability on some popular computer systems. Most of the function names are followed by an argument in parentheses. To be used, these functions need only be referred to by name in a LET, PRINT or IF statement and, if necessary, followed by arguments in parentheses.

Concatenation, Substrings and Character Counting Revisited— +, LEN, LEFT\$, RIGHT\$ and MID\$

The extraction of substrings from a large string or the combination of two or more strings are important in manipulating non-numeric data. In Section 3.4 the concatenation operator + and the LEN, LEFT\$, RIGHT\$ and MID\$ functions were briefly introduced. Recall that concatenation is the only string operation allowed in BASIC. It joins two strings to form a new string. For example,

```
500 LET A$ = 'ABC' + 'DEF'
```

assigns A\$ the value ABCDEF. The second string is joined to the right end of the first string to form the result, which is then assigned to A\$. More than one concatenation operator may appear in a single assignment statement. For example, if X\$ =

151

TABLE 9.1   String Functions Common to Most BASIC Systems*

Function	Function Value	Apple	COMMO-DORE	DEC Rainbow	DEC VAX-11	IBM PC and Macintosh	TRS-80
ASC(C$)	Returns a two-digit numeric value that is equivalent in ASCII code to the single character C$.	Yes	Yes	Yes	ASCII(C$)	Yes	Yes
CHR$(N)	Returns a single string character that is equivalent in ASCII code to the numeric argument N.	Yes	Yes	Yes	Yes	Yes	Yes
DATE$	Returns the date as a string in the form mm-dd-yyyy.	No	Yes	No	Yes	Yes	Yes
INKEY$	Provides for a program to accept a single character from the keyboard without the Enter key being pressed.	No	GET C$	Yes	No	Yes	Yes
INPUT$(N)	Provides for a program to accept N number of characters from the keyboard without the Enter key being pressed.	GET C$	No	No	No	Yes	No
INSTR(P,X$,S$)	Returns the beginning position of the substring S$ in string X$. P indicates the position the search begins in X$ and may be omitted from the argument list. If the search for S$ in X$ is unsuccessful, INSTR returns a value of 0.	No	No	Yes	Yes	Yes	No
LEFT$(X$, N)	Extracts the leftmost N characters of the string argument X$.	Yes	Yes	Yes	Yes	Yes	Yes
LEN(X$)	Returns the length of the string argument X$.	Yes	Yes	Yes	Yes	Yes	Yes
MID$(X$,P,N)	Extracts N characters of the string argument X$ beginning at position P.	Yes	Yes	Yes	Yes	Yes	Yes
RIGHT$(X$, N)	Extracts the rightmost N characters of the string argument X$.	Yes	Yes	Yes	Yes	Yes	Yes
SPACE$(N)	Returns N number of spaces.	No	No	Yes	Yes	Yes	No
SPC(N)	Displays N spaces. May only be used in a PRINT statement.	Yes	Yes	Yes	No	Yes	No
STR$(N)	Returns the string equivalent of the numeric argument N.	Yes	Yes	Yes	Yes	Yes	Yes
STRING$(N,"C")	Returns N times the character C within quotation marks.	No	No	Yes	Yes	Yes	Yes
TIME$	Returns the time of day in 24-hour notation as a string in the form hh:mm:ss.	No	Yes	No	Yes	Yes	Yes
VAL(X$)	Returns the numeric equivalent of the string argument X$.	Yes	Yes	Yes	Yes	Yes	Yes

* Check the specifications on your BASIC system in the user's manual for the format of the value returned by these functions. Some of the computer systems designated as not having a particular function may in fact have the function under some other operating system.

RESISTb and Y$ = THE URGEb and Z$ = TO CODE, then

```
600 LET T$ = X$ + Y$ + Z$
```

assigns T$ the string RESIST THE URGE TO CODE.

The function LEN returns the length of the argument. The argument may be a string constant, string variable or string expression. Table 9.2 and Program 9.1 illustrate the use of the function LEN.

TABLE 9.2   Examples of the LEN Function

Value of Variable	The Statement	Results In
S$ = IBM PC	100 LET L1 = LEN(S$)	L1 = 6
X$ = APPLE	200 LET L2 = LEN(X$)	L2 = 5
	300 LET L3 = LEN("TRS-80")	L3 = 6
	400 LET L4 = LEN("")	L4 = 0
Y$ = null	500 LET L5 = LEN(Y$)	L5 = 0

```
100 REM PROGRAM 9.1
110 REM EXAMPLES OF THE USE OF THE FUNCTION LEN
120 REM ****************************************
130 LET B$ = "STRUCTURED"
140 LET C$ = "PROGRAMMING"
150 LET L = LEN(B$)
160 PRINT B$; " HAS"; L; "CHARACTERS."
170 PRINT C$; " HAS"; LEN(C$); "CHARACTERS."
180 PRINT B$ + " " + C$; " HAS"; LEN(B$ + " " + C$); "CHARACTERS."
190 END

RUN

STRUCTURED HAS 10 CHARACTERS.
PROGRAMMING HAS 11 CHARACTERS.
STRUCTURED PROGRAMMING HAS 22 CHARACTERS.
```

Program 9.1

The string functions LEFT$, MID$ and RIGHT$ may be used to extract **substrings** from a string constant, string variable or string expression. A substring is a part of a string. For example: some substrings of RETURN OF THE JEDI are RETURN, JEDI, OF T and ED. All three functions reference substrings based on

TABLE 9.3   Examples of the LEFT$, RIGHT$ and MID$ Functions

Assume S$ is equal to: IF SOMETHING CAN GO WRONG, IT WILL

The Statement	Results In
100 LET C$ = LEFT$(S$, 12)	C$ = IF SOMETHING
200 LET F$ = LEFT$(S$, 1.4)	F$ = I
300 LET H$ = LEFT$(S$, 0)	H$ = null
400 LET J$ = RIGHT$(S$, 7)	J$ = IT WILL
500 LET P$ = RIGHT$("TO BE", -1)	Illegal function call
600 LET R$ = RIGHT$(S$, 50)	R$ = S$
700 LET T$ = MID$(S$, 3 + 4, 6)	T$ = ETHING
800 LET U$ = MID$(LEFT$(S$, 4), 2, 1)	U$ = F
900 LET V$ = MID$(S$, 75, 4)	V$ = null
950 LET X$ = MID$(S$, 18, 200)	X$ = GO WRONG, IT WILL

the position of characters within the argument string, where the leftmost character of the argument string is position 1 and the next position 2 and so on. For example, in the string RETURN OF THE JEDI, the substring RETURN begins in position 1 and the substring JEDI begins in position 15. Program 3.7, on page 42, makes use of the string functions: LEFT$, MID$, RIGHT, and LEN.

Table 9.3 illustrates the use of the functions LEFT$, RIGHT$ and MID$.

In line 200 of Table 9.3, the argument 1.4 is rounded to the value of 1. In line 300, the numeric argument 0 causes the system to return the null string. In line 500, the negative argument results in an illegal function call. Line 500 is invalid. Lines 600 and 950 of Table 9.3 also show that if the length argument is greater than the length of the string argument, the function returns a substring that begins at the specified position and includes the remaining portion of the string. Line 800 shows that you may include a string function as the string argument. Finally, line 900 illustrates that a null string is returned when the position P specified in the MID$ function is greater than the length of the argument string.

Substring Searching and Replacement— INSTR Function and MID$ Statement

Some BASIC systems include the function INSTR, which searches the string argument for a particular substring. The function INSTR (P, X$, S$) returns the beginning position of the substring S$ in X$. The search begins at position P of X$.

For example, if V$ is equal to TO BE OR NOT TO BE, the following statement assigns C a value of 4:

```
500 LET C = INSTR(1, V$, "BE")
```

Line 500 assigns C the position of the first character of the substring BE in string V$. If there are no occurrences of the substring, INSTR returns the value zero.

The function INSTR always returns the leftmost position of the first occurrence of the substring. The following statement,

```
600 LET C = INSTR(5, V$, "BE")
```

assigns C a value of 17. The first occurrence of BE is by-passed because the search began at position 5.

The position argument P may be omitted from the list of arguments. For example, the following statement is identical to the previous line 500:

```
500 LET C = INSTR(V$, "BE")
```

That is, the search begins at position 1 (by default) and assigns C a value of 4. Table 9.4 illustrates some additional examples of the function INSTR.

TABLE 9.4   **Examples of the** INSTR **Function**

Assume S$ is equal to: RALLY 'ROUND THE FLAG, BOYS, RALLY ONCE AGAIN

The Statement	Results In
`100 LET A = INSTR(1, S$, ",")`	A = 22
`200 LET B = INSTR(A, S$, "RALLY")`	B = 30 (assume A = 22)
`300 LET C = INSTR(S$, "'")`	C = 7

Some BASIC systems also include the MID$ statement for the purpose of substring replacement. Do not confuse the MID$ statement with the function MID$. The function MID$ returns a substring, but the MID$ statement replaces a series of characters within a string with a designated substring. The general form of the MID$ statement is given in Table 9.5

TABLE 9.5 **The** MID$ **Statement**

General Form:	MID$(X$, P, N) = S$
	where X$ is the string in which the replacement takes place
	P is the position at which the replacement begins
	N is the number of characters to replace
	S$ is the replacement substring
Purpose:	To replace a substring within a string.
Examples:	100 MID$(X$, 3, 4) = S$
	200 MID$(C$, 1, 5) = "Y" (only 1 character replaced)
	300 MID$(F$, 30, 2) = "ABCDE" (only 2 characters replaced)
	400 MID$(E$, 4, 5) = A$ + B$
Caution:	This statement is found on systems using Microsoft BASIC. It is not available on the Apple, COMMODORE or DEC VAX-11.

As illustrated by the general form in Table 9.5, a substring of X$, specified by the beginning position P and the length N, is replaced by the substring S$. For example, if X$ is equal to INPROCMENT and S$ is equal to VEST, then the following statement

```
100 MID$(X$, 3, 4) = S$
```

assigns X$ the value IN**VEST**MENT. The substring VEST replaces the substring PROC.

In Table 9.5 line 200 shows that if the replacement substring is shorter than the substring designated by the length argument in the MID$ statement, then only those characters designated by the replacement substring are actually replaced. For example, if C$ is equal to BEAST, then the statement

```
200 MID$(C$, 1, 5) = "Y"
```

assigns C$ the value YEAST.

If the replacement substring has a length greater than that specified by N in the MID$ statement, then the system replaces only N characters. The rightmost excess characters in the replacement substring are not used.

Program 9.2 on page 156 modifies a line of text through the use of the function INSTR and the MID$ statement. The program searches for all occurrences of the substring NE. Each time the substring is found, it is replaced with the substring IN.

Line 150 in Program 9.2 assigns R the value 7, which is the beginning position of the first occurrence of the substring NE. Line 170 replaces the substring NE that begins in position 7 with the substring IN. Line 180 searches for the next occurrence of the substring NE. The search begins one position to the right of the previous occurrence. The next occurrence of the substring NE begins at position 16. Therefore, the function INSTR assigns R a value of 16. The loop continues with line 170 making the next replacement.

```
100 REM PROGRAM 9.2
110 REM SEARCHING AND REPLACING STRINGS
120 REM *******************************
130 LET A$ = "THE RANE IN SPANE STAYS MANELY IN THE PLANE"
140 PRINT "OLD TEXT - "; A$
150 LET R = INSTR(A$, "NE")
160 WHILE R <> 0
170    MID$(A$, R, 2) = "IN"
180    LET R = INSTR(R + 2, A$, "NE")
190 WEND
200 PRINT
210 PRINT "NEW TEXT - "; A$
220 END

RUN

OLD TEXT - THE RANE IN SPANE STAYS MANELY IN THE PLANE

NEW TEXT - THE RAIN IN SPAIN STAYS MAINLY IN THE PLAIN
```

Program 9.2

This process continues until all the occurrences of NE have been changed to IN. At this point, line 180 assigns R a value of zero and the loop terminates. The modified value of A$ is then displayed by line 210.

If A$ is assigned a value without the substring NE, the While loop (lines 160 through 190) will not execute. The function INSTR in line 150 returns a value of zero when the substring is not found. With R equal to zero, the WHILE statement in line 160 causes execution to continue at line 200. In this case, the next text and old text are identical.

Converting Character Codes—ASC and CHR$

Each character in BASIC has a corresponding ASCII numeric code that the computer uses for storing the character in main memory or on auxiliary storage. For example, the character "A" has an ASCII code of 65, the character "B" has an ASCII code of 66, and so on. The functions ASC and CHR$ facilitate the manipulation of individual characters. The function ASC(C$) returns a two-digit numeric value that corresponds to the ASCII code for the single character argument C$. The function CHR$(N) can be described as the reverse of the function ASC. It returns a single string character that is equivalent in ASCII code to the numeric argument N.

A total of 256 different characters are represented by the ASCII code.* Only characters with codes in the ranges 32–126 and 128–255 can be entered in response to an INPUT statement or defined as a string constant. The function CHR$ allows you to by-pass this restriction and use any of the 256 characters. For example, the partial program

```
300 FOR I = 1 TO 10
310    PRINT CHR$(7);
320 NEXT I
```

causes the system to beep ten times. That is because the ASCII code 7 corresponds to the character BEL (Bell).

The function ASC is used to convert a single character string into a numeric value which can later be manipulated arithmetically. For example, the following

---

* Some computer systems use only 128 different characters, represented by the numeric codes 0–127.

partial program changes the single character string assigned to U$ from uppercase to lowercase:

```
490 LET U$ = "A"
500 LET U = ASC(U$)
510 LET L = U + 32
520 LET L$ = CHR$(L)
530 PRINT "UPPERCASE: "; U$
540 PRINT "LOWERCASE: "; L$
       .
       .
       .

RUN

UPPERCASE: A
LOWERCASE: a
```

In this partial program, the ASCII code for a lowercase character is equal to the corresponding uppercase numeric code plus 32. Line 500 assigns the variable U the numeric value 65 that is equal to the ASCII code for the character "A." Line 510 assigns L the value 97. Line 520 assigns L$ the character "a," which has a ASCII code of 97. Lines 530 and 540 display the values of U$ and L$ respectively.

TABLE 9.6   Examples of the ASC **and** CHR$ **Function**

Value of	The Statement	Results In
	100 LET C = ASC("5")	C = 53
C$ = null	200 LET D = ASC(C$)	D = 00
D$ = ABC	300 LET E = ASC(D$)	E = 65
	400 LET X$ = CHR$(75)	X$ = K
D = −3	500 LET Y$ = CHR$(D)	Fatal Error

Table 9.6 illustrates several examples of the functions ASC and CHR$, and the following BASIC at Work Problem makes use of both functions to decipher a coded message.

Messages are often coded by having one letter represent another. The coded message is called a **cryptogram**, and an algorithm is used to decipher the message into readable form.

BASIC at Work

Deciphering a Coded Message

The objective here is to take a coded message and have the computer display the corresponding deciphered message. The algorithm calls for subtracting 3 from the numeric code representing each character in the coded message. Obviously the algorithm can be, and usually is, more complex.

The coded message is

W K H # V K D G R Z # N Q R Z V

Program 9.3 on page 158 accepts a coded message, deciphers it one character at a time and displays the corresponding message one character at a time.

In line 160 the function LEN determines the terminal value for the For loop. Line 170 determines the numeric value that corresponds to the ASCII code for the character selected by the MID$ function. It is valid to have a string function as part of

```
100 REM PROGRAM 9.3
110 REM DECIPHERING A CODED MESSAGE
120 REM ***************************
130 INPUT "CODED MESSAGE"; C$
140 PRINT
150 PRINT "THE MESSAGE IS: ";
160 FOR I = 1 TO LEN(C$)
170     LET N = ASC(MID$(C$, I, 1))
180     LET N = N - 3
190     LET M$ = CHR$(N)
200     PRINT M$;
210 NEXT I
220 PRINT
230 PRINT "----------------"
240 END

RUN

CODED MESSAGE? WKH#VKDGRZ#NQRZV

THE MESSAGE IS: THE SHADOW KNOWS
----------------
```

Program 9.3

the argument for another string function. Line 180 subtracts 3 from the value of N and in line 190 the function CHR$ returns the corresponding character.

Program 9.3 can be shortened by replacing lines 170 through 200 with the following statement:

```
170 PRINT CHR$(ASC(MID$(C$, I, 1)) - 3);
```

Modifying Data Types—STR$ and VAL

In Chapter 3 it was mentioned that strings and numeric values are stored differently inside the computer and that the computer cannot add a numeric and string value. The functions STR$ and VAL allow this restriction to be circumvented. The function STR$(N) returns the string equivalent of the numeric value N. The function VAL(X$) returns the numeric equivalent of the string X$. Thus, STR$(52.3) returns the string 52.3 and VAL("310.23") returns the numeric value 310.23. If the argument for the function STR$ is negative, the function returns a leading negative sign. If the argument for the function VAL does not represent a number, the function returns a value of 0. For example, the value returned by the following statement

```
500 LET V = VAL("IBM")
```

is zero.

TABLE 9.7   Examples of the STR$ and VAL Function*

Value of	The Statement	Results In
	100 LET A$ = STR$(34)	A$ = 34
B = 64.543	200 LET S$ = STR$(B)	S$ = 64.543
C = −3.21	300 LET Z$ = STR$(C)	Z$ = −3.21
	400 LET F = VAL("766.321")	F = 766.321
K$ = 12E−3	500 LET Q = VAL(K$)	Q = 12E−3
P$ = STR	600 LET W = VAL(P$)	W = 0

*Note that any numeric value assigned to a string variable is actually a string and not a number.

Table 9.7 illustrates examples of both the STR$ and VAL functions. The functions VAL and STR$ are primarily used in instances where a substring of numeric digits within an identification number, like a credit card number or invoice number, need to be extracted for computational purposes and the result transformed back as a string value.

Displaying Spaces—SPC

The function SPC is similar to the space bar on a typewriter. The function SPC is used in a PRINT statement to insert spaces between column headings or other results that are displayed as part of a report. The form of the function SPC is SPC (N) where the argument N may be a numeric constant, variable, expression or function reference. Consider the following:

```
240 PRINT "COLUMN 1"; SPC(3); "COLUMN 2"; SPC(5); "COLUMN 3"
```

The SPC (3) causes the insertion of three spaces between COLUMN 1 and COLUMN 2. The SPC (5) inserts five spaces between COLUMN 2 and COLUMN 3. The spaces inserted between results displayed are often called **filler**. The SPC function may only be used in a PRINT statement, but it may be used any number of times in the same PRINT statement.

Duplicating Strings—SPACE$ and STRING $

The functions SPACE$ and STRING$ are used to duplicate string data. The function SPACE$ (N) returns N spaces or blank characters. It is similar to the function SPC. For example, the two statements

```
300 PRINT "DEC"; SPC(4); "RAINBOW"
```

and

```
300 PRINT "DEC"; SPACE$(4); "RAINBOW"
```

display identical results. The advantage of the function SPACE$ over the function SPC is that SPACE$ may be used in statements other than the PRINT statement. For example, the statement

```
400 LET A$ = SPACE$(25)
```

assigns A$ a string value of 25 spaces. If the argument is equal to or less than zero, the function returns the null string.

The function STRING$ (N, "C") returns the character C, which is within quotation marks, N times. The function STRING$ may be used to duplicate any character. For example, the statement

```
500 PRINT STRING$(72, "*")
```

displays a line of 72 asterisks. The second argument may also be represented in ASCII code. That is, the statement

```
500 PRINT STRING$(72, 42)
```

is identical to the previous one, since 42 is the ASCII code representation for the asterisk character.

Table 9.8 illustrates examples of both the SPACE$ and STRING$ functions.

TABLE 9.8   **Examples of the** SPACE$ **and** STRING$ **Functions**

Value of	The Statement	Comment
N = 50	100 PRINT SPACE$(N); "A"	Displays the character A in position 51.
	200 LET X$ = SPACE$(12)	Assigns 12 spaces to X$.
	300 LET Y$ = SPACE$(0)	Assigns Y$ the null string.
S = 45	400 PRINT STRING$(S, "-")	Displays 45 minus signs.
	500 LET X$ = STRING$(5, 65)	Assigns X$ the string value AAAAA.
	600 IF Z$ = SPACE$(15) THEN 900	Transfers control to line 900 if Z$ is equal to 15 spaces.

Date and Time—DATE$ and TIME$

Many BASIC systems include the function DATE$ and TIME$. The function DATE$ returns the current system date as a string value in the form mm-dd-yyyy. The first two characters, mm, represent the month. The fourth and fifth characters, dd, represent the day. The last four characters, yyyy, represent the year. For example, if the system date is initialized to December 25, 1986, then the statement

        300 LET D$ = DATE$

assigns D$ the string 12-25-1986.

The function TIME$ returns the time of day, in 24-hour notation, as a string value in the form hh:mm:ss. The first two characters, hh, represent the hours (range 00-23). The fourth and fifth characters, mm, represent the minutes. The last two characters represent the seconds. If the internal clock is equal to 11:35:42 *at the instant* the statement

        400 PRINT "THE TIME IS "; TIME$

executes, then the system displays

        THE TIME IS 11:35:42

The key phrase in the last sentence is "at the instant," since the computer's internal clock automatically maintains the time after it is entered by the operator as part of the start up procedures.

Table 9.9 illustrates examples of both the DATE$ and TIME$ functions.

TABLE 9.9   **Examples of the** DATE$ **and** TIME$ **Functions***

Assume DATE$ = 09-15-1986 and TIME$ = 15:26:32

The Statement	Results In
100 LET A$ = DATE$	A$ = 09-15-1986
200 LET B$ = TIME$	B$ = 15:26:32
300 LET C$ = MID$(DATE$, 1, 2)	C$ = 09
400 LET D$ = MID$(DATE$, 4, 2)	D$ = 15
500 LET E$ = MID$(DATE$, 9, 2)	E$ = 86
600 LET F$ = MID$(TIME$, 1, 2)	F$ = 15
700 LET G$ = MID$(TIME$, 4, 2)	G$ = 26
800 LET H$ = MID$(TIME$, 7, 2)	H$ = 32

*Note that any numeric value assigned to a string variable is actually a string and not a number.

The function DATE$ and TIME$ are often used to display the date and time as part of report headings, or to verify that a payment date, birthdate or hire date is valid.

Accepting String Data—LINE INPUT Statement and the INKEY$ and INPUT$ Functions

Some BASIC systems include an alternative input statement, the LINE INPUT string statement, that accepts a line entered from an external source like a keyboard as the string value and assigns it to a specified string variable. The string value may include quotation marks and commas. That is, if the string value

```
SHE SAID, "TERMINATE THE PROGRAM!"
```

is entered, and the Enter key is pressed in response to the statement

```
300 LINE INPUT "WHAT DID SHE SAY? "; A$
```

then A$ is assigned the entire string of characters

```
SHE SAID, "TERMINATE THE PROGRAM!"
```

including the comma and quotation marks.

The general form of the LINE INPUT statement is shown in Table 9.10.

TABLE 9.10   The LINE INPUT Statement

General Form:	LINE INPUT string variable or LINE INPUT "input prompt message"; string variable
Purpose:	Provides for the assignment to a string variable of a line, including commas and quotation marks, entered from a source external to the program.
Examples:	*Input Statements* *Data from an External Source*
	`100 LINE INPUT A$` `1 219 844 0520`
	`200 LINE INPUT "WHAT? "; S$` `"DON'T DO IT", SAID AMANDA`
	`300 LINE INPUT "WEIGHT? "; W$` `126.5 LBS.`
Caution:	Not available on the Apple and COMMODORE. On the DEC VAX-11 use the LINPUT statement.

The major differences between the LINE INPUT statement and the INPUT statements are:

1. The LINE INPUT statement does not prompt the user with the question mark and trailing space that the INPUT statement does.
2. The LINE INPUT statement may only have at most one string variable in the list. The INPUT statement may have multiple variables in the list and they may be either numeric or string.

When executed, an INPUT or LINE INPUT statement instructs the system to suspend execution of the program until the Enter key is pressed. That is, with these two statements, we must always signal the system by pressing the Enter key when we have finished entering the data requested.

Some BASIC systems include two functions, INKEY$ and INPUT$, that do not require that the Enter key be pressed for the program to accept input. The function INKEY$ *does not* suspend execution of the program but instead checks the keyboard to determine if a character is pending—that is, if a key was recently pressed. The function INKEY$ has no argument.

The following statement

```
300 LET A$ = INKEY$
```

assigns A$ the character that corresponds to the last key pressed. If no character is entered, then INKEY$ assigns the null string to A$. Since this function accepts one character from the keyboard but does not suspend execution of the program, the function is normally located in a statement within a loop. For example, the following partial program displays the value of X and 2 * X either until the user presses a key or until the value of X exceeds 1E + 38 (an **arithmetic overflow** occurs):

```
500 LET X = X + 1
510 LET C$ = ""
520 WHILE C$ = ""
530    PRINT X, 2 * X
540    LET X = X + 1
550    LET C$ = INKEY$
560 WEND
```

Line 510 assigns C$ the null string which allows control to pass into the While loop. Line 530 displays the value of X and 2 * X. The variable X is incremented by one in line 540. Line 550 checks to determine if the user has recently pressed a key. If no character is pending from the keyboard, C$ is assigned the null string and control once again passes through the loop. The system will continue to execute the loop until the user presses a key or the value of 2 * X causes an arithmetic overflow.

The function INKEY$ is useful for applications that require a program not be interrupted and yet accept responses from the keyboard. This method of processing is essential for video game programs, like Space Invaders or Missile Command, which are moving objects constantly on the display device, but must also constantly check for user input, like the firing of a phaser.

The function INPUT$ (N) is even more sophisticated than the function INKEY$, because it accepts N characters from the keyboard. However, unlike INKEY$, INPUT$ suspends execution of the program until the user has pressed N number of keys. For example, the statement

```
300 LET C$ = INPUT$(1)
```

causes the system to suspend execution of the program (like the INPUT and LINE INPUT statements) and wait until a key is pressed. However, the character entered is not displayed on the screen. To display the response, the statement containing INPUT$ must be followed with a PRINT statement. For example,

```
400 LET C$ = INPUT$(5)
410 PRINT C$
```

displays the five characters entered by the user.

Table 9.11 illustrates examples of the functions INKEY$ and INPUT$.

TABLE 9.11   Examples of the INKEY$ **and** INPUT$ **Functions**

The Statement	Keyboard Response	Results In
`100 LET X$ = INKEY$`	J	X$ = J
`200 LET V$ = INKEY$`	No Response	V$ = null
`300 LET W$ = INPUT$(4)`	A1B2	W$ = A1B2
`400 LET Z$ = INPUT$(1)`	3	Z$ = 3

A common use of the function INPUT$ is to suspend the execution of a program at the conclusion of a task so that the information on the screen may be read before it disappears. For example, if a program is displaying a long list of items, you may want to suspend execution of the program after every 20 or so lines are displayed. The message

```
PRESS ANY KEY TO CONTINUE
```

is often used in this situation. The INPUT$ simplifies the entry by not requiring that the Enter key be pressed. The following partial program shows how to incorporate this technique into a BASIC program.

```
1000 PRINT "PRESS ANY KEY TO CONTINUE"
1010 LET A$ = INPUT$(1)
```

The most common numeric functions supplied with BASIC systems are listed in Table 9.12.

9.2 NUMERIC FUNCTIONS

TABLE 9.12 Numeric Functions Common to Most BASIC Systems

Function	Function Value
ABS(X)	Returns the absolute value of the argument X.
ATN(X)	Returns the angle in radians whose tangent is the value of the argument X.
COS(X)	Returns the cosine of the argument X where X is in radians.
EXP(X)	Returns e(2.71828⋯) raised to the argument X.
FIX(X)	Returns the integer portion of the argument X.
INT(X)	Returns the largest integer that is less than or equal to the argument X.
LOG(X)	Returns the natural log of the argument X where X is greater than 0.
RND	Returns a random number between 0 (inclusive) and 1 (exclusive).
SGN(X)	Returns the sign of the argument X: -1 if the argument X is less than 0; 0 if the argument X is equal to 0; or, $+1$ if the argument X is greater than 0.
SIN(X)	Returns the sine of the argument X where X is in radians.
SQR(X)	Returns the positive square root of the argument X.
TAN(X)	Returns the tangent of the argument X where X is in radians.

In the discussion that follows, several examples of each numeric function are shown.

Arithmetic Functions—ABS, FIX, INT and SGN

The functions classified as *arithmetic* include ABS (absolute value), FIX (fixed integer), INT (integer) and SGN (sign).

The function ABS takes any numeric expression and returns its positive value. For example, if X is equal to -4, then ABS (X) is equal to 4. Additional examples of the function ABS are shown in Table 9.13 on page 164.

The function FIX(X) returns the integer portion of the argument X. For example, if X is equal to 13.45, then FIX(X) returns 13. When the argument is positive, the function FIX is identical to the function INT. However, when the argument is negative the two functions return a different result. For example, if X is equal to -4.45, then FIX(X) returns -4 and INT(X) returns -5. The function INT returns an integer that is less than or equal to the argument. Additional examples of the function FIX and INT are shown in Table 9.13

The function SGN (X) returns a value of +1 if the argument X is positive; 0 if the argument is 0; and −1 if the argument X is negative. Table 9.13 also shows examples of the function SGN.

TABLE 9.13   Examples of the ABS, FIX, INT and SGN Functions

Value of Variable	The Statement	Results In
K = −3	100 LET P = ABS(K)	P = 3
Q = 4.5	200 LET C = ABS(Q)	C = 4.5
C = 4, D = −6	300 LET A = C + ABS(D)	A = 10
G = 25.567	400 LET F = FIX(G)	F = 25
G = −25.567	500 LET F = FIX(G)	F = −25
G = 25.567	600 LET I = INT(G)	I = 25
G = −25.567	700 LET I = INT(G)	I = −26
D = 4	800 LET E = SGN(D)	E = 1
P = −5	900 LET F = 5 + SGN(P)	F = 4

Exponential Functions—SQR, EXP and LOG

The functions classified as exponential include the SQR (square root), EXP (exponential) and LOG (logarithmic).

The function SQR (X) computes the square root of the argument X.

Table 9.14 shows several examples of computing the square root of a *non-negative* number.

TABLE 9.14   Examples of the SQR Functions

Value of Variable	The Statement	Results In
Argument = 9	100 LET X = SQR(9)	X = 3
E = 0	110 LET Z = SQR(E)	Z = 0
R = 25	120 LET D = SQR(R)	D = 5
Q(1) = 1.15129	150 LET C = SQR(Q(1))	C = 1.23
X = 3, Y = 4	500 LET P = SQR(X^2 + Y^2)	P = 5
D = −49	650 LET U = SQR(ABS(D))	U = 7

The symbol e in mathematics represents 2.718281828459045 · · · , where the three dots show that the fractional part of the constant is not a repeating sequence of digits. In BASIC, the keyword EXP is used to represent this constant, which is raised to the power given as the argument in parentheses following the function name. The function EXP can be used, for example, to determine the value of $e^{1.14473}$. The following BASIC statement

```
110 LET Y = EXP(1.14473)
```

results in a Y value of 3.14159.

The natural log ($\log_e$ or ln) of a number can be determined by using the LOG function. For example, the value of X in the equation

$$e^x = 3$$

can be determined by using the following statement:

```
110 LET X = LOG(3)
```

The resulting value of X is 1.09861 and, therefore,

$$e^{1.0961} = 3$$

This function can also be used to determine the logarithm to the base 10 by multiplying the LOG function by .434295. For example, in the statement

```
110 LET Y = 0.434295 * LOG(3)
```

Y is assigned the value 0.477122, the base 10 logarithm of 3.

Trigonometric Functions—SIN, COS, TAN and ATN

In BASIC the functions SIN, COS and TAN can be used to determine the sine, cosine, and tangent of the angle X expressed in radians. Since angles are usually expressed in degrees, the following statements relating angles and radians should prove helpful:

1 radian = $180/\pi$ degrees = 180/3.14159 degrees
1 degree = $\pi/180$ radians × 3.14159/180 radians

When using these three functions remember that if the argument is in units of degrees it must first be multiplied by 3.14159/180 in order to convert it into units of radians before the function can evaluate it. In mathematics, if the equation X = sin 30° is evaluated, then X = 0.5. However, evaluating the same equation in BASIC requires the following:

```
110 LET A = 30 * 3.14159/180
120 LET X = SIN(A)
```

or

```
110 LET X = SIN(30 * 3.14159/180)
```

Most BASIC systems do not have corresponding functions for the cosecant, secant and the cotangent. These three trigonometric functions must be evaluated by combinations of the SIN, COS and TAN functions. Table 9.15 illustrates the combinations.

TABLE 9.15   Determining the Cosecant, Secant and Cotangent

To find the	Use
Cosecant	1/SIN(X)
Secant	1/COS(X)
Cotangent	1/TAN(X)

The fourth trigonometric function available in BASIC is the arctangent. The function ATN returns a value that is the angle (in units of radians) that corresponds to the argument in the function. For example,

```
110 LET V = ATN(1)
```

results in V being assigned the value of .785398 radians. Multiplying this number by 180/3.14159 yields an angle of 45°.

Random Number Function and the RANDOMIZE Statement

The function RND is important to the programmer involved in the development of programs simulating situations that are described by a random process. The owners of a shopping mall, for example, may want a program written to simulate the number of cars that will enter their parking lots during a particular period of the day. Or a grocery store may want a program to model unpredictable values that represent people standing in line waiting to check out. The unpredictable values can be supplied by the function RND. Actually, the random numbers generated by the computer are provided by a repeatable process, and for this reason they are often called **pseudo-random numbers**.

The function RND returns an unpredictable decimal fraction number between 0 (inclusive) and 1(exclusive). Each time the function is referenced, any number between 0 and <1 has an equal probability of being returned by the function. For example, the statement

```
100 LET Y = RND
```

assigns Y a random number. Program 9.4 illustrates the generation of five random numbers.

Program 9.4

```
100 REM PROGRAM 9.4
110 REM GENERATING RANDOM NUMBERS
120 REM ************************
130 FOR I = 1 TO 5
140    PRINT RND,
150 NEXT I
160 END

RUN

 .887512      .983185      .496765      .717194      .417542
```

Each time the function RND is referenced in line 140 of the loop, a number between 0 and <1 is displayed.

The functions INT or FIX and RND can be combined to create random digits over a specified range. The following expression allows for the generation of random digits over the range C ≦ n ≦ D:

```
INT((D - C + 1) * RND + C)
```

For example, to generate random digits over the range 1 to 10 inclusive, change line 140 in Program 9.4 to:

```
140 PRINT INT((10 - 1 + 1) * RND + 1)
```

or

```
140 PRINT INT(10 * RND + 1)
```

Program 9.5 simulates tossing a coin twenty times. The expression INT(2 * RND) returns a zero (heads) or one (tails). The expression in line 160 returned 13 zeros (heads) and 7 ones (tails).

```
100 REM PROGRAM 9.5
110 REM SIMULATION OF COIN TOSSING
120 REM 0 IS A HEAD AND 1 IS A TAIL
130 REM THE COIN IS TOSSED 20 TIMES
140 REM ***************************
150 FOR I = 1 TO 20
160    X = INT(2*RND)
170    PRINT X;
180 NEXT I
190 END
```

Program 9.5

```
RUN

1  0  1  0  0  0  1  1  0  1  0  0  0  0  1  0  0  1  0  0
```

```
100 REM PROGRAM 9.6
110 REM SIMULATION OF COIN TOSSING
120 REM 0 IS A HEAD AND 1 IS A TAIL
130 REM USER ENTERS NUMBER OF TIMES COIN IS TOSSED
140 REM H = NUMBER OF HEADS, T = NUMBER OF TAILS
150 REM ********************************************
160 LET H = 0
170 LET T = 0
180 INPUT "HOW MANY TOSSES"; N
190 FOR I = 1 TO N
200    LET X = INT(2*RND)
210    IF X = 0 LET H = H + 1 ELSE LET T = T + 1
220 NEXT I
230 PRINT "NUMBER OF HEADS====>"; H
240 PRINT "NUMBER OF TAILS====>"; T
250 END
```

Program 9.6

```
RUN

HOW MANY TOSSES? 500
NUMBER OF HEADS====> 259
NUMBER OF TAILS====> 241
```

Program 9.5 can be enhanced to allow a user to enter the number of simulated coin tosses desired and to display the total number of heads and tails. This is illustrated in Program 9.6.

When executed, Program 9.6 requests that the user enter the number of coin tosses to be simulated. Line 210 increments H (head counter) or T (tail counter) by 1 depending upon the value assigned to X. At the conclusion of the For loop, lines 230 and 240 display the total number of heads H and total number of tails T. As illustrated by the results of Program 9.6, out of 500 simulated coin tosses, 259 were heads and 241 tails.

Every time Program 9.6 is executed on the same system, it will display the same results, because the system generates random numbers for a starting value called the **seed**. Unless the seed is changed, the system continues to generate the same set of random numbers in the same sequence each time the same program is executed. Once a program containing the function RND is ready for production, the statement RANDOMIZE can be used to instruct the system to generate random numbers from a different seed each time the program is executed. The general form of the RANDOMIZE statement is shown in Table 9.16 on page 168.

The rule for the execution of the RANDOMIZE statement in a program is

RANDOMIZE **Rule 1:** The RANDOMIZE statement must be executed prior to any reference to the RND function.

TABLE 9.16   **The** RANDOMIZE **Statement**

General Form:	RANDOMIZE
Purpose:	To supply a new seed for the generation of random numbers by the function RND.
Example:	100 RANDOMIZE
Caution:	With the Apple and COMMODORE, a new seed is supplied based on the value of the argument to the right in the function RND. The statement RANDOMIZE is not available with these two systems. With the TRS-80, use the statement RANDOM.
	With the DEC Rainbow, IBM PC, Macintosh and Microsoft BASIC in general, you may include a parameter following the keyword RANDOMIZE. With these systems, if a parameter is not included, the RANDOMIZE statement suspends execution and requests a value. The value must be between -32768 and 32767.

Program 9.7 simulates a popular guessing game in which the player attempts to guess a number between 1 and 100. The RANDOMIZE statement is included so that the function RND will return a new set of random numbers each time the program is executed.

When the RUN command is issued for Program 9.7, line 130 ensures that the program does not generate the same set of random numbers as the last time the program was executed. In line 130, the seed is based on the seconds portion of the function TIME$ and therefore, chances are 1 in 60 that the same seed will be used.

Line 140 assigns N the number to be guessed (8). Line 150 sets a counter C to 1. The counter C keeps track of the number of guesses. Line 160 through 250 display the instructions for the game. Line 260 accepts a guess G from the user. If G is equal to N, the program terminates after 1 guess. If G does not equal N, the system executes the While loop and displays an appropriate message before requesting the next guess and incrementing the counter C. When the user finally guesses the number, control passes to line 320 and a message and the value of C are displayed.

Table 9.17 shows the modifications to Program 9.7 for some popular computer systems.

TABLE 9.17   **Variations to the** RANDOMIZE **Statement and Function** RND **in Program 9.7**

Computer System	Modification
Apple	Delete line 130 and change the function RND in line 140 to RND (1).
COMMODORE	Delete line 130 and change the function RND in line 140 to RND (−1).
DEC Rainbow, IBM PC, Macintosh and Microsoft BASIC in general	No modifications.
DEC VAX-11	Delete the parameter from the RANDOMIZE statement.
TRS-80	In line 130, replace RANDOMIZE with RANDOM.

```
100 REM PROGRAM 9.7
110 REM GUESS A NUMBER BETWEEN 1 AND 100
120 REM ******************************
130 RANDOMIZE VAL(MID$(TIME$, 7, 2))
140 LET N = INT(100 * RND + 1)
150 LET C = 1
160 CLS
170 PRINT
180 PRINT "*************************************"
190 PRINT "*                                   *"
200 PRINT "* GUESS A NUMBER BETWEEN 1 AND 100. *"
210 PRINT "* I WILL TELL YOU IF YOUR GUESS IS  *"
220 PRINT "* TOO HIGH OR TOO LOW.              *"
230 PRINT "*                                   *"
240 PRINT "*************************************"
250 PRINT
260 INPUT "GUESS A NUMBER"; G
270 WHILE G <> N
280     IF G > N THEN PRINT "TOO HIGH" ELSE PRINT "TOO LOW"
290     INPUT "GUESS A NUMBER"; G
300     LET C = C + 1
310 WEND
320 PRINT
330 PRINT "YOUR GUESS IS CORRECT."
340 PRINT "IT TOOK YOU"; C; "GUESSES."
350 END

RUN


*************************************
*                                   *
* GUESS A NUMBER BETWEEN 1 AND 100. *
* I WILL TELL YOU IF YOUR GUESS IS  *
* TOO HIGH OR TOO LOW.              *
*                                   *
*************************************

GUESS A NUMBER? 50
TOO HIGH
GUESS A NUMBER? 25
TOO HIGH
GUESS A NUMBER? 5
TOO LOW
GUESS A NUMBER? 15
TOO HIGH
GUESS A NUMBER? 10
TOO HIGH
GUESS A NUMBER? 7
TOO LOW
GUESS A NUMBER? 8

YOUR GUESS IS CORRECT.
IT TOOK YOU 7 GUESSES.
```

Program 9.7

9.3 USER-DEFINED FUNCTIONS

In addition to numeric and string functions, BASIC allows you to define new functions that relate to a particular application. This type of function, known as a **user-defined function**, is written as a one-line statement directly into the program.* User-defined functions can be referenced only in the program in which they are included. The BASIC system recognizes a user-defined function by the keyword DEF, which is incorporated in the function statement just to the right of the line

*Some systems allow for multiple line user-defined functions. Check the specifications on your BASIC system in the user's manual.

number. As an example, the DEF statement

```
150 DEF FNA(X) = X * (X + 1)/2
```

defines a function, $X(X + 1)/2$, whose name is FNA. The parentheses following the name of the function surround a simple variable known as a **function parameter**. The expression to the right of the equal sign indicates the operations that are to be performed with the value of X when the function is referenced in such statements as LET, ON–GOTO and IF.

The DEF statement is non-executable; that is, the system treats the statement in much the same way it treats a DATA statement. It is used only if referenced in another statement. For example, either

```
900 LET B = FNA(R) + 5
```

or

```
910 PRINT FNA(P + 3)
```

found in the same program with line 150 will reference the function FNA.

The DEF Statement

Table 9.18 shows that the DEF statement permits the creation of user-defined functions. The name of the function follows DEF, and it must begin with the two letters FN followed by a variable name that is consistent with the rules used for naming variables.

TABLE 9.18   **The DEF Statement**

General Form:	DEF FNx(p, . . . , p) = expression
	where x is a simple variable which must agree in type with the expression
	p is a simple variable.
Purpose:	To define a function that is relevant to a particular application that can be referenced as often as needed in the program in which it is defined.

Examples:	`100 DEF FND(Y) = Y^3`
	`200 DEF FNC$(A$) = MID$(A$, 2, 5)`
	`300 DEF FNG(N, E) = INT(N * 10^E + 0.5 * SGN(N))/10^E`
	`400 DEF FNR(Z) = INT(10 * RND)`

Caution:	With the Apple and COMMODORE, only numeric functions may be defined.

Table 9.19 lists some invalid DEF statements and some possible valid counterparts.

TABLE 9.19   **Invalid DEF Statements and Corresponding Valid DEF Statements**

Invalid DEF Statements	*Error in the Invalid DEF Statements*	*Valid DEF Statements*
`100 DEF(X) = X^2`	Missing function name.	`100 DEF FNA(X) = X^2`
`150 (X) = X * X + C`	DEF and Name mandatory.	`150 DEF FNC(X) = X * X + C`
`220 DEF FN5(V) = V * V * V`	Invalid name.	`220 DEF FNF(V) = V * V * V`
`300 DEF FNA(X$) = LEFT$(X$, 2)`	Function name must have an appended $ since expression is a string.	`300 DEF FNA$(X$) = LEFT$(X$, 2)`

The parameters in a user-defined function are sometimes called **dummy variables**, since they are assigned the values of the corresponding arguments when reference is made to the function. For example, the following partial program contains a user-defined function that rounds the value assigned to the argument X.

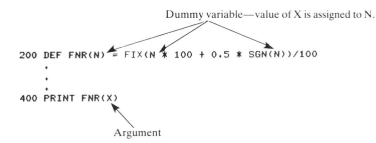

Dummy variable—value of X is assigned to N.

```
200 DEF FNR(N) = FIX(N * 100 + 0.5 * SGN(N))/100
      .
      .
      .
400 PRINT FNR(X)
```

Argument

This partial program displays the value of X rounded to the nearest hundredths place, whether X is positive or negative.

The dummy variables assigned as parameters are local to the function definition. That is, they are distinct from any variables with the same name outside of the function definition. For example, in the following partial program:

```
200 DEF FND(A, B, C) = A * B * C
      .
      .
      .
410 READ A, B, C
```

The dummy variables A, B and C in line 200 *are not affected* when A, B and C are assigned values due to line 410.

It is possible to define functions using variables other than the parameters. For example, in the following partial program

```
200 DEF FNC(A) = A * B * C
      .
      .
      .
410 READ A, B, C
```

the variables B and C in line 200 are the same as the variables B and C in line 410. That is, when line 410 is executed, the variables B and C in line 200 are assigned values. The dummy variable A in line 200, however, is not assigned a value when line 410 is executed.

A function that does not use the parameter list in the expression may be defined. Such functions may be used to define constants or expressions that do not require a variable. Each of the following functions includes a parameter that is not used in the expression.

```
100 DEF FNP(Z) = 3.14159
200 DEF FNC(Z) = 2.54
300 DEF FNR(Z) = INT(10 * RND + 1)
```

Line 100 defines FNP equal to pi (π). Line 200 defines FNC equal to the number of centimeters in an inch. Line 300 defines FNR so it returns a random number between 1 and 10. In each case, the parameter Z is not used in the expression. The parameter Z (or any other variable name) is necessary because of the syntax required to write a user-defined function.

User-defined functions may be referenced in statements in the same manner as numeric and string functions. The number of arguments following the reference should agree with the number of dummy variables in the DEF statement.

1. Consider the valid programs listed below. What is displayed if each is executed?

a.
```
100 REM EXERCISE 9.1A
110 LET N$ = "MISSISSIPPI"
120 FOR I = 1 TO LEN(N$)
130     PRINT LEFT$(N$, I)
140 NEXT I
150 END
```

b. Assume that the system time is equal to 15:34:56.
```
100 REM EXERCISE 9.1B
110 LET B = VAL(MID$(TIME$, 1, 2))
120 IF B < 12 THEN 130 ELSE 160
130     LET A$ = "A.M."
140      IF B = 0 THEN LET B = 12
150 GOTO 180
160     LET A$ = "P.M."
170      IF B <> 12 THEN LET B = B - 12
180 LET C$ = STR$(B) + MID$(TIME$, 3, 6) + SPACE$(1) + A$
190 PRINT "THE TIME IS "; C$
200 END
```

c.
```
100 REM EXERCISE 9.1C
110 LET C$ = "08<NC74N0AA>FN20A45D;;H"
120 PRINT "CODED MESSAGE:  "; C$
130 PRINT
140 PRINT "THE MESSAGE IS: ";
150 FOR I = 1 TO LEN(C$)
160     LET N = ASC(MID$(C$, I, 1))
170     LET N = N + 17
180     LET M$ = CHR$(N)
190     PRINT M$;
200 NEXT I
210 END
```

d.
```
100 REM EXERCISE 9.1D
110 FOR K = 1 TO 24
120     FOR J = 1 TO 10
130         PRINT "WAKE UP";
140         FOR I = 1 TO 5
150             PRINT CHR$(7);
160         NEXT I
170     NEXT J
180     PRINT
190 NEXT K
200 END
```

2. Evaluate each of the following. Assume C$ is equal to the following string: IF I HAVE SEEN FURTHER IT IS BY STANDING UPON THE SHOULDERS OF GIANTS.

a. LEN(C$)
b. RIGHT$(C$, 100)
c. LEFT$(C$, 5)
d. MID$(C$, 11, 4)
e. VAL("36.8")
f. ASC(MID$(C$, 4, 1))
g. CHR$(71)
h. STRING$(14, "A")
i. STR$(-13.691)
j. INSTR(C$, 5, " ")
k. MID$(C$, 64, 7) = "MIDGETS"
l. SPACE$(4)

3. Evaluate each of the following. Assume Y is equal to 2 and A$ is equal to the following string: GOTO IS A FOUR LETTER WORD.

a. LEN(A$)
b. RIGHT$(A$, 4)
c. RIGHT$(A$, 30)
d. LEFT$(A$, 50)
e. LEFT$(A$, 0)
f. LEFT$(A$, Y)
g. MID$(A$, Y, 3)
h. MID$(A$, Y^3, 2)
i. MID$(A$, 1, 5 * Y)
j. INSTR(A$, "IS")
k. INSTR(Y, A$, "T")
l. INSTR(2 * Y, A$, "GOTO")

4. Evaluate each of the following.

a. VAL("99")
b. ASC("+")
c. CHR$(63)
d. STR$(48.9)
e. LEN("PROGRAM")
f. CHR$(37)
g. ASC(":")
h. VAL("-3.1416")
i. SPACE$(10)
j. STRING$(5, " ")

5. Assume that the system time is exactly 11:59:59 P.M. and the system date is September 15, 1986. Evaluate each of the following.

   a. `100 LET A$ = TIME$`
   b. `110 LET B$ = DATE$`

6. What does the following program display when executed? Explain the algorithm used in this program.

```
100 REM EXERCISE 9.6
110 PRINT "PRIME NUMBERS"
120 PRINT "BETWEEN 1 AND 100"
130 PRINT 2
140 FOR I = 3 TO 100
150     LET M = INT(SQR(I))
160     FOR K = 2 TO M
170        IF I = K * INT(I/K) THEN 20C
180     NEXT K
190     PRINT I
200 NEXT I
210 END
```

7. What is the numeric value of each of the following?

   a. `INT(-18.5)`
   b. `ABS(-3)`
   c. `INT(16.9)`
   d. `ABS(6.7)`
   e. `EXP(1)`
   f. `LOG(0)`

8. Write a single BASIC statement for each of the following. Use numeric functions wherever possible. Assume the value of X is a real number.

   a. $p = \sqrt{a^2 + b^2}$
   b. $b = \sqrt{|\tan X - 0.51|}$
   c. $q = 8 \cos^2 X + 4 \sin X$
   d. $y = e^x + \log_e (1 + X)$

9. Explain the purpose of the RANDOMIZE statement.

10. Write a program that will generate and display 100 random numbers between 1 and 52 inclusive.

Purpose: To become familiar with the use of the functions LEN and MID$ and the LINE INPUT statement.

Problem: A palindrome is a word or phrase that is the same when read backward or forward. For example, "noon" is a palindrome, but "moon" is not. Write a program that requests the user to enter a string of characters and determines whether the string is a palindrome. The string of characters may include quotation marks. Use a sentinel value of EOE to terminate the program.

Input Data: Use the following sample data:

I
9876556789
ABLE WAS I ERE I SAW ELBA
"BOB DID BOB"
WOW LIL DID POP
OTTO
RADAR
!@#$$@#!
()
A PROGRAM IS A MIRROR IMAGE OF THE MIND

**9.5
BASIC
PROGRAMMING
PROBLEMS**

**1:
Palindromes**

Output Results: The following partial results are shown:

```
STRING? I
I IS A PALINDROME.

STRING? 9876556789
9876556789 IS A PALINDROME.
        .
        .
        .
STRING? WOW LIL DID POP
WOW LIL DID POP IS NOT A PALINDROME.
        .
        .
        .
STRING? EOE
JOB COMPLETE
```

2:
Time to Double an Investment Compounded Quarterly

Purpose: To become familiar with the use of numeric functions and user-defined functions.

Problem: Write a program that will determine the time to double an investment compounded quarterly for the following annual interest rates: 6%, 7%, 8% and 9%. The formula for computing the time is:

$$N = \frac{\log 2}{M(\log(1 + J/M))}$$

where N = the time in years
     J = annual interest rate
    M = number of conversion periods

Once the time has been determined for a given interest rate, round the answer to two decimal places. Define the formula in a user-defined function in your program.

Input Data: None

Output Results: The following results are displayed:

```
TIME TO DOUBLE AN INVESTMENT
   COMPOUNDED QUARTERLY
------------------------------

ANNUAL          YEARS TO
INTEREST        DOUBLE
--------        --------
  6%             11.64
  7%              9.99
  8%              8.75
  9%              7.79

JOB COMPLETE
```

3:
Cryptograms

Purpose: To become familiar with concatenation, table searching and string manipulation of cryptograms.

Problem: In Section 9.2, you were introduced to a method of substituting characters in a coded message and determining the contents of the message. The direct substitution method, based on a table of substitutes, may also be used with cryptograms. Write a program that uses the following table of substitutes to decode a given message. The character ƀ represents the space character.

Regular characters— A B C D E F G H I J K L M N O P Q R S T U V W X Y Z – ƀ .
Coded characters — 9 G Q 6 V L P N W X A 8 T # H Z J M (U 3) R I S B F K D

Input Data: Use the following sample coded message:

```
LW╪6W╪PKUNVK6VVZK(WTZ8WQWUWV(KW╪K9K
QHTZ8WQ9UV6KQH88VQUWH╪KHLKUNW╪P(K
UHKGVK6H╪VKW(KUNVKQMV9UW)WUSKW╪K
ZMHPM9TTW╪PKFKND6DTW88(
```

Use the LINE INPUT statement to accept each of the four lines and assign them to four different string variables. Use the concatenation operator to join the four strings.

Output Results: The following is shown for the first line of the coded message:

```
THE MESSAGE IS: FINDING THE DEEP SIMPLICITIES IN A
```

4:
Payroll Problem VI—
Spelling Out
the Net Pay

Purpose: To become familiar with table utilization, the functions INT and STR$, and spelling out numbers.

Problem: Construct a program that spells out the net pay for check writing purposes. For example, the net pay $5,078.45 results in the phrase:

FIVE THOUSAND SEVENTY-EIGHT DOLLARS AND 45 CENTS

Assume that the net pay does not exceed $9,999.99.

Hint: Use the function INT to separate the integer portion of the net pay into single digits. Use the single digits to access the words from one of two positionally organized tables. If the digit represents the thousands, hundreds or units position, then access the word from the following table:

Digit	Word	Digit	Word
0	Null	10	TEN
1	ONE	11	ELEVEN
2	TWO	12	TWELVE
3	THREE	13	THIRTEEN
4	FOUR	14	FOURTEEN
5	FIVE	15	FIFTEEN
6	SIX	16	SIXTEEN
7	SEVEN	17	SEVENTEEN
8	EIGHT	18	EIGHTEEN
9	NINE	19	NINETEEN

If the digit represents the tens position, then access the word from the following table:

Digit	Word	Digit	Word
0	Null	5	FIFTY
1	TEN	6	SIXTY
2	TWENTY	7	SEVENTY
3	THIRTY	8	EIGHTY
4	FORTY	9	NINETY

Use the functions INT and STR$ to determine the fraction portion of the net pay. Use the concatenation operator to string the words together.

Input Data: Use the following sample data:

Employee Number	Net Pay	Employee Number	Net Pay
123	$8,462.34	127	$1,003.39
124	987.23	128	4,037.00
125	78.99	129	4.67
126	6,000.23	130	0.42

Output Results: The following results are displayed:

```
EMPLOYEE
NUMBER      NET PAY    NET PAY SPELLED OUT
--------    -------    --------------------
   123     $8,462.34   EIGHT THOUSAND FOUR HUNDRED SIXTY-TWO DOLLARS AND 34 CENTS
   124      $987.23    NINE HUNDRED EIGHTY-SEVEN DOLLARS AND 23 CENTS
   125       $78.99    SEVENTY-EIGHT DOLLARS AND 99 CENTS
   126     $6,000.23   SIX THOUSAND DOLLARS AND 23 CENTS
   127     $1,003.39   ONE THOUSAND THREE DOLLARS AND 39 CENTS
   128     $4,037.00   FOUR THOUSAND THIRTY-SEVEN DOLLARS AND 0 CENTS
   129        $4.67    FOUR DOLLARS AND 67 CENTS
   130        $0.42    42 CENTS
```

APPENDIX A
DEBUGGING
TECHNIQUES

Although the top-down approach and structured programming techniques help minimize errors, they by no means guarantee error-free programs.

Due to careless or insufficient thought, program portions can be constructed which do not work as anticipated and give erroneous results. When such problems occur, techniques are needed to isolate the errors and correct the erroneous program statements.

Many BASIC systems can detect hundreds of different grammatical errors and display appropriate diagnostic messages. However, there is no BASIC system that can detect all possible errors since literally thousands of possible coding errors can be made. Some of these errors can go undetected by the BASIC system until either an abnormal end occurs during execution or the program terminates with the resulting output in error.

There are several techniques for attempting to discover the portion of the program that is in error. These methods are **debugging techniques**. The errors themselves are **bugs**, and the activity involved in their detection is **debugging**.

Tracing (TRON and TROFF)

Many BASIC systems provide a means of tracing the path of execution through a BASIC program in order to determine which statements are executed.

The most popular trace instructions for personal computers are TRON (**TR**ace **ON**) and TROFF (**TR**ace OFF). These instructions may be inserted into a BASIC program as BASIC statements or they may be used as system commands before the RUN command is issued.

The TRON instruction activates tracing and the BASIC system displays the line number of each statement executed. The line numbers appear enclosed in square brackets to prevent them from being confused with other output the program may produce.

For example, if the BASIC system with tracing activated executes a program portion consisting of lines 250, 260, 270 and 280, the output display will be as follows:

[250][260][270][280]

The TROFF instruction deactivates tracing. Both the TRON and TROFF instructions may be used any number of times in a BASIC program, as shown:

```
200 TRON
    .
    .
    .
290 TROFF
    .
    .
    .
550 TRON
    .
    .
    .
700 TROFF
```

Program A.1 has the TRON and TROFF statements in lines 125 and 195. When the RUN command is issued, all statements between lines 125 and 195 are traced, and their line numbers and corresponding output are displayed accordingly.

```
100 REM PROGRAM A.1
110 REM ILLUSTRATING USE OF THE TRACE INSTRUCTIONS
120 REM *********************************************
125 TRON              'SET TRACE ON
130 LET S = 0
140 LET I = 1
150 WHILE I <= 4
160    LET S = S + I
170    LET I = I + 1
180    PRINT S; I
190 WEND
195 TROFF             'SET TRACE OFF
200 END

RUN

[130][140][150][160][170][180] 1    2
[190][160][170][180] 3    3
[190][160][170][180] 6    4
[190][160][170][180] 10   5
[190][195]
```

Program A.1

Program A.2 is similar to Program A.1. When this program is executed, the computer displays the value of 1 over and over. The program has a bug which results in an infinite loop when the program is run.

```
100 REM PROGRAM A.2
110 REM THIS PROGRAM CONTAINS A BUG
120 REM ****************************
130 LET S = 0
140 LET I = 1
150 WHILE I <= 4
160    LET S = S + I
170    LET T = I + 1      '***ERROR*** - T SHOULD BE I
180    PRINT S
190 WEND
200 END
```

Program A.2

If the TRON instruction is used as a system command, the following output occurs during tracing:

```
TRON

RUN

[100][110][120][130][140][150][160][170][180] 1
[190][160][170][180] 1
[190][160][170][180] 1
[190][160][170][180] 1
[190]...
```

From the output we can see the repetition of the following sequence of line numbers:

```
[190][160][170][180]
```

This output reveals that the program executes lines 160, 170, 180 and 190 repeatedly in the While loop.

The WHILE statement cannot be satisfied, since the value of I will always be less than four. Line 170 has been incorrectly written. In order to satisfy the WHILE statement, line 170 should be written as:

```
170     LET I = I + 1
```

Examining Values (STOP, PRINT and CONT)

Another useful debugging technique is to stop a program, examine the values of various variables within the program, and then continue the execution of the program. All this can be accomplished through the use of the STOP, PRINT and CONT (continue) statements.

Consider the partial Program A.3:

```
100 REM PROGRAM A.3
110 REM ILLUSTRATING USE OF STOP, PRINT AND CONT
120 REM ****************************************
130 .
    .
    .
300 LET V1 = 10 * 12.15
310 LET A1 = 2 * 24.3
320 LET S1 = 36.9/3
325 STOP
330 .
    .
    .
```

Program A.3

```
RUN

BREAK IN 325            (Displayed when STOP is executed)

PRINT V1                (Entered by user)

 121.5                  (Displayed result from PRINT statement)

PRINT A1; S1            (Entered by user)

 48.6   12.3            (Displayed result from PRINT statement)

CONT                    (Entered by user)
```

When the STOP statement is executed in line 325, the program will stop and the message

```
BREAK IN 325
```

will be displayed.

Now the values of various variables can be examined by using a PRINT statement written without a line number.

When a BASIC statement like the PRINT statement is written without a line number it is executed immediately. This is the **calculator mode** of BASIC; it is also called the **Immediate mode**. (See also p. 56.)

After the values of V1, A1 and S1 are displayed, the CONT is issued and the remaining program is executed. CONT should not be placed directly into a BASIC program. Instead, it should be entered as a command from the keyboard by the user.

Intermediate Output

In some instances, including intermediate PRINT statements as a part of the program may be preferable to using STOP statements and displaying the values of variables in calculator mode.

Appropriate PRINT statements are inserted after each one or each group of statements involving computations. This technique is called **source language debugging** or the **intermediate output method**.

Intermediate results are displayed until the specific portion of the program that is in error can be deduced.

If a program produces little output to begin with, the intermediate output method should be used, since the outputs from the intermediate PRINT statements will be easy to distinguish from the regular output. If a program produces a great deal of output, then the technique using the STOP, PRINT and CONT should be used to minimize the amount of output to the display unit.

ANSWERS TO BASIC SELF-TEST EXERCISES

2. The basic subsystems of a computer are input, main storage, central processing unit, auxiliary storage and output.

   Input—a device that allows programs and data to enter into the computer system.

   Main Storage—a subsystem that allows for the storage of programs and data for the **CPU** to process at a given time.

   Central Processing Unit—the **CPU** controls and supervises the entire computer system and performs the actual arithmetic and logical operations on data specified by the stored program.

   Auxiliary Storage—a subsystem that is used to store programs and data for immediate recall.

   Output—a device that allows the computer system to communicate the results of a program to the user.

4. A terminal and a magnetic disk unit both serve as input and output devices.

6. a. 7   b. 0   c. 8

2. a.
```
CALCULATE DISCOUNT
ORIGINAL PRICE 4162.5
DISCOUNT 416.25
SALE PRICE 3746.25
END OF PROGRAM
```
   b.
```
THE VALUE OF A IS-2
THE VALUE OF B IS -3

THE VALUE OF C IS 6
```

4. a.
```
100 LET Y = 21
110 PRINT Y
120 END
```
   b. `110 PRINT S`

   c. `120 END`

   d. `105 PRINT S`

   e.
```
110 PRINT A1
120 END
```
   f. `110 PRINT Z`

6. RUN—instructs the computer to execute the current program in main storage.

   LIST—instructs the computer to list the source statements of the current program.

   NEW—instructs the computer to delete the current program.

8. Yes.

CHAPTER 3

2. 8962482E3

   The error is 176.

4. a. **11**   b. **˙1**   c. **−.666666**   d. **262,144**   e. **17**   f. **2320**

6. a. `110 LET Q = (D + E)^(1/3)`

   b. `120 LET D = (A^2)^3.2`

   c. `130 LET B = 20/(6 - S)`

   d. `140 LET Y = A1 * X + A2 * X^2 + A3 * X^3 + A4 * X^4`

   e. `150 LET E = X + X/(X - Y)`

   f. `160 LET S = 19.2 * X^3`

   g. `170 LET V = 100 - (2/3)^(100 - B)`

   h. `180 LET T = (76234/(2.37 + D))^(1/2)`

   i. `190 LET V = 1234E-4 * M - (.123458^3/(M - N))`

   j. `200 LET Q = ((F - M * 1000)^(2 * B))/(4 * M) - 1/E`

8. a, b, c, d, f, g, i

CHAPTER 4

2. a.
```
100 REM EXERCISE 4.2A SOLUTION
110 READ S, B
120 LET D = S - B
130 PRINT D
140 DATA 4, 6
150 END
```
   b.
```
100 REM EXERCISE 4.2B SOLUTION
110 DATA 1, 2, 5, 6, 8, 7, 1, 3, 2
120 READ X, Y, Z
130 LET X1 = X * Y
140 LET X1 = X1 * Z
150 PRINT X1
160 GOTO 120
170 END
```

4. a. `120 DATA 1, 2, 3, 4, 5`   c. `140 DATA 1, 2, 3, 4`

   b. `130 DATA 1, 2`   d. The READ statement is invalid.

6.
```
110 PRINT A
120 PRINT
130 PRINT
140 PRINT B
```

8. b

10.
```
 vvvvv
X     X
X  o o  X
X       X
X   U   X
X ( ) X
X   -   X
 X     X
  XXXXX
```

CHAPTER 5

2.
```
100 LET X = 0
110 LET T = 10
```
   a.
```
130 LET X = X + 1
140 LET T = T + 1
```
   b.
```
150 LET X = X + 7
160 LET T = T + 7
```
   c.
```
170 LET X = X + 2
180 LET T = T + 2
```
   d.
```
190 LET X = 2 * X
200 LET T = 2 * T
```
   e.
```
210 LET X = X - 1
220 LET T = T - 1
```

4. a. Q value greater than 8

   b. Q value greater than or equal to −3

   c. Q value less than 27

   d. Q value not equal to 3

6. a.
```
200 IF A >= 21 THEN LET C = C + 1
210 LET S = S + 1
```
   b.
```
300 IF S$ = "M" THEN LET M = M + 1 ELSE LET F = F + 1
```

8.
```
100 REM EXERCISE 5.8 SOLUTION
200 IF U < V THEN 210 ELSE 230
210    IF U < W THEN LET S = U ELSE S = W
220 GOTO 240
230    IF V < W THEN LET S = V ELSE S = W
240
```

10.   a. X   b. C = 3; S = 320   c. 5   d. 356   e. 4

12.
```
100 REM EXERCISE 5.12 SOLUTION
110 IF C = 0 THEN 120 ELSE 140
120    IF D = 0 THEN LET A = -1 ELSE LET A = -3
130 GOTO 150
140    IF D = 0 THEN LET A = -3 ELSE LET A = -2
150
```

CHAPTER 6

2.   a. True   d. False   g. False
     b. False   e. True   h. True
     c. True   f. False

4.   a.   b.

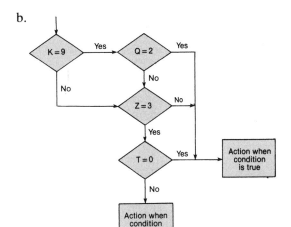

6.   a. 12   b. 3   c. 12

CHAPTER 7

2.   a. L(2, 2)   e. L(3, 4)
     b. L(3, 3)   f. L(2, 1)
     c. L(3, 2)   g. L(1, 3)
     d. L(5, 2)   h. L(5, 1)

4.   a. c
     b. c
     c. e, a fatal error is caused by accessing elements outside the range of the array.
     d. a

6.
```
190 REM EXERCISE 7.6 SOLUTION
200 FOR I = 1 TO 50
210    IF A(I) >= B(I) THEN 240
220       LET C(I) = -1
230       GOTO 250
240    IF A(I) = B(I) THEN LET C(I) = 0 ELSE LET C(I) = 1
250 NEXT I
```

8. The following are invalid:

b. the value of the subscript cannot be negative.

d. subscripted subscripts are not permitted.

CHAPTER 8 2.
```
100 REM EXERCISE 8.2 SOLUTION
110 LET K = 0
120 LET T = 0
130 OPEN 'I', #1, 'SALES.DAT'
140 PRINT 'STOCK', 'SELLING', 'DISCOUNT'
150 PRINT '-----', '--------', '----------'
160 INPUT #1, S$, S, C
170 WHILE S$ <> 'EOF'
180    LET K = K + 1
190    LET T = T + S
200    PRINT S$, S, C
210    INPUT #1, S$, S, C
220 WEND
230 CLOSE #1
240 PRINT
250 PRINT USING 'TOTAL NUMBER OF RECORDS====> ###'; K
260 PRINT USING 'AVERAGE SELLING PRICE======> ###.##'; T/K
270 PRINT
280 PRINT 'JOB COMPLETE'
290 END
```

4. The ON ERROR GOTO 0 statement is used to return control to the system following a branch to an error or end-of-file routine when the branch is due to an unexpected error. The system terminates execution of the program following the display of an appropriate diagnostic message.

Following the detection of an error by an ON ERROR GOTO statement, the RESUME statement is used in an error-handling routine or end-of-job routine to transfer control to any line in a program.

6.
```
200 INPUT 'ENTER THE FILENAME'; N$
210 OPEN 'I', #1, N$
```

8. Yes.

10. a, the parameters are out of order.
    b, the variable M should be M$.
    e, a comma should follow the filenumber.
    f, the trailing comma is invalid.
    g, the keyword CLOSE should be followed by a filenumber.
    h, the ON ERROR GOTO statement should not transfer control to itself.
    i, the number sign (#) is invalid.

CHAPTER 9 2.

a.	68	g.	G
b.	The entire string	h.	AAAAAAAAAAAAAA
c.	IF Ib (where b indicates a blank or space follows I)	i.	−13.691
		j.	Invalid
d.	SEEN	k.	GIANTS is replaced by MIDGETS in C$.
e.	36.8	l.	Four spaces.
f.	73		

4.

a.	99	c.	?	e.	7	g.	58	i.	Ten spaces.
b.	43	d.	48.9	f.	73	h.	−3.1416	j.	Five spaces.

6. The program displays the prime numbers between 1 and 100. Any whole number greater than 1 that has no factors other than 1 and the number itself is

called a **prime number**. In number theory it can be proved that if a number has no factors between 2 and the square root of the number, then the number is prime. The algorithm utilizes this method of finding the prime numbers between 1 and 100.

8.   a. `100 LET P = SQR(A^2 + B^2)`

    b. `200 LET B = SQR(ABS(TAN(X) - 0.51)`

    c. `300 LET Q = 8 * (COS(X))^2 + 4 * SIN(X)`

    d. `400 LET Y = EXP(X) + LOG(1 + X)`

10.
```
100 REM EXERCISE 9.10 SOLUTION
110 FOR R = 1 TO 52
120     PRINT INT(52 * RND + 1)
130 NEXT R
140 END
```

INDEX